Hilary du Pré
and
Piers du Pré

HILARY AND JACKIE

(formerly titled *A Genius in the Family*)

BALLANTINE BOOKS • NEW YORK

A Ballantine Book
Published by The Ballantine Publishing Group

Copyright © 1997 by Jacqueline du Pré Ltd.

All rights reserved under International and Pan-
American Copyright Conventions. Published in the
United States by The Ballantine Publishing Group, a
division of Random House, Inc., New York. Originally published in slightly different form in Great
Britain by Chatto & Windus in 1997 under the
title *A Genius in the Family*.

Discography by Andrew Keener first published in
Jacqueline du Pré: A Biography by Carol Easton ©
1991. This revised and updated Discography with
new introduction © Andrew Keener 1997.

http://www.randomhouse.com/BB/

A CIP catalog record for this book is found at the
Library of Congress

Manufactured in the United States of America

First American Edition: November 1998

10 9 8 7 6 5 4

Our heartfelt thanks to

Jan Younghusband

without whose tireless guidance this
book could not have been written

These are our memories

This book is not a biography nor an account of Jackie's career

It is simply what happened

We offer the reader the story of our family, from within

This book was written with love
and is dedicated with love to:

Theresa, Clare, Nicolette, Orlando

and

Rollo, Diccon, Adam, Tobias

This is how it was . . .

Contents

PROLOGUE

Hilary

October 1987

Jackie died on a Monday and the funeral was two days later.

My brother Piers, his wife Lin, and I drove to Rock House in Buckinghamshire to collect Dad. He greeted us at the door wearing his bowler, as the Rabbi had requested he should bring a hat. Since none of us had been to a Jewish funeral before, we had no idea what to expect. Squashing into the car, we all set off for Golders Green, allowing plenty of time to find our way through north London.

We arrived far too early and the cemetery seemed deserted. We parked as near as possible, and while Piers lifted Dad from the car and lowered him into his wheelchair, I wandered into the graveyard and found the hollow tomb where Jackie was to go. It was covered but lay waiting, cold and empty.

One after another, bouquets were being delivered and I suddenly realized, with horror, that I had forgotten the flowers I had picked from the garden for Jackie. They were still on the kitchen table at home.

I asked for the nearest florist and was directed down the road. Leaving Piers and Lin to look after Dad, I ran and ran through the miserable, gray day to the main road, under the railway bridge, and to the right. At last, ahead of me, was the shop, bursting with flowers, glorious bouquets spilling on to the pavement, making a blanket of color.

I picked my way between them. "This is incredible, all these flowers . . ."

"Oh, yes," came the reply. "There's a big funeral today. The great cellist, Jacqueline du Pré, has died, and I just can't keep up with the orders . . . Can I help you?"

The florist looked aghast as tears streamed down my face.

Through my sobs, I tried to explain that I needed a flower for my sister. I could hardly see but eventually chose one pale, creamy-pink rose with a gorgeous scent that Jackie would have loved. Still in tears, I put my hand in my pocket and found I had left my purse at home, too.

The florist simply gave me the rose. I tried to thank her properly, but could only whisper.

I was desperately anxious to find Jackie, and ran wearily back to the cemetery. The caretaker welcomed me at the gate and promised to put my rose with the family flowers. I asked him where the funeral service would be and he pointed to the little synagogue. I opened the door.

There, on a trolley in the peaceful, wooden room, was Jackie's coffin, covered with a black shroud. I don't know how long I was with her but we were alone again, at last, and I was able to say so much. Silently, I told her I loved her, and said goodbye.

After a while I heard a sound, and turned to find a rabbi waiting quietly at the door. He had one of the kindest faces I have ever seen. He walked over and put his arm round me.

"Many will claim they were her best friend," he said. "Many will claim they alone understood what she needed. But your memories of your sister are unique. They are your own. Let no one interfere or take them from you." He hugged me and whispered, "Never forget that."

I wanted to thank him but, as I tried to speak, the doors opened and in poured the great and illustrious. We were completely surrounded.

In the beginning

CHAPTER ONE

Hilary

After Jackie died, all the press cuttings, letters, diaries and family photographs, which Dad had so carefully collected for the family archives, were left untouched. We had no desire to look at any of them: it would be far too painful.

As the years went by, we gradually found ourselves taking on the roles of ambassadors for the Jacqueline du Pré Appeal. We attended various charitable events, including the unveiling of plaques, celebrations of anniversaries and special tributes. Longer-term projects were set up in her memory and have only recently come to fruition: a new concert hall at St. Hilda's College, Oxford, and the Jacqueline du Pré Cello Competition, initially sponsored by EMI Records, which aims to inspire young performers by providing a showcase for the finest cellists of today. These projects enabled us to continue our involvement with Jackie in a positive way. But they were always centered around Jackie the icon, allowing us to function at a superficial level, keeping the pain at bay. We had not yet begun to realize we were running away from very powerful emotions.

Five years after her death, the volatile nature of our suppressed feelings surfaced for the first time when an author came to my house and asked if she could take all the letters and documentation referring to Jackie, to use as research for a book. When my brother and I explained how vast our collection was, the only comment was that there might be sufficient for one chapter.

I looked at Piers. I could see he was thinking the same as me. "One chapter!" We both knew we just couldn't be parted from our hoard of treasures; and neither could we bear the thought of someone rummaging through them, now or in the future.

In 1994, we went to a fund-raising event at Claridge's. During the evening, a new film about Jackie was screened. The director, Christopher Nupen (Kitty) had met Jackie in her late teens and had made several films of her when she was in her early twenties. This latest film presented Jackie during the golden years of her career, performing with the "Jewish musical mafia" as they were nicknamed: her husband, the conductor and pianist Daniel Barenboim, the violinists Itzhak Perlman and Pinchas Zukerman, and the conductor and double-bass player, Zubin Mehta.

The moment Jackie appeared on the screen I froze. The commentary spoke of her genius and glorious talent, but the look in her eyes shattered me. I didn't see Jacqueline du Pré, the great cellist; I saw my sister behind a professional façade. I was struck by Jackie's appalling vulnerability in stark contrast to the security and vibrancy of her music-making.

At dinner afterward I was so upset I could hardly speak. Few people could see how isolated Jackie's talent had made her. She had always presented a bold, brave-hearted personality to the public, yet inside she was struggling with herself and her role as one of the world's finest cellists. While I completely understand the desire to revel in the bliss of great artistry, I could no longer bear to witness my sister being publicly enshrined because of her genius—a genius which had been destructive not only to her personally but also to our family.

On the way home from Claridge's, Piers and I talked openly for the first time about our feelings and the powerful emotions we had repressed for so long. We decided we simply had to protect our family memories. We would have to burn everything. We agreed to meet at his house to have one last look through the boxes.

When the day arrived I set off with my boxes of photographs, letters and papers, but my mood of thoughtful anticipation gradually turned to dread as I wove my way along the narrow country lanes to Piers's house in Upper Bucklebury. By the time I arrived, I felt so sick with apprehension I could hardly move.

Piers

The very thought of looking at the vast amount of family material was already bringing memories to the surface. Beautiful memories, but oh, so painful. Painful because I was beginning to discover I had never really grieved for Mum, Jackie or Dad: it had all happened far too quickly, and in Jackie's case, far too publicly.

But now Hilary was on her way to share the task of opening the family archives. When I heard her pull into the driveway, I stood by the front door ready to greet her. For a long time she didn't get out of the car but stared into the distance. Eventually, she turned, saw me, and appeared to struggle out of a dream as she opened the car door. As we hugged each other, we both began weeping at the thought of what lay ahead of us.

In the cellar we opened the box labeled "J's letters—Box 1": Dad had certainly kept things in order. The first letter was addressed to me. I recognized the envelope, and the memory of opening it for the first time rushed back. Neither of us spoke, but in a charged silence we read:

Dearest Bar . . .

There—in Jackie's writing—was her favorite nickname for me.

I have been thinking about you a lot and wondering
what's been happening in your crazy life . . .

Another letter started, "Dear Fart Face." Another, written on toilet paper, finished: "P.S. Unused!" So many letters to Gran, Mum, Hilary and me. One after another, they tumbled out. Suddenly it was as if Jackie was actually talking to us. Her exuberant personality, her roguish sense of humor, her crazy observations about people and life were with us anew. It seemed we were all laughing together once again.

On and on we read, reliving every moment. Suddenly, we both stopped laughing and looked at each other.

"Hil," I said, "burning this would be the same as burning Jackie."

The next box was full of press cuttings:

Callas may have sung Tosca, Horowitz may have returned to the recital platform, Charles Ives's 4th Symphony may have achieved its première at last, but what I shall remember about the 1964–65 Season in New York is Jacqueline du Pré. She is divine. At twenty she already inhabits the lofty world of the few supreme artists. As soon as she started playing this very quiet and very English work (the Elgar Concerto), a rapt and unprecedented silence descended over the Carnegie Hall audience. Afterward, tears were to be seen in many eyes. "It restores your faith," a man behind me muttered.

Bernard Jacobson
Music and Musicians

Hilary

The past came flooding back with violent intensity. Piers and I batted memories back and forth in a frenzy. Do you remember this? Do you remember that? And then I paused. A torrent of confusing emotions swept through me. I was happy to remember our laughter; I would have loved to have been able to perform as Jackie did; I was angry about her death; I felt guilty; and I was frightened to look back in case we found why she had been taken from us.

After that day we couldn't talk about Jackie without tears streaming down our faces. Gradually I began to realize that through all the years of illness and suffering we had lost touch with the essential core of our sister. Rather than burn and forget, we knew then we had to go back, even if it meant facing many agonizing memories.

Hilary and Piers

By retracing our lives through this story, we hope we will be able to create an honest portrait of Jackie, the sister we knew behind the public image; and in so doing, rediscover the sister we lost so many years ago.

CHAPTER TWO

Hilary

My earliest memories of music are of listening to Mum's broadcasts. The wireless was on the sideboard and I remember Gran's obvious excitement as she hoisted me in her arms and gently settled me next to it. "Come on, Hilary, we're going to listen to Mummy playing the piano." Gran hushed me when the announcer said: "Today's recital will be given by the young English pianist, Iris Greep, in a program including Bach, Schumann and Brahms."

Listening to Mum on the wireless was a source of wonder to me: I knew it was important, and I knew it was Mum playing as I had heard her practicing those pieces many times before. Sometimes I could hear her breathing, some breaths deeper and noisier than others. Everything in the house came to a standstill and I was aware of a sense of almost holy awe. Gran sat completely still in the chair. I wondered how on earth Mum and the piano could fit inside such a small box—a thought that puzzled me for years. She seemed so close to me that I expected to see her climb out of the wireless when she had finished.

Mum (Iris) came from a Devonshire family. Her mother was the seventh child of a seventh child, the last and youngest of a seafaring family. Hard up, they lived extremely frugally in a small house "down" in the Barbican in Plymouth. Gran's father caught fish which they ate and also dried and salted. Gran was often sent to do the shopping and fetch the milk, which she collected in a large jug. Nothing was wasted: even chickens' feet were made into a meal by scraping the meat off the bones. All clothes were passed down, including shoes, which caused squashed toes and awful bunions. Baking was done in the local baker's oven—a goodly batch of bread and fruit cakes, all baked together. Although they had no toys and certainly no money to buy any, Gran said they were always busy and happy and the child that brought in the first celandine of spring received a farthing.

At five, she went to a local school which at first she loved but, being a bright child, rapidly outpaced the rest of the class and became frustrated. Gran thought it would be good for her to learn the piano, so she bought an old upright and found a teacher. Iris took to it immediately and her progress was astonishingly swift. Very soon she was entered for festivals which she always won. I am not sure whether Gran had fully realized just how gifted Iris was, but at one of the festivals, the adjudicator, Professor Weekes, recognizing the girl's potential, told Gran she should find a more advanced teacher for her talented daughter. Gran explained they could not afford more expensive lessons, so he offered to teach Iris himself. Gran accepted with gratitude. As time went on, it was suggested Iris should try for a scholarship to Devonport High School. She won it, and her life was transformed. At last she was receiving academic stimulus, and having enormous successes with both musical and scholastic studies.

Mum's piano playing improved in leaps and bounds, and successes rolled in. Gran and Grandpa were immensely proud of their daughter who became well known in and around Plymouth. But, despite her achievements, it was assumed that when she left school she would work in the local draper's. Gran and Grandpa had not contemplated a musical career for her and did not want her to go away. Theirs was a tight family unit; all relations lived near to one another, helping with everything, including births and deaths, which always happened at home.

Iris took her performing degree, the Licentiate of the Royal Academy of Music (LRAM) when she was seventeen and still at school. She passed the exam with flying colors and was inspired and excited by the whole experience. Having had a taste of London and, above all, the Royal Academy of Music, she knew she wanted music as her career. But with another year to go at school, this could only be a dream.

Her teacher, Miss Watts, wanted Mum to study Dalcroze Eurhythmics, a fresh and, at first, controversial form of teaching music. It was developed around 1900 by Émile-Jaques Dalcroze, a superb mime artist and Professor of Music at the Conservatoire in Geneva, Switzerland. He discovered that when children are taught to use movement as well as hearing, their responses to music become infinitely more vital and their progress astonishing. He spent fifty years evolving and perfecting his ideas.

Miss Watts was tireless in her persuasion, and eventually managed to convince Gran and Grandpa that Iris should audition for a scholarship at the London Dalcroze school—which, of course, she was awarded.

Although Mum loved her Dalcroze lessons, she really wanted to play and perform. One day, desperately longing for fine piano teaching, she wandered into the Royal Academy of Music and just stood in the entrance hall. After a while, a porter approached and asked if he could help.

Mum burst into tears and explained that she wanted to be a student at the RAM.

He told her he knew just the person to help and led her upstairs to Room 33 where Eric Grant was teaching.

By extraordinary coincidence Eric Grant had been on the examining jury when Iris had taken her LRAM, and he remembered her. She told him about her Dalcroze scholarship but explained that her dream was to study at the Royal Academy. He took her to the top floor to meet Theodore Holland, who had also been on the LRAM panel.

Mum completed her Dalcroze course in two years instead of three and in 1934 went to the Royal Academy to study piano with Eric Grant, composition with Theodore Holland and viola with Rowsby Woof.

She flourished, winning most of the available prizes for both piano and composition, including the Challen Gold Medal, the Janet Duff Greet Prize and the Anthonia D. Murdoch Prize. Soon she was a deputy professor, and earning money by teaching the piano and eurhythmics.

Had Mum's performance in the LRAM exam been less vital, Eric Grant might not have remembered her, and she might never have gone to the RAM. Had the porter not taken it upon himself to introduce her to Eric Grant, and had Eric Grant not taken her

to see Theodore Holland, she might never have made contact
with the Hollands. As it was, Theodore Holland and his wife, Is-
ména, took the girl from Peverell under their wing, and a lifelong
friendship began.

Mrs. Holland, an Austrian, was a wealthy woman in her own
right. The Hollands had no children of their own—a conscious decision, since they were cousins. Instead they acquired an "adopted"
family of talented students, who needed shelter and encouragement, and to whom they were extremely generous. Mum was
quickly welcomed into the fold and spent much of her time
performing and listening to music at their house in Eldon Road,
Kensington.

A large man, with a kindly face, Mr. Holland sat at a big desk,
with the Blüthner grand piano behind him—the piano that would
one day become a part of our family life, when Mrs. Holland gave
it to Mum.

Piers

Dad (Derek) was the younger of two boys born to Florence
Gertrude Shaw-Green (Gannie) and James Wilfred du Pré (Pondles); du Pré is a Jersey name, and the family had lived there for
generations, their roots traceable back to 1480.

Pondles and his brother Harold owned Luce's, a scent-making
company based in Jersey. Harold was a perfumier of outstanding talent, and perfected Luce's own eau-de-cologne, frequently
winning gold medals in Cologne, much to the annoyance of his
local German competitors. Later he produced cologne in the form
of a stick, calling it "Frozen Cologne." Pondles, tall, handsome
and flamboyant, promoted and marketed the business. Luce's was
extremely successful, with shops in Jersey, Southampton, Liverpool, London and Cape Town; and factories in Southampton and
Cape Town.

Pondles had a fixed idea about Dad's future. The choice was
simple: the bank or the Army. As joining the Army meant leaving
his beloved Jersey, Dad chose the bank and started at Lloyds Bank
in St. Helier on November 1, 1926 at the age of eighteen. But after two years, he was transferred to London. They "needed" him

there. Although it was the last thing Dad wanted, the move was seen by Gannie and Pondles as a good promotion with future potential.

For Dad, it was a disaster. He hated London and knew he would miss Jersey desperately. When he took up his new appointment in 1928, he was profoundly unhappy, but he persevered. He stayed with Lloyds for eleven years, eventually leaving on October 30, 1937 to take up a new job as assistant editor of *The Accountant*.

Hilary

In 1938 Dad won a raffle prize, a ticket to Germany. As the atmosphere in Germany was threatening and unpleasant, he asked to go to Poland instead. There was, as well, an ulterior motive for choosing Poland: two years earlier he had befriended a young Ukrainian violinist on a train when he and his first cousin Norman were traveling to the Czech side of the High Tatra mountains for a climbing expedition. Since then, Derek had dreamed of walking across Poland to visit his Ukrainian friend and to explore the mountains on the Polish side of the border.

It was the height of summer, and he was full of the thrill of solo adventure. His equipment list was short: an old pair of boots, well oiled and nailed for climbing, an equally old water bottle (filled with tea and milk, which soon curdled and smelled horrible), a stout canvas rucksack, and his piano accordion, which worked overtime when he was traveling through Europe—a chorus was never lacking for Bavarian yodeling songs. On the train he teamed up with some German students, one of whom had a guitar. Together they played English, French and German songs, with everyone in the carriage joining in, all singing lustily. He quickly picked up Polish folk-songs from the local people, playing and singing with them. His self-taught skill on the accordion, his innate musical ability and excellent ear made him a charismatic communicator. Although he couldn't read music, he could harmonize any tune with ease.

After two nights in Cracow, he set off for the mountain town of Zakopane which was to be his climbing center. He squeezed into the train crammed with bearded priests, soldiers, peasants, officials, Polish trippers, black-robed Jews, and stood in the tightly packed corridor all night.

He found being unable to speak Polish a strain, but soon learnt that there was a girl who spoke English staying in Zakopane. He determined to find her address and it didn't take him long to locate the villa on the outskirts of the town. He knocked expectantly and heard footsteps on a tiled floor. A maid appeared, but before Dad could speak she said in Polish, but with unmistakable emphasis, "Go away!" and shut the door. Although night was approaching, he was undeterred. He slept under the hedge until morning.

Bright and early, he woke, and knocked again. The same footsteps came toward him but, before she could utter a word, Dad pleaded in a flood of English to be allowed to speak to the girl who spoke English. The maid retreated, only to return with the message, "Too busy." Yet again, the door was firmly shut.

Dad went in search of breakfast. Revived by a meal of brown bread and honey, strawberries and cream, he found a stream where he had a cold wash. He was ready, now, for his third attempt.

This time the footfall responding to his knocking was different, and the door was opened by a gentle-faced girl. Dad was over the moon, his elfin face beaming with relief and success. After chatting for a while he congratulated her on the ease with which she spoke English. His surprise was as great as hers when she replied, "But I *am* English." The girl was Iris Greep—Mum—who as a music student had won a scholarship to study the piano with Egon Petri, the leading Polish pianist.

They went indoors to a room with a piano, and Mum, who was shy in everything except her playing, immersed herself in an impromptu performance of Busoni. Dad then launched into Polish folk-songs with his accordion.

And—what luck—she loved walking, too. Mum, who usually never allowed anything to interfere with her piano practice, abandoned it immediately for her walking boots, and unplanned adventures with this exciting visitor from Jersey. Off they went into the mountains, walking much too far to return that night. They stayed in a shepherd's hut, along with other walkers, all sleeping in a row on the floor.

Walking and exploring for a further four days, they met, sang and danced with Polish peasants and were welcomed into their homes to eat with them. Mum wrote down the folk-songs as they were sung, and Dad accompanied on the accordion.

Two years later, on July 25, 1940, Mum and Dad were married in a register office in London. She was twenty-six and he was thirty-two. Their marriage certificate showed they shared an address, but I don't know if they were living together before they were married.

For their honeymoon, they stayed with Gran and Grandpa in their home in Devon, spending their days in idyllic happiness exploring Dartmoor, and their nights in the concrete shelter listening to the air raids.

CHAPTER THREE

Hilary

Dad signed up on July 21, 1941. Within two weeks, his enlistment papers had arrived and he departed for the Royal Military Training Camp at Lockerbie in Scotland. He was immediately popular with everyone, playing his accordion and leading sing-songs in the barracks. He found the training harsh and the separation from Mum almost intolerable, but was cheered by the fact that she was pregnant. She was busy teaching and broadcasting, and visited him as often as she could.

Two months later, with an impressive report, he went to Sandhurst.

I was born on April 25, 1942. Mum and I lodged with a Mrs. Macleod, in her large house in Woking, Surrey, and Gran was usually there too, helping to look after me. The Macleods grew all their own vegetables, made jam and kept chickens.

It was in Mrs. Macleod's garden that I first experienced the conscious feeling of love. There were wonderful borders bursting with color and I have a clear memory of Mum kneeling on the path, leaning over the blooms. I must have been very small as I remember looking up at her while she was picking the flowers, and can still see her young profile. She was wearing a blue and white striped dress and I was suddenly overwhelmed by a strong surge of love for her.

Shortly after I was born, Dad joined the Coldstream Guards and became a captain. Early in 1944, he heard he was to be transferred to Oxford, where he became a member of the Senior Common Room at Worcester College. The new post started on June 10, "in plain clothes." With a secure base, Dad was at last able to buy a house. We moved into 33 Beech Croft Road in Oxford on June 29. To celebrate, he bought a clarinet so he and Mum could play together. Dad loved college life. Wartime rationing was still severe, but he thrived on college dinners, and intellectually stimulating conversations with "highborn people."

Mum was unable to conceive a second child, so she went to the doctor for advice. Dr. Fraser prescribed mare's serum, a form of estrogen. While giving Mum the injections, Dr. Fraser joked, "This child will be a racehorse winner!"

The night before Jackie was born was the coldest for fifty years. Dad wrote in his diary:

January 25, 1945
To the doctor in the morning as the baby moved greatly during the night. Iris has to take castor oil tomorrow morning followed by two hot cups of tea.

January 26, 1945
At about 3 a.m. the pains started and we looked at the clock regularly until 3:45 a.m. I then lit the stove in the kitchen, made a cup of tea and we got dressed. We walked to the nursing home through the snow, admiring the silvery trail in the road. I left Iris with a jolly nurse and went home to do the chores, the fire and dustbins etc. until 5:30 a.m. Then to bed, but sleepless because I'd drunk too much tea. Up as usual, Matron kept me waiting. I telephoned at 9:15 a.m. for news—None. Was rung by Dr. Fraser at 11:30 a.m. to say, "A girl and all well." Cheers in the office. I saw Iris at 12:30. Jackie sweet and opened her eyes to talk to us.

I was two and three-quarters when Jackie was born. The day after her birth, Dad took me to Plymouth to stay with Gran. He planned to return the same day, but as I had a nasty cough which was worsening, he decided to stay overnight. In the event, he delayed his departure for a week. Grandpa had been complaining of stomach pains for some time and the diagnosis was indigestion. However, he suddenly became much worse and had to be taken into hospital. No reason for the illness could be found. Gran was naturally extremely distressed. I have often thought that looking after me must have been the last thing she wanted at that time but, nevertheless, I stayed with her for a further two weeks.

Then Grandpa slipped into a coma. Gran went to the hospital every day, leaving me with Auntie Em, her oldest sister. Gran was sitting at his bedside when he suddenly opened his eyes, looked at her and said:

"You don't need to worry, Maudie, I've been to a wonderful place which is full of angels, and they are waiting for me now."

He smiled at her, squeezed her hand, closed his eyes, and died.

The post-mortem revealed that he had a perforated duodenal ulcer.

Jackie was only twelve days old when Grandpa died and Mum was still in the nursing home. Although Dad knew that Mum would be profoundly upset, there seemed to be no best time to tell her. Without delay, he went to see her. She was breast-feeding Jackie when he arrived. The news was like a thunderbolt. Desperately shocked and confused, she could not believe her beloved father had gone. And yet, despite the numbness, she was elated and in love with her little baby girl. I think that the utter devotion Mum had had for her father was, at that point, transferred to Jackie. Her emotions were in excess of the normal softnesses and attachments that follow the birth of a child. An intense tie was formed in that moment, an extraordinary bond of love and dependency.

When Gran brought me home, Mum was completely absorbed with Jackie. Gran ran the house and looked after us all. Dad was back at work, but he made sure he had enough time to play with me, to go for walks and to build snowmen. He also washed Jackie's nappies every evening: twenty-four of them, all soaking in a bath tub. He was exhausted by the chores although he did them happily.

One of my earliest memories of Jackie was at her christening. As Dad was a member of the Senior Common Room of Worcester College, the Provost granted permission for Jackie to be baptized in the chapel.

While Mum was helping me put on my best dress, she told me what was going to happen: "I want you to be a very good girl today because there are lots of important people coming. It will be very quiet in the chapel. You'll hear the organ playing and if you look up at the roof, you'll see some very pretty patterns. But keep as quiet as a mouse. And at teatime afterward, you can tell me which colors you saw."

"Will I be sitting next to you, Mummy?"

"No, darling, I shall be holding Jackie. Auntie Vera will sit next to you, so you must stay with her." Aunt Vera was my godmother and Dad's boss. She was strict and I was frightened of her.

It was a beautiful, early autumn day and my friend Judith Herrin and I were having a wonderful time chasing each other on the grass in the quadrangle. Auntie Vera called in her crackly voice:

"Hilary, darling, it's time to come and say a prayer for Jackie. Let's go into the chapel with everyone."

She took my hand and led me toward the sounds of the organ. Mum was ahead of me, carrying Jackie, and Gran was with her. Dad was talking to Jackie's godparents.

I sat next to Auntie Vera and could see Jackie and Mum on the other side of the chapel. Suddenly the organ stopped and, in the momentary hush, Jackie chortled. Mum was flipping the pages of a book, making her laugh, but the organ started again and everyone stood and sang. Auntie Vera lifted me on to the pew and I became captivated by the mingling sounds. I caught Mum's eye as she pointed to the roof, and my gaze traveled back and forth across the pretty mosaics. I felt overwhelmed by the atmosphere and was totally absorbed.

Jackie was passed to a man in a white robe who was surrounded by the godparents. I heard the man say, "Name this child."

Quickly I struggled down from my perch next to Auntie Vera and ran across the chapel to Mummy. "It's Jackie," I announced, just as Jackie's godmother said, "Jacqueline Mary." There was a startled pause, and the vicar did not repeat her name.

When Dad was discharged from the Army a year later, in June 1946, he returned to his job in London as assistant editor of *The Accountant*. Soon we were on the move again, this time to 99 Beechwood Avenue, St. Albans, Hertfordshire, which was within easier commuting distance for Dad. He used to take me to kindergarten in the mornings on his bicycle, in a special seat on the back. I disliked going on the bridge over the railway track because I was

terrified of the noise and whistling of the approaching steam-
trains. The afternoons were spent playing or going for walks with
Mum, pushing Jackie in the pram.

In September 1947, Aunt Vera announced her retirement. Dad
was offered her job and was proud to become the editor of *The
Accountant.*

Despite his new responsibilities, he always had time for us. One
day we were in the kitchen, playing with Dad's collection of Jersey
granite and shells. I was swirling them around in a bowl of warm
water and watching as the pinks, grays, blues and yellows intensi-
fied. They were my special treasures. Mum, with the eighteen-
month-old Jackie on her knee, was singing a medley of nursery
rhymes, quietly harmonized by Dad. Just as Mum started "Baa Baa
Black Sheep," Jackie suddenly sat upright and joined in. Mum
stopped and Jackie carried on:

". . . have you any wool? Yes sir, yes sir, three bags full . . ." and
continued to sing the whole song to the end, on her own and perfectly in tune. At that time, I didn't understand why this was so
extraordinary but, as Mum told everyone about it with such pride,
I realized it must be important.

CHAPTER FOUR

Hilary

From as early as I can remember, Mum entertained us with music. She was always singing, playing the piano, clapping and stepping rhythms. Music was a wonderful game. As she played, we would skip and dance around the room, making shapes in the air according to the phrase shapes. We curled into the tiniest forms when the music was soft, and burst out jumping into the air when it was loud. We tiptoed and crouched for creepy music and skipped to dotted rhythms. We had to convey ferocity or tragedy and all as a spontaneous reaction to her playing.

When I was four, Mum started to teach me the piano. I would clamber on to the piano stool and line my tummy button up to middle C. My piano book with its black and white giraffes had something new on every page. Each time I mastered a piece with correctly shaped hands and fingering, I performed it from memory to Mum, Dad, Mrs. Latimer, our next-door neighbor—and sometimes the milkman. When Gran and Auntie Em were staying, we had a concert every evening after tea. I loved the performing, the delight it seemed to give, and being told to learn the next piece quickly, ready for another concert.

When learning a new piece, I wasn't allowed to look at my fingers, but had to concentrate on looking ahead at the music. However, when playing from memory, I could watch my fingers as much as I liked. Mum would talk to me about the contrast between making big sounds and little sounds, encouraging me to be aware of the different touches. I had to listen very carefully as every piece had to tell a story.

Playing the piano became second nature to me. I loved it and took it completely for granted. It was my time with Mum and she always seemed pleased with me, stopping anything she was doing to come and listen.

At the end of our garden in St. Albans, behind the runner beans, we had a large sandpit. I loved playing there. I had a metal bucket and spade, and shells of many different colors, sizes and shapes which I had collected in Jersey. I had, too, my special collection of granite pebbles, my rocks, which I stuck together with soggy sand. I made rows of purple top shells with yellow-golden winkle shells in between, and fairy circles of the pinky-white cowries.

One day, when I was five, Mum gave me three buckets of different sizes and a new spade with a red handle. I was thrilled and ran down the garden path, the buckets clattering within one another. I gathered all my shells into my old bucket and ran back to Auntie Em to ask her to wash them for me.

"Wait a minute, Hilary, and you can take them back with you."

But I couldn't wait, so Auntie Em, holding the three-year-old Jackie by the hand, brought my precious shells to me, cleaned and gleaming.

I was having a wonderful time. I had swept my rocks away and was making rows of castles in three different sizes. I had collected dandelion heads, buttercups and daisies, and was carefully decorating each castle. I planned to make a daisy chain, too, and thread it between them. But the shells were what I needed now, particularly the purple ones.

"Thank you, Auntie. Please take Jackie away. Don't tell Mummy what I'm doing. I want to give her a surprise."

They departed and left me to my world. I stuck the shells to the sides of the castles and made a cowrie path up to the main front door. I was so absorbed I did not hear Jackie returning and suddenly realized she was standing and watching me.

"Don't touch anything, Jackie, they're for Mummy."

"I want that bucket," she said, and launching herself into the sandpit, tripped over and smashed several of my precious castles. I screamed furiously, reached for my metal spade and hit her across the knuckles with all the force I could muster.

"Get off! Go away!" I shouted, as I rapped her knuckles again.

Jackie struggled to her feet, her dress and legs covered with damp sand. She was screaming and trampling her way out of the sandpit. She ran as fast as she could up the garden path, rubbing her eyes with her sandy hands, sobbing and calling, "Mum-my, Mum-my!"

I was left, surveying my broken world in fury and despair. I had to tell Mummy what Jackie had done: she shouldn't have done it, and I knew that Mummy would be cross.

Jackie was indoors, sobbing in Mummy's arms. The red, quickly bruising and swelling knuckles had already been discovered. Auntie Em was filling a bowl with warm water and Gran, as always, was fetching the butter to rub into the bruises.

"Mummy, she's bashed down all my special castles which I was—"

"Go straight outside, Hilary, and wait until I've made Jackie better."

I couldn't believe it. It was Jackie's fault, not mine. I tried protesting but was firmly guided outside and the door was shut. I burst into frustrated tears.

Jackie was calming down inside, responding to the murmurings, the warm-water bathing and the butter. I knew I couldn't repair my castles, and I didn't even want to try. All I could do was wait. Eventually, Auntie Em came out. She was the personification of gentleness.

"Come on, Hilary, let's go for a walk together. I've got a nice dry hankie in my pocket and a red sweetie. Come on."

She took my hand and we walked down the road to my special grassy patch, where the grasses grew taller than me. We sat down.

"Hilary, why did you hurt Jackie?"

"But, Auntie, she smashed my castles and spoilt my special present for Mummy."

"Darling, she's only three and I'm sure she didn't mean to do it. But you *did* mean to hurt her and you're bigger than she is. You must never, never do that again. Promise me you won't? . . . Poor Mummy, too."

Auntie Em took me on to her lap and gave me a cuddle. "Promise me you won't?"

"I promise."

She unwrapped the red sweetie and popped it into my mouth.

I was so restored by Auntie Em's softness toward me that the next morning I took Jackie by the hand and led her down to the sandpit.

"Jackie, let's make a surprise for Mummy. You have that end, I'll have this end, and we'll have a path down the middle."

We spent an extremely happy morning creating our highly decorated castle city. Occasionally, Auntie Em appeared just to see that we were all right but each time we asked her to leave us alone. We were making a surprise and she was not allowed to see it until it was finished.

The completion of the surprise and the admiration of the audience that surrounded us made Jackie and me fast friends. It was the first time we had worked side by side and achieved a successful goal. Thereafter, we did everything together; we became dependent on each other, indeed inseparable.

CHAPTER FIVE

Hilary

Piers was born in May 1948 and, with three children to accommodate, we needed a bigger house. In November, a month after Piers's christening in St. Alban's Abbey, we moved to Pine Lodge, 14 The Bridle Road, Purley, Surrey. Our new home was a 1930s semi-detached house, distinguished by a huge copper beech in one corner of the front garden. The house was spacious yet cozy, and provided everything we needed: three roomy bedrooms, two attic rooms and a cubby-hole office for Dad. Downstairs, a good-sized sitting room where the piano lived, a dining room and the kitchen. There was a fairly large garden, with my Wendy house at the end and, behind that, a wild area of scrub and flowers.

Jackie and I attended Laleham Lea pre-preparatory school. The friends we made there rarely came to our house. At home, Jackie and I always played together, creating our own world of adventure and fun. We shared a bedroom, her bed at one end and mine at the other, and in the security of our room we built camps and made imaginary journeys together. Dad made a huge doll's house, modeled on our house, with real electric lights, which stood in the center of the room. He also painted a large, friendly, fantastical creature, the Keekeewalapus, which started life as a telephone doodle but now hung proudly on our wall.

There was always something exciting to look forward to when we came home from school. I loved my daily piano lessons with Mum, after which we played musical games together.

We had been swaying about like sailors on a rough sea when Jackie said: "Mummy, can I be a soldier?"

"Of course, darling, and while you're on parade, Hilary can step quavers to each of your strides."

As soon as the speed was established, Jackie strode about the room while I, on tiptoe, ran two steps to each of her strides, keeping carefully in time with Mum's beat.

"Listen carefully," said Mum, "I'm going to alter the speed and, Hil, you change to semi-quavers."

The music slowed down and I fitted in four steps to each one of Jackie's.

"It's my turn now," said Jackie. "Hil, you be a soldier and I'm going to skip."

Mum continued playing, while we took it in turns to skip and march, still to the same beat and always in time together.

"I have another game for you now," said Mum. "I want you both to run in circles. Jackie in twos to my beat and Hil in threes. And, Hil, don't race too far ahead. Your steps will have to be shorter. When I say 'now,' swap over."

After a few bars, Jackie and I decided it was time for us to lead.

"Come on, Jacks," I whispered. "Let's be kangaroos and see if Mummy keeps up with us."

We suddenly leapt around. Mum immediately changed and followed us with bouncy music. It was impossible to catch her out.

"Who am I now?" said Jackie, putting her hands above her head and striding along.

"A giraffe?" I shouted with glee.

"No, silly. I'm Daddy!"

Mum's ability to involve us in music came directly from her own training in Dalcroze Eurhythmics. I don't think it was a conscious decision, but rather a completely spontaneous process for a mother to share the things she loved with her children. As our musical games progressed, it became natural for us to express emotion and tell stories through the language of music.

Every evening Mum bathed us and Dad always came to say goodnight. He told us stories and we planned adventures together. Mum could now have her precious moment of the day, when she sat at the piano and played uninterrupted. Jackie and I would lie in our beds, talking of Aladdin's cave and trunks of gold, while the strains of Mum's playing filled our room. We must have eventually drifted off to sleep because I never remember the music stopping.

A year after we had moved to Purley, Jackie had to go into hospital to have her tonsils removed. Gran was staying with us but Mum was having difficulty in keeping calm. She had been advised not to tell Jackie about the operation for fear of frightening her. Jackie was only four and running around thinking she was going on an outing. Mum's agitation was spilling into everything. Gran disliked it when Mum worried.

"What's for lunch, Gran?" I asked hopefully. Gran in the house meant delicious food on the table.

"I don't know, my little Hil. What would you like for lunch?"

"Roast chicken and potatoes with gravy," I said, without hesitation.

"Well, I don't know about that. Let's go and see what's in the larder."

At that moment, Jackie bounced into the kitchen looking perfectly fit and well.

"Mummy," she said, "I want to sing to you."

Mum was trying to read calmly to Piers, but paused while Jackie drew a deep breath and poised herself to begin. As Gran and I emerged from the larder, Jackie burst into song.

Away in a manger, no crib for a bed,
The little Lord Jesus lay down his sweet head . . .

Mum and Gran stood motionless as Jackie sang all the verses with startling emotion: it was a deeply felt performance. The moment she had finished, she smiled and ran off, leaving Mum and Gran in tears at the maturity of her singing.

Mum took Jackie by taxi to Purley Hospital. There, Jackie was delivered into the care of the ward sister, and Mum was told to leave. Furthermore, she was advised she would not be able to see Jackie for a week. No parents were allowed to visit for fear of upsetting their children.

Mum was distraught with worry. When the interminable week was over and the time came to collect Jackie, she found her in a state of deep shock: she had been abandoned, was terrified and lonely. Why had Mummy left her alone with strangers? Why had she left her in such a horrible place with other children who were all crying? Why had the doctors and nurses hurt her so much?

"I called for you, Mummy, again and again, but you didn't come."

Understandably, the whole appalling experience made Jackie insecure. She had become withdrawn and tearful. By contrast, I was so excited Jackie was home again I became too exuberant. Gran took me to Devon to allow Mum time alone with Jackie, and to give Jackie the peace and love in which to recover.

I remember our early childhood as being extremely happy, except that I was terrified of dogs. When I was four, I was walking with Gran and had run up a little path on my own. Suddenly I was attacked and knocked over by a large black dog which trampled on me, barking loudly. Gran heard my screams and came running to rescue me. The sight of Gran waving her arms and shouting made the dog run away, but my heart still pounds to this day at the sound of barking dogs.

There was always plenty to do. Our indoor camps were for wet days and we used furniture, blankets, and sheets in any arrangement. Chairs were piled on tables, covered with blankets and secured with heavy books. Sheets were slung and tied over the stairs. Gran made special feasts for us and we would hide in our private world for hours. We had a dressing-up box, and were occasionally allowed to use Mum's evening dresses.

When the weather was good we were always outside. One of our adventures involved an old pram. We would climb aboard and sail the oceans, coping with all kinds of dangers. There were pirates, sharks and shipwrecks, but somehow we managed to find our way home again—starving! Gran always had a favorite meal ready on our return.

One wet day, I had been sent upstairs for taking Jackie's chocolate biscuit and eating it. Mum's uncharacteristic outburst surprised me, but despite my protestations, I had to go to my room. While Mum was dispatching me, Jackie took Piers's biscuit and was caught as she gulped it down. Now it was Jackie's turn to be admonished. Mum guided the complaining four-year-old out of the kitchen and into the hall, shutting the kitchen door firmly behind her. Jackie's complaints instantly changed to desperate screams.

Hearing her cries, I rushed downstairs and found her banging the door with her right hand. The fingers of her left hand were trapped in the closed door.

"*Mummy*," I screamed. "Open the door. *Quickly* . . ."

Mum opened it immediately, to find Jackie's fingers squashed and white. As she comforted Jackie, Mum feared that she had ruined any hope of Jackie ever playing an instrument.

One day Jackie was in the kitchen at home with Mum who was ironing. The wireless was on and *Children's Hour* was presenting a program about the instruments of the orchestra. Mum was moving the iron in time to the music and Jackie was swaying from side to side in time with Mum's strokes. The flute, oboe and clarinet all had their turn, followed by the violins. As the sound of a cello filled the room, Jackie became completely still and attentive. She listened transfixed until the end, leapt up, clutched Mum's leg and said, "Mummy, I want to make *that* sound."

Mum was thrilled and, on the eve of Jackie's fifth birthday (January 1950), crept into her room and left a three-quarter-size cello at the end of her bed. In the morning an astonished Jackie woke the whole household as she rushed out of her room, shouting at the top of her voice.

"Mummy . . . Mummy."

She ran across the corridor into Mum's and Dad's bedroom.

"Mummy, wake up. Come and see. There's a whopping creature in my room!"

Jackie had never seen anyone play the cello and didn't know what to do with it. There were shrieks of delight and excitement as Mum sat her on a chair and placed the instrument in front of her for the first time. The fact that it nearly obliterated her with its size did not seem to matter at all. She was impatient for help. Mum put the bow in her right hand and Jackie took a great swipe at the strings. The cello grunted. "Gently, gently!" laughed Mum. "Stroke the string with the bow, like this." Mum guided Jackie's hand, drawing the bow slowly across the D string. The cello began to sing. For a while, the sound seemed suspended in silence. No one moved until Jackie beamed with joy.

"I can do it, I can do it!"

She was immediately in love with the instrument which soon became her favorite toy.

Mum had met Mrs. Garfield Howe, mother-in-law of the well-known pianist, Denis Matthews, when they were both adjudicating a music festival. Mrs. Garfield Howe agreed to come to our house on Saturday afternoons to give a string class. We were joined by our friends Margaret and Winifred Beeston. Margi and I learned the violin while Jackie and Freddie played the cello. From the beginning it was obvious that Jackie could easily do whatever was asked of her. She seemed to know the kind of sound she was after and how to produce it, having no apparent technical difficulties. I, on the other hand, could never make the violin sound lovely, and found it extremely uncomfortable.

In the absence of suitable cello music for very small children, Mum decided to compose pieces for Jackie. Mum had had several of her compositions performed by both amateurs and professionals: she had written a ballet, a viola sonata, an opera, piano pieces and some songs. Now she set about her task with enthusiasm, composing little tunes which she wrote in a notebook, calling the collection: "Jackie's First Cello Book." Each piece was illustrated with a drawing and a story: rhymes about the weather, a visit to the zoo, feeding the sea-lions, tales about witches, elves, jumping frogs, and many others all suited to five-year-olds. The words were set to the music.

Mum left the notebook at the end of Jackie's bed while she was asleep. In the morning, Jackie would find her new piece and Mum was woken by an excited child, tugging at her nightdress.

"Mummy, Mummy, wake up. I want to try my new piece! I want to play 'Brumas'."

Brumas was the new polar-bear cub we had seen the previous day at London Zoo. Mum struggled out of bed and put on her dressing gown.

First, Mum had to tune the cello.

"Play the A, Jackie, and tell me when it matches."

Jackie went straight to the piano, played the A and listened until it was perfectly matched.

"Stop, Mummy. That's right."

Mum quickly adjusted the other strings.

Jackie settled eagerly behind the cello, while Mum read aloud the poem which she had set to music:

"Have you seen Brumas, the new polar bear,
He's the sweetest wee pet you could find anywhere,
He's often in mischief and covered in dirt,
But his mother stays near him in case he gets hurt."

Each piece involved a new fingering or technical difficulty and Mum wrote the music to fit the rhymes, thus teaching Jackie how to find the emphasis.

"Brumas" was an exercise for the first finger and for string crossing, requiring Jackie to move the bow from one string to another, cleanly, and to make each note sound individually and clearly. Jackie imagined the words as she played and launched into the exercise with great gusto, playing it again and again and again.

By the time we came down for breakfast, Jackie, still in her nightie, was ready to give a performance.

Mum accompanied her on the piano. "Come on," she said. "Let's sing it with her." We all joined in, with Dad harmonizing.

Shortly after Jackie began playing the cello, Mum entered her for her first music festival in London. As soon as we arrived, Jackie raced down the corridor. The doorman stopped her.

"I can tell that you have just finished playing!"

"Oh, no," she replied. "I'm just about to play!"

She could hardly contain herself and was not in the least bit nervous. She was going to play her favorite new piece, the one Mum had left on the end of her bed three days before.

At last it was her turn. She passed her teddy to me.

"Rock him to sleep while I'm playing, Hil, and look after him."

Mum carried the cello as Jackie ran up on to the platform. The stool adjusted and the cello tuned, Mum handed her the instrument and she immediately started to play from memory:

Sleep, sleep, Teddy Bear . . .

Mum, who had not even reached the piano, returned to Jackie, and said quietly: "Hang on, Jackie, wait for me!"

Dear <u>MuMMy</u>

I Hope you are well. it was very Funny wher. daddy was Teaching me

From Jackie

Jackie looked up.

"Wait for me to sit down, and then I'll accompany you."

Jackie waited. Mum announced the title and they began together. From the first open G of the music, Jackie was totally absorbed. At the end of the little piece, Mum was just about to get up when Jackie started again. Mum sat down immediately and accompanied her again. One repeat was not enough for Jackie, but Mum was ready as Jackie went back to the beginning for a third time. Jackie obviously felt that three performances were just right, and looked up to a burst of applause and laughter from the audience. She handed her cello to Mum and skipped back to me and her teddy.

"Is he asleep, Hil? Give him to me gently."

Meanwhile, in our Saturday string classes, Jackie was advancing in leaps and bounds, while I was still struggling with the violin. Although I could play it, I disliked the sound and always found it uncomfortable. I loved the piano.

Early mornings in our house became hectic. Dad seemed to be working harder and harder and was usually up at the crack of dawn, sitting at the dining room table with his cup of tea, catching up on his paperwork. For a while now, in addition to Gran, we had had an au pair girl who cooked the breakfast of porridge, toast, eggs and bacon which we all ate together before setting off for the day. Gran helped with Piers so that Mum could spend time with Jackie and the cello.

When Jackie and I became more capable of practicing on our own, we started at 7 a.m.—Jackie at the top of the house, me in the sitting room. The neighbors were not pleased and began to thump on the wall. In due course, a compromise was reached: we could start practicing at 7:30 a.m. but if we started a minute too early, the thumps would fly. It must have been extremely irritating for the neighbors, but we wanted to practice and Mum would not allow anything to stop us. The older we became, the fiercer Mum was in her protection of us.

Practice times became a battle for me with the violin and I began to loathe the approach of the next lesson. Meanwhile, Jackie was rocketing ahead and attracting great interest. Fortunately it soon became clear that Jackie would need individual tuition so the

string classes with Mrs. Garfield Howe stopped, and I was allowed
to put away the violin forever.

Every morning on our Devonshire holidays at Gran's house,
Piers, Jackie and I piled into bed with Mum and Dad, and took it
in turns to dunk Rich Tea biscuits in their morning cups of tea.
Dad invented gripping stories, which he told us in instalments.
Gradually the smells of breakfast wafted upstairs: cereal with rich
Devonshire milk, bacon, eggs, tomatoes, mushrooms, toast with
golden butter, marmite or jam.

We set off after breakfast, as soon as the rucksacks were packed,
Dad in his hiking boots, clutching various maps and guides. We
left everything in a mess behind us, and never had to worry about
making our beds or tidying up. Gran and Auntie Em looked after
the house. They always packed a picnic for us: pasties wrapped in
newspaper and Auntie Em's homemade fruit cake. By the time we
returned in the evening, the house was organized and clean again,
and full of appetizing smells of supper, usually chicken with plenty
of vegetables and roast potatoes, and an old-fashioned rice pudding or junket for dessert. If we came back in time for tea, there
were scones, clotted cream (homemade, of course), jam and cakes.

One of our favorite places was Crazy Well Pool: a hundred-
meter-wide lake, which is said to be bottomless. Being difficult to
find, it was usually deserted, apart from Dartmoor ponies and
sheep. The water was always freezing, but Jackie could swim and
splash for hours and never feel the cold.

One day, we were walking back to the car when Jackie suddenly
burst into tears. Mum embraced her immediately.

"Whatever is the matter, Jackie?"

"I miss my cello," she sobbed. Leaving it at home was like aban-
doning a favorite toy or a comforter. From that moment on, the
whopping creature accompanied us everywhere.

It was Mrs. Holland who told Mum about the London Cello
School, at 34 Nottingham Place. Its patron was Pablo Casals, its
president Sir John Barbirolli, who had started his career as a cellist.
The principal was Herbert Walenn. There were three terms of
twelve weeks a year, and the fees ranged from £4.4s. to £12.12s.
per term, according to the length of lesson and the professor with

whom the student studied. The entrance fee was 10s.6d., and the school provided cellos.

Following Mrs. Holland's suggestion that Jackie should have an audition with Mr. Walenn, Mum, Jackie and I went to London. Jackie was five and a half and very excited.

When Jackie finished playing to him, Mr. Walenn lifted her on to his knee.

"I know the best person in the world to teach you, Jackie," he said, in a quiet, kindly voice. "She's called Miss Alison Dalrymple and she's waiting to see you."

He led us to Miss Dalrymple's room, where I waited outside. There was an air of solemnity and importance, and I seemed to wait for ages. Eventually they emerged, Mum carrying a different cello. Miss Dalrymple had replaced Jackie's whopping creature with a quarter-size instrument. Jackie was not entirely happy about this. She was, however, excited about her new achievements and the music she had been given. It was a lively journey home.

The moment we arrived, Jackie and Mum disappeared into the sitting room and, some while later, an exuberant Jackie ran out.

Jackie, Piers and I were all in the bath when Dad returned from work and as soon as Jackie heard the door latch she clambered out, splashing water and making puddles all over the floor.

"Daddy, Daddy . . . quick."

She ran out of the bathroom, pursued by Mum and a large towel. Dad was already on his way up the stairs. He caught the towel and wrapped Jackie up as she leapt wetly into his arms.

"Take me downstairs, Daddy, I want to show you—"

"Hang on, hang on, Jeetz, let me dry you first and put on your nightie, and then I'll have a look."

"But I want to play it to you now. Mummy, please will you tune it? Daddy, you mustn't look until I've got it. Wait here."

There followed an excited, happy concert, full of the possibilities and achievements of the day. An extremely contented Jackie went to sleep that night.

The cello school held regular concerts at Queen Mary Hall, Great Russell Street, London, where I usually performed as well. These were formal occasions, taking place in a large room with paintings which had been turned round to face the wall to hide their

nude subjects. Jackie and I wore our party frocks which were made
of translucent material with short puffed sleeves. The lining in
Jackie's was pink, with a broad satin sash, and mine was green.

On November 24, 1951, when she was six, Jackie took part in a
demonstration program by Alison Dalrymple's junior pupils. She
had long since mastered the art of vibrato and was thrilled by the
far-reaching world of new sound colors which this technique offered her.

She played three pieces: Andantino by Florembassi, Russian
Song by Fitzenhagen and *Wiegenlied* by Schubert. There was a
hush of anticipation when it was her turn. Taking her place in
front of the assembled group in an unassuming way, she paused
and slipped into a deep concentration before beginning. The focus
between Jackie, the cello and everyone in the room was direct and
powerful. She was speaking to me with her cello and the sound
which she loved so much had become her voice. It sent shivers
down my spine.

In December 1952, a month before her eighth birthday, Jackie received a letter from a secret benefactor. The letter said that since
she had been making such good progress with her cello-playing
and had worked so hard, she was to be given a new cello which
Mr. Walenn had helped to choose. It was a three-quarter size and
suitable for playing concertos.

CHAPTER SIX

Hilary

At the end of our garden, behind the Wendy house and underneath the old apple tree, was a rather rickety fence. Jackie and I discovered a loose strut which could easily be pushed aside. This was the gateway to our own secret world. We called it the bomb patch. It had been left alone since the war and was completely wild. For us it was a haven. No one used it, and we knew that we could not be seen. In spring and summer we could slip unnoticed through the fence and disappear among escaped garden blooms and myriad wild flowers growing in uninhibited profusion.

It was a haven, too, for caterpillars, and multi-colored butterflies. Feeling awfully brave, we would set off armed with sandwiches and jam jars with punctured paper lids. It was silent there and we talked only in whispers. First, we would set up camp. Our favorite was underneath the clematis because it smelt so delicious when in flower, and was so cozy inside. We found logs to sit on. Then, with our sandwiches carefully hidden in an old tin, we started the serious business of caterpillar hunting. The aim was to find as many different kinds as possible. We avoided the stinging nettles, but carried dock leaves in our pockets, just in case. We carefully took the lids off our jam jars and laid fresh leaves inside to make a cool mat for our colorful prisoners. With string tied tightly round the rim and a loop for a handle, we secured the paper lids with elastic bands. We loved watching the butterflies sunning themselves; the varieties and kaleidoscopic colors were a constant source of wonder. It seemed so strange that those delicate and fragile creatures had begun their lives as squelchy, soft, wriggling crawlers. As we moved forward, sprays of iridescent wings leapt silently ahead of us, and in the undergrowth, crawling under the stems, unsuspecting caterpillars were gently nudged into our jars.

Sometimes we ventured into the more densely wooded area, but that was rather frightening. In our favorite nursery-rhyme book there was a desperately sad picture of the Babes in the Wood, lost and clinging to each other. They never found their way home, so lay down and died and were covered with leaves by the birds. We could hear silence in the wood, so our visions of being lost forever were greatly heightened and sometimes more than we could bear, and we would rush out into the open and the sun again.

Often we crept along the perimeter fence to spy on other people in their gardens. There was a lady who wore make-up, a source of amazement to us, and we always peered through a hole in her fence, hoping for a glimpse of this elegant and opulent person. We were sure she must be very important with her bright red lipstick and long painted nails. She certainly would not be able to play the piano: our nails were always kept very short. A little further on lived a man with a huge nose which had rough bumps on it. His garden was well behaved and the flowers grew in straight lines. There was a pond in the middle, but we couldn't see what was inside.

When we were tired of spying, we picked bunches of flowers for Mum, but they had to wait for their water until after we had had our feast. And so we went back to the safety of our camp, and our picnic. The tin had guarded our spread well: Marmite and cheese sandwiches, with a tomato and, oh joy, a bar of chocolate each, rapidly softening in the heat.

"No rats here, Jack. Anyway, they couldn't gnaw through our tin. But listen:

> "In Hans's old mill, his three black cats
> Watch . . ."

And Jackie joined in:

> ". . . the bins for the thieving rats . . ."

Instantly we began acting as we recited in duo, each trying to out-perform the other.

> "Then down they pounce, now in, now out . . .
> At whisking tail and sniffing snout . . ."

"One line each now, your go . . ."

> "While lean old Hans, he snores away . . ."
> " 'Til peep of light at break of day . . ."

"Jack? Do you think we could stay here all night? If we had a torch we could carry on reading *Peacock Pie*. We'll ask Mum, but let's have our chocolate first."

We peeled the paper open and licked off the sticky chocolate, smudging it on our noses and lips. Suddenly we heard a voice from another world.

"Hil-lar-ry . . . Jack-kie . . . Time to come home . . ."

Gran sang her call and it traveled down the garden, over the fence and through the undergrowth.

"Come on, Jack, we must run."

Quickly we gathered our bags, our limp flowers, our jam jars with the caterpillars pressing on the punctured lids, and stumbled out of our camp. We ran as fast as we could with all our possessions and arrived home as triumphant hunters from the other world.

We had forgotten about staying the night, and were glad to settle into our cozy beds. As we lay in the darkness, Jackie whispered:

"Hil?"

"Yes?"

"Frogs in bed, frogs in bed . . ."

"All the way to strawberry jam. Frogs in bed."

And then we chanted it, on and on, as loudly as we could, kicking our legs on the bedclothes:

"FROGS IN BED, FROGS IN BED, ALL THE WAY TO STRAWBERRY JAM. FROGS IN BED."

On June 18, 1953, Jackie and I took part in the Coulsdon and Purley Festival. I was eleven and Jackie eight. We both won all our classes, including singing and reciting poetry, but Jackie had higher marks than me. Mum was walking on air. The vice-president told Dad that he had never known anyone, adult or child, to receive such high marks in a competition before.

The prize-winners gave a concert. It was on July 23, a day of great excitement for us, but we were kept calm and quiet, saving our energy for the playing itself. Our matching party frocks needed ironing and were hanging from the mantelpiece, and our sashes—one blue, one yellow—were in a heap.

As usual on concert days, Jackie and I were bundled upstairs for a good rest immediately after lunch. The curtains were drawn and we had to try to sleep. Gran was washing up downstairs; her splashing and singing had such a soporific effect we both drifted off.

I awoke first, and it was time for Mum to hear my pieces. She was very clever at keeping our pieces simmering, ensuring they would reach their peak just in time for the performance. First of all I had, as usual, to use the dining room table as an imaginary keyboard. Taking away the framework of the keyboard and the sounds of the piano tested my knowledge of the music.

"Let's play the Bach Invention first, Hilbil! Make me 'hear' all the shapes, and be sure you know where you are."

I set off on my journey through the F Major Invention. All the shapes, the spacing and the expression had to be there. It needed complete concentration to achieve a performance that Mum could "hear." She watched carefully and listened for the varieties of touch.

"Lovely, Hil! Now you can play it on the piano."

What a relief! And how easy the piano was after the table. Mum always had a suggestion for me to keep my performance fresh and alive: "Make those voices chatter, Hil . . . They keep on interrupting each other. That's it! And listen to them giggling now . . . Go on, make your audience laugh."

As soon as I had finished, I ran down to the bottom of the garden for a swing. I loved that. I swung high and looked over our secret bomb patch. From the sitting room I could hear Jackie and Mum playing and I knew that, in a moment, Jackie would want a turn on the swing.

At the concert hall, Dad found seats near the front and put programs on them for reservation. There was lively chatter as families arrived, the prize-winners in their best clothes, everyone jostling for seats and scanning programs to see when they were playing. Gradually, as people settled, a hush descended over the packed hall. The diminutive Mr. Bluett, Chairman of the Festival, walked on to the stage to welcome the great Dorothy Grinstead, who was to present the prizes. The concert began.

My turn came and I went excitedly on to the platform. I couldn't wait to play. I adjusted the height of the piano stool, and began. This was the culmination of all the preparation, the moment I had been waiting for, and I loved it.

First, the Minuet in G by Bach. I had to paint a picture of the dancers, where they were dancing, and who they were. I instantly found myself in my own musical world, unaware of anyone or anything else. I felt free and totally involved in what I was doing. I was in charge and the piano and the music were there for me.

Next came the Bach Invention and I embarked on my gossipy conversation running around the keys, listening to the sounds and the story in my head. It worked.

My pieces came to an end and I bowed to noisy applause and ran back to my glowing parents. The clapping continued.

"Go and bow again, Hil, go on," Mum said, as she pushed me back toward the platform.

Up I ran, my heart pounding with the thrill of success, and gave a sweeping bow to a sea of beaming faces. I knew I had played well and now *I* was walking on air, and Mum was extremely pleased with me. I *had* enjoyed myself.

I was in such a state of elation that, instead of returning to my seat beside Mum and Dad, I skipped off the platform and down to the end of the hall. Shortly after my turn, it was Jackie's. She was to perform the set piece, Purcell's Air in D minor. Mum climbed on to the platform with her and played the "A" on the piano for Jackie to tune. Silence descended, and Jackie began. Her concentration was so intense that it seemed as though the whole hall had stopped breathing while she was performing for them.

I loved her playing and had already heard this piece while I was on the swing, but now there was an electric feeling in the air. As the final note died away, the audience burst into spontaneous cheering.

When the clapping died down, the talking about her took over. Jackie returned to her seat, and she and Mum and Dad were quickly surrounded by a press of people offering their praises and asking questions. I knew that Dad would be the proudest man in the world that night and I wanted to be with them but was too shy to push my way through the crowd.

Dorothy Grinstead was now on the platform. What a commanding presence she was, towering above us in a glamorous long, green evening dress, the color set off by her silvery white hair. Mr. Bluett stood next to her and called out the winners' names. One by one, we received our prizes, shook Miss Grinstead's hand, and bowed. I was still so excited that, again, I skipped off the platform and carried on to the back of the hall.

And then it was Jackie's turn. Instead of immediately giving her the medals, Miss Grinstead beamed and launched into a speech about this remarkable child, her outstanding and rare playing and how lucky we were to hear her. A photographer was called on to the stage and Jackie was surrounded by important people as she was presented with her medals and a special prize for outstanding achievement. The audience rose to its feet as the cameras clicked.

Why wasn't I there too? Mummy was pleased with me and I knew that I had played well. Surely I should be there for the photos? Miss Grinstead must have forgotten to make a speech about me. Why didn't she call me back now? But she didn't. I stood on tiptoe, hoping to make myself seen, but no one saw me. Suddenly I felt very alone. Every muscle in my body was straining for recognition but it didn't come.

All eyes and all attention were on Jackie. We had always done everything together, but now we were separated and I felt frantic. I turned and ran: ran out of the door at the back of the hall, and along a dark corridor. Applause seemed to follow me but no one was calling me back. I was crying and felt bereft and completely forgotten. I dashed through an open door into a huge kitchen and shot under a table, dropping my medals on the floor. I buried my head against my knees and sobbed and sobbed. My mind raced in a whirl of loneliness, dismay, failure. I was lost.

I don't know how long I stayed there, but after a while my crying lessened and I knew the only way I could cope would be to go back, smiling and joining in. I came out from under the table, shook my frock to uncrumple it and drank some cold water. Gran had always given me a glass of water and washed my face if I had been crying. So I did that now. I gathered up my medals and re-traced my steps.

The concert and prize-giving were over, and there was a jostle of people chatting and preparing to leave.

No one had missed me.

When eventually I found Mum and Dad, I told them I had a headache—which was true. I don't think they ever found out what had actually happened.

Although at the time it was ghastly for me, this experience stood me in very good stead for the future. I had been acutely aware of the speed with which Jackie learned and progressed: people had already begun to say, "Hello Hilary, how's your wonderful sister?" The shock of the Purley concert taught me how to enjoy and take part in the overwhelming interest in Jackie, and it made me more mindful of what she was doing. It also made me very conscious of my own capabilities and limitations. I learned to protect myself against attacks of envy and misery, but became fearful of not suc-ceeding, of not being good enough. In my heart of hearts I knew that Jackie was speeding ahead of me and I couldn't keep up.

CHAPTER SEVEN

Hilary

Jackie and I disliked school. Neither of us was a successful class or team member. We had no pack instinct and made no effort to be one of the crowd. Uninspired by academic subjects, we just coasted along without any dedicated input. Although it is said that maths and music go together, it certainly was not the case with us. We abandoned math at an elementary level—when we were confronted with square roots.

Mum had no compunction about taking us out of school for any kind of musical activity and, as we much preferred being involved with rehearsing and performing, we were only too happy to be withdrawn. One day one of the teachers, Miss Mounsey, called Jackie to the front of the form and said, "We have a girl in this class who thinks she's very special and different from the others, but I can tell you that she isn't."

Jackie began to be difficult in the mornings.

"Come, on darling, eat up. We need to get going or we'll all be late."

Jackie looked quiet but determined. "Hil and Piers can go, but I'm staying at home today."

"Not today, Jackables, it's a school day."

"I'm not going."

Mum knew the signs well and tried to coax her. "Come on, darling. You'll be fine once you're there and Rebecca will be waiting to play with you. We mustn't let her down."

It was Piers's turn now. "I want to stay at home too, Mummy. Please. I don't like school either."

"Barzi, darling, have a race up to the bathroom with Gran . . .

Mother, will you take Piers upstairs and help him get ready, please?"

"Of course I will, bless his little heart. Come on, darling, we must put your tie on and you can choose one of my sweeties." That was always a successful bribe.

Mum put her arm round Jackie. "I tell you what, we'll have a *special* tea when you come home. How about chocolate cupcakes?"

But Jackie was still determined.

"Mummy, I'm not going. I don't want to go."

And she burst into tears.

"No one likes me at school. It's horrible. They all tease me."

"Don't cry, darling, you'll make your eyes all sore. Here, blow your nose."

I didn't want to go to school either, so I joined in. "Mummy, there's no point in me going to sch-"

"Hilary, run upstairs and do your teeth. Quickly, now, I don't want you to miss the bus."

"But, Mummy . . ."

"Look, Hullaballoo, don't make it more difficult. Just go and do as I've asked and let me cope with Jackie."

As I ran upstairs, I could hear Mum trying to cajole Jackie, but to no avail.

". . . Anyway," Jackie pleaded. "I want to learn my new pieces and play them with you."

That always worked.

I reappeared.

"Have you put everything in your satchel, Hil? It's time to go."

We all went down to the bus stop together and waited. Piers and I climbed on the bus, and waved goodbye to Jackie, Mum and Gran.

Jackie became aware of how successfully she could communicate through music and how accurately her emotions and feelings could be heard and understood. This was made evident by the deep emotional reactions so often shown by her audience.

Near the end of term, she was waiting to play three short pieces in the Junior School concert. Mum was there to accompany her. Miss Mounsey was sitting near the front with several important guests, and Jackie had chosen a seat where she could keep a careful

eye on her. I sat next to Jackie and, as we listened to the many so-
los, duets and ensembles, we wrote messages to each other on the
back of the program, and drew caricatures of Miss Mounsey.

At last it was Jackie's turn to play. As Mum squeezed past me,
smiling and wrinkling her nose, Jackie leaned over and whispered
in my ear: "You watch, Hil, I'm going to make Miss Mounsey cry."

One of the pieces was from Saint-Saëns's *Carnival of the Animals*.
Even before the accompaniment had started, Jackie's concentration was so intense, she was already in another world. Mum began
with the soft, floating introduction on the piano, setting the scene
of a still lake. When the swan floated into the music, the serene,
majestic theme on the cello immediately penetrated our senses,
and the entire audience became still, as if our hearts had stopped
beating.

It wasn't long before several people were dabbing their faces
with handkerchiefs . . . including Miss Mounsey.

In March 1954, Jackie and I were entered for several classes in the
Bromley Festival: Jackie in the string section and me in the piano
section. We had also learnt the Sonatina by Beethoven for the
chamber music class. Mum always put a lot of emphasis on the
importance of listening to our accompaniments carefully, but this
piece was to be played as a duo, both parts being of equal importance. She taught us to treat the duo as a conversation, and to
recognize musical give-and-take.

We climbed on to the platform together and bowed; Jackie po-
sitioned her chair, tuned, and we played. Despite Mum's teaching,
the moment Jackie was on stage, the piece was no longer a duo
but a solo. I had no option but to follow as her accompanist.

The adjudicator, Herbert Withers, gave a perceptive and pro-
phetic appraisal: ". . . A great pleasure again to hear sisters playing
together. If this arrangement is supposed to be chamber music, the
cellist should not play from memory and sit as if she were playing
a solo. They both played very well but it was not chamber music.
The pianist must not be pushed into the background."

During our annual summer holiday in Jersey, we were singing and
making music after tea as usual, when Pondles, who had been
playing his flute, suddenly handed it to me.

"Here, Hil. See if you can make a sound on this."

Having never been allowed to touch his beautiful dark wooden flute, I could hardly believe I was now holding it.

"Can I?"

"Yes, of course."

As I had watched Pondles so often, there was no difficulty in putting my fingers in the correct positions. I lifted the flute, blew across the mouth hole and instantly made a sound. He was astonished and I was electrified. Without thinking, I began experimenting with fingerings and playing simple tunes. Pondles had just been playing *Jesu, joy of man's desiring*, so now I played it to him. He was overcome by my instant ability and obvious love for his beloved instrument.

"Hilary . . . . I'd like you to keep it."

I just looked in disbelief.

"I mean it, you should have it. Learn to play it and enjoy it."

He was in tears.

During the autumn term Mum searched for a flute teacher and found Samuel Foster, an elderly gentleman who lived nearby. Unfortunately, Pondles's flute was high-pitch, which didn't match the current tuning requirements. I needed to learn on a modern, low-pitch instrument, but continued to play Pondles's flute until another could be found. Later it was reserved for holidays when we played and sang together.

Mr. Foster made inquiries of Rudall, Carte and Co. in London about the cost of a new sterling silver Boehm flute (low-pitch) and a fitted case. The price quoted was £190.8s.—far more than Mum and Dad could afford at that time. Yet I was not without a modern flute for long. One day, I came home from school to find a brand-new Rudall Carte flute, a gift from Jackie's cello benefactor. I was more excited than I had ever been. My sights were set and I could start my lessons.

Mum's supreme gifts were teaching and fostering musical ability. When Jackie began to reveal her talent and passion for the cello, the whole focus of the family changed. In her playing, Jackie demanded everything and gave with total generosity. It was the same with her relationships. And Mum was devoted to fulfilling all those needs.

Jackie's need for Mum was so great that anyone close to her was perceived as a threat. This included Dad, and a tussle for Mum's attention and affection was established between Jackie and Dad.

I maintained my closeness to Mum through music, but Dad became more and more isolated. Although he was musical, he was not trained in music, couldn't express himself through it on the same level, and had no comprehension of the background requirements. However, we adored it when he played his accordion at our parties, and loved listening to him playing and singing Ukrainian folk-songs. Mum tried to teach him to read music but as he played so well by ear he found it unnecessary. Even though Dad often felt left out of the music-making, he was incredibly proud of us, and his role was in keeping information about our concerts and achievements, and answering correspondence. He trusted Mum to make all the musical decisions.

Piers had a great struggle. It was easier for Jackie and me: we were both willing and natural musicians and therefore on a direct wavelength with Mum. Piers had musical talent, and his ear and ability were as keen as ours. But because he resisted, he lost out, and it took him much longer to find a platform from which to shine. Watching his sisters must have been very hard for him.

Of course it was understandable that Jackie should be dependent on Mum while she was small, but, as she grew, the affinity between them became so powerful that they were almost inseparable. I mentioned earlier how I believed it was Mum's father's death at that crucial moment after Jackie's birth that laid the foundations for the strength of their bond. Recently, I was talking with a child psychiatrist at the Tavistock Clinic who told me that many psychological conditions are triggered by an event in very early life, often around birth. A baby senses if its mother is grieving or depressed and as a result clings to the mother, and she in turn, clings to the child; the baby is in effect protecting and nurturing the mother for its own sake, for, of course, the baby's need of the mother is paramount.

As Dad's feeling of isolation increased, he relied more on his friends, particularly Arthur Mourant, known to us as Lalla. He was my godfather and a very beloved one, too. He came to our house almost every weekend. A Pied Piper figure, he willingly joined in our games and listened to us playing our pieces. He was the first person we had encountered who couldn't sing, and it was a source of astonishment and disbelief to hear his tuneless groanings.

Theirs was an unlikely friendship: Dad loved sailing and climbing mountains; Lalla disliked such activities. However, geology was a common interest and Lalla, as in most things, was an expert.

Happy to scramble through bushes or climb trees, Lalla paid no heed to rips in his clothes. One day we took him through the fence behind the Wendy house.

"Promise you won't tell anyone, Lalla?" I said. "This place is just for Jackie and me."

He entered into our world with a child's excitement, allowing us to lead him through the undergrowth to our camps. "Look at the butterflies, Lalla. There are millions of them!"

"Do you know their names ?" he asked.

"Yes. Mum showed us in her book. That's a purple emperor—there—look!"

"Did you know," said Lalla, softly, "that butterflies have been living here since before man was created—they were around with the dinosaurs, forty million years ago."

"How do you know that?" I asked.

"Because a scientist found a fossil of a butterfly in a lake in Colorado, and by doing certain tests, was able to tell its age."

He was about to give us a natural history lesson when he heard Dad calling him.

"Coming Derek," he shouted. "Just a minute . . ."

And turning to us asked, "Would you like these Jersey toffees in your camp?"

He departed, crashing his way clumsily toward the fence and leaving us on our own.

It was in the intensity of our scented camp that we shared our deepest thoughts and observations which we vowed we would never divulge. We talked profoundly about the future, too, although we were in no hurry to get there. Grown-ups had to do so much they didn't enjoy. We knew Dad didn't like going to work, and that Mum loathed the social functions he had to attend. She was supposed to go with him, but he usually went alone. Jackie and I were certainly in no rush to grow older.

The toffees were becoming sticky and the paper had to be peeled off. We sucked and chewed until several had been consumed. Unwrapping the last one, Jackie suddenly looked at me with an intense expression, and confided a whispered secret.

"Hil?"

"Mmm . . ." I responded, my jaws clamped together by toffee.

"Don't tell Mum but . . . when I grow up, I won't be able to walk or move."

Neither of us stirred or spoke. We just stared at each other.

CHAPTER EIGHT

Piers

Someone suggested that Hilary should appear on the television program *All Your Own*, produced by Cliff Michelmore and presented by Huw Wheldon. We didn't have a television at home but Mum wrote to register Hilary's name.

She was invited to audition on Friday, December 31, 1954, at the television studios in Lime Grove, Shepherd's Bush. She had to prepare a five-minute program and wear something that wouldn't require changing-room facilities. Later that day, the BBC telephoned to say that Hilary had been successful.

Early in the New Year, a formal contract arrived: Hilary would receive a fee of one guinea to play the piano. They would pay traveling expenses of 12s.6d. and a meal allowance of 6s. If the program was repeated, Hilary would receive 10s.6d. for each repetition.

The day before the broadcast, the *London Evening Standard* printed a picture of the three of us: Hilary at the piano, Jackie with her cello, and, to complete the trio, Hilary's cast-off violin under my arm. I have never played the violin and certainly had not the faintest desire to do so, but the photographer had insisted. My dismay is clear in the pictures, and I am asked to this day if I still play the violin. *The Times* newspaper quoted Mum saying "Hilary's ambition is to be a concert pianist."

Hilary only had one rehearsal on the day of the recording, and she was the last to play. As the others finished, they all looked so miserable that Mum began encouraging Hilary to be cheerful and enjoy it. Hil was unaware that the program was going out live and played her pieces brilliantly: Humoresque by Bantock and Solfeggietto by Bach. The interview with Huw Wheldon afterward went so well that the producer in the control room sent a message to keep her talking. As a result, they ran overtime.

Outside the studio, when Hilary was asked for her autograph, Dad whispered, "Don't sign your name, write Anne Meadows."

Dad had always been fiercely protective of Hilary and Jackie at concerts. He was concerned that they might sign their names unknowingly to something and later be taken to court. Consequently, Hilary became Anne Meadows while Jackie was Mary Meadows, derived from their middle names with "Meadows" as a translation of du Pré, which means "of the field."

Mum and Dad received hundreds of letters complimenting Hilary on her performance and Dad replied to them all.

Hilary

As a result of my TV appearance on *All Your Own*, other opportunities presented themselves. Mum was asked to rehearse and conduct Haydn's *Toy Symphony* using her pupils as players. As the minimum legal age for a musician to perform on television was twelve, Jackie, at ten, was too young to play her cello. However, a loophole in the rules was discovered: the toy drum didn't qualify. I played the piano and Mum's pupils played the string parts and the other toy instruments. Rehearsals were great fun, but I was astonished to find how strict and authoritative Mum could be when training us all together.

On the day of the performance we were ferried to London in various cars. As usual our excitement was controlled, but, on arrival at the studio, we were overcome by the bright lights, the men sitting on huge moving cameras, yards of cables all over the floor. First we had to do a microphone test. One by one we played our instruments: the piano first, followed by the violins, cello, cuckoo, quail, toy trumpet, warbling bird and, last of all, drum. Jackie gave it an enthusiastic thwack and went right through! There was a gasp, followed by laughter, and a studio runner was sent off to find a more resilient drum.

The rehearsal over, there was a rush for the canteen where we were allowed to choose our lunches—what a treat!—and we knew we were sitting among the famous. Afterward, it was time to wash, brush and change. The make-up lady decided that Jackie and I had to have our eyebrows darkened, otherwise, on black and white television, we would appear to have none.

We assembled in the studio in our places, tuned carefully and sat in silence waiting for the red light. All went as planned and we gave a lively performance which was so successful that we were asked to perform Reinecke's *Toy Symphony* four months later.

Early in 1955, Jackie was feeling rather restricted by her lessons with Miss Dalrymple, and Mum knew it was time to find another teacher. Mum had never forgotten the cellist Bill Pleeth, whom she had met when they were students. She hadn't been in touch with him since, but she knew he was now a professor at the Guildhall School of Music and was much in demand as a teacher. She had to muster all her courage to telephone him and decided she would try only once. If he was not there, she would look elsewhere. After many days of hesitating, she telephoned. He was in. There had been a last-minute alteration to his teaching schedule that day. So it was by lucky coincidence that one of the great teacher–pupil partnerships of this century was formed.

Jackie was ten when Mum took her to Bill's house in Finchley. He had expected her to be precocious but, instead, found her both unaffected and unspoilt. For a child, she made an unique impression of simplicity and quietness. He sensed that she might have been held in check by a family that was possibly strait-laced, but when she played he knew that inside this little girl was something musically explosive and unending. He couldn't wait to let her off the reins to see where she would lead.

In September 1955, when I was thirteen, I was invited to play the Bach F minor Piano Concerto on television with the Royal Philharmonic Orchestra conducted by Eric Robinson. It was my first opportunity to play with a professional orchestra and I was delighted. I didn't need any persuading.

Although there was only one orchestral rehearsal on the day itself, Mum had frequently rehearsed with me, playing the accompaniment on another piano, making me well aware of the background. Fortunately, a near neighbor in Rose Walk had four pianos in one room, and allowed us to rehearse there.

What a day it was! Another adventure to the studio. For me,

these occasions were pure joy. Mum and I left home early in the morning, and I was so excited I couldn't wait to arrive. In the canteen, I found myself gazing in awe at the actors in their costumes, the presenters, the musicians, and technicians: I was glimpsing another world. An arm round my shoulders brought me back again.

"You must be Hilary du Pré? I'm Eric Robinson."

We shook hands.

"How are you? Not nervous, I hope?"

"Will there be a chance for Hilary to try the piano?" Mum asked.

"Well, actually, I thought you might like to have a run-through now, before the orchestra finishes its break."

"Oh, yes please. I'd love to."

The three of us walked down long corridors to the studio. In front of the empty orchestral seats was a piano: a huge Steinway concert grand. I'd never played one that size before.

Mum stood beside me as we worked through the score, picking out excerpts to demonstrate my speeds. Mum had warned me that the conductor might request different tempi or dynamics, but he didn't. As we were finishing, the orchestra began to return and the studio was quickly filling with musicians. I stopped playing and sounds of tuning and warming up took over. A tap on the conductor's stand silenced everyone.

"Gentlemen, may I introduce Hilary du Pré?"

There was a clattering of bows on music stands in welcome.

"Hilary, would you give us an A, please . . . Thank you. We'll go from the beginning."

He raised his arms and we were off. How different and how much more thrilling the orchestral background sounded in comparison with the piano accompaniment. I kept my own tempi and Eric Robinson followed.

At the end of the rehearsal, there were more tappings from the orchestra and I was whisked away to have my eyebrows darkened.

As I was so used to playing to an audience, the fact that the program was live didn't inhibit me at all. The broadcast began with Eric Robinson interviewing me. He had his arm round my shoulders while he was chatting and he was shaking all over—I felt I was propping him up.

Once at the piano, I disappeared into my world of Bach. I was in seventh heaven.

Later Mum explained that Eric Robinson was nervous. It was the first time I had come across nerves. Performing was such a habit for us—it was as natural as eating a meal. Being nervous was something I did not apply to myself at that time.

Early in 1956, Bill suggested that the eleven-year-old Jackie should be entered for the Suggia Gift, a new source of funding for young cellists. He knew that Mum and Dad needed financial help to pay for Jackie's lessons, and, although the award was intended for older students, felt Jackie stood a chance.

Guilhermina Suggia, the flamboyant mistress of Pablo Casals, was one of the few women cellists to rise to fame this century. She died in 1950, and in her will stated that her Stradivarius cello should be sold to fund a trust for talented cellists. The Arts Council of Great Britain was appointed to administer the fund for the benefit of students of any nationality and in particular players aiming to become soloists. A distinguished panel, led by the conductor, Sir John Barbirolli, was formed and included eminent figures from the music world: Ambrose Gauntlett, Ivor Newton, Bernard Shore, Lionel Tertis. Suggia had instructed that no women should be on the panel.

Bill wrote a letter of recommendation about Jackie:

Apart from one other, Jacqueline du Pré is the only child cellist to pass into my teaching classes. She is the most oustanding cellistic and musical talent that I have met so far, to which she adds incredible maturity of mind. I am of the opinion that she will have a great career, and deserves every help to this end.

Mum accompanied Jackie in a recital of pieces which had been carefully selected by Bill. A few minutes into the performance, Sir John Barbirolli leaned over to Lionel Tertis and whispered in his gravelly voice:
"This is it. This is it."

One of the conditions of the award was to practice for four hours a day and, as a result, Jackie virtually left school at the age of eleven.

At first her teachers tried to persuade Mum and Dad that she should continue to attend school full time, but she was profoundly unhappy there and her misery was becoming too heavy and constant for Mum to bear. Often Jackie came home in tears, complaining of bullying and teasing, and of being on the receiving end of cruel rhymes.

The opportunities that the Suggia Gift offered were too important to be ignored. Mum, knowing that Jackie could no longer flourish in a "normal" situation, was only too relieved that her gift and astonishing ability had been recognized by celebrated professionals.

The headmistress of Croydon High School agreed that Jackie should reduce her academic timetable to four subjects only: Math, German, English and French. Mum drove Jackie to school for her lessons, waited, and returned with her immediately afterward, which sometimes necessitated as many as four return journeys a day. Jackie was delighted with this arrangement. Although leaving school narrowed her horizon in one direction, it freed her from the torment of school life and released her to her music, allowing her the time and space to progress with astonishing speed.

I, too, had few interests in common with my peers. I loathed popular music and stupidly made it clear to everyone. When my class started bringing their transistors to school to play between lessons, I would go out of the room. Eventually transistors were banned: someone had complained, and it was assumed to be me. It wasn't.

To my great joy, it was decided that I should reduce my school timetable on the same basis as Jackie. I was fourteen and studying for O levels, but had already missed a great deal of school, having had twenty-six days off during the previous term alone for various musical activities. It was agreed that I should study English language, English Literature, French and Scripture only, and that Mum would coach me for music O level at home.

On Wednesdays and Saturdays, Mum took Jackie to London for her lessons with Bill: one at the Guildhall School of Music, the other at his home. The journeys to London each week were made in our new car, a dark green Wolseley 12 which had been given to us by Uncle Bill, Gran's surviving brother, who adored his musical niece. The journey took a long time as Mum's maximum speed was twenty-five miles an hour. The Suggia Trust paid for the fuel and, during the Suez Crisis, when petrol was rationed, Mum was given extra coupons to ensure the London journeys would not be jeopardized.

Mum could be delightfully absent-minded and disappear into daydreams. One day she was driving us all to the Guildhall School for Jackie's lesson and we were late. We arrived at a junction where the traffic lights had failed and a policeman was on point duty. Somehow Mum didn't see him. Edging her way forward to turn right, there was a bump. As Mum looked round to see what had happened, the policeman picked himself up, walked round to the driver's side, and knocked on the window. Winding it down, Mum said: "I'm frightfully sorry, I simply don't have time to chat." She wound the window up, and drove off, blissfully unaware that she had knocked the poor man over.

Bill wasn't surprised to learn that Jackie hardly ever practiced.

He says: "You cannot regiment certain temperaments against what that temperament, by instinct, feels it has to do. There is a naturalness which mustn't be destroyed. You would be surprised at how much tension is created by saying to someone that they have to practice for five hours a day. It's like a doctor prescribing the same pill for every illness. Sometimes just thinking about the music can be enough. It's the quality of the practice that matters and not the duration."

Jackie had two physical problems which needed resolving. Two fingers of her left hand were the same length, making certain hand positions awkward. The other problem was that her third finger caved in at the top joint. An adjudicator at one of the festivals had pointed this out and felt it should be corrected. Bill was unconcerned, but where necessary he was inventive. To prevent her from gripping the bow and causing tension in her arm, he suggested she should put her little finger behind the frog of the bow, a trick which worked well and one which she used throughout her career.

Jackie had been thoroughly grounded by Miss Dalrymple and had no bad habits, which meant that Bill had a clean canvas to work on. The ingredients were all there: a passionate desire to learn and absorb any music put in front of her, a vivid and colorful imagination, the ability to understand and express deep and often complex sentiments in the music, and a fearless love of performing.

Bill was probably the only person who could let Jackie "off the reins." He offered her a freedom which allowed her to gallop with breathtaking speed. She was a wild horse, cleverly guided through a unique journey of discovery.

The world is full of copies created by teachers whose over-developed egos are efficiently imposed upon their unsuspecting and receptive pupils. Bill never forced any dogma or restrictions on Jackie, but constantly opened pathways and fed her unspoilt imagination with new ideas. Her innocence and natural pliability were ideal for Bill's style of teaching.

Often, lessons were filled with conversation which fueled the vital dreaming and inspired her playing. Jackie spent remarkably little time practicing, but her music was always racing around her head. She was fortunate in having no technical barriers, allowing her "thoughts" to be immediately voiced with her cello.

Bill taught the whole Jackie. There were no divisions, no seams, but a complete melding of all the elements, the ingredients of which grew into a oneness, a circle, which had no start and no finish. Bill's and Jackie's partnership was perfect.

In the meantime, I was improving so quickly on the flute that Mum decided I should attend the junior department of the Royal Academy of Music to study the flute with Derek Honner, and the piano with her former professor, Eric Grant, who had already given me some lessons on my Bach F minor Concerto.

The flute lessons were the highlight of my week. Derek Honner was the ideal teacher for me, giving me exactly what I needed at that time, and enabling me to race ahead. He stretched me by giving me advanced music which I loved and responded to eagerly. He taught me technique by encouraging me to listen critically to what I was playing, and to be aware of how it was achieved. He was skilled at binding technique and music together so there was no separation between the two, and took it for granted that I would be able to do anything he asked. This alone gave me increasing confidence.

I traveled to London on my own, by Greenline coach or by train. Although I was fourteen, the journey frightened me and I always sat next to the alarm chain. After my lessons, Dad would meet me at Victoria Station and we would return home together. These journeys I loved; we always had Horlicks and peanuts at the station as we waited for the train.

In January 1957, I was invited to perform in the Vivaldi Concerto for four pianos in a Young Persons' Concert on BBC Children's Television. Mum chose the other three pianists, three girls we had met at Festivals: Diana Knowles, Hilary Page and Caroline Richards. We all learned our parts and had weekly rehearsals with Mum. Keeping four excited girls together and teaching them to play without one of them hurrying ahead or lagging behind, was quite a task. The four pianos gleamed under the spotlights and the conductor, Stanford Robinson, Eric's brother, seemed to enjoy himself too. We were followed by the same concerto performed on violins by four boys.

That summer we had a Jersey holiday, staying with Gannie and Pondles. Our first day was scorchingly hot and we spent it at Archirondel, swimming, building sand fortresses and having races up the breakwater. Dad sculled his small white rowing boat, *Dodo,* into the bay and Jackie and I took turns to row to St. Catherine's breakwater where we moored, and dived over the edge to swim to the slipway. The huge granite stones were warm and the sea was gently lapping against them. We couldn't spend too long there as we had promised to meet Gannie and Pondles at Mrs. Lecouteur's for tea. So we scrambled back into *Dodo* again and headed for Archirondel.

Gannie and Pondles were waiting at our usual round table with its cream-colored sunshade. We arrived pink from the day's sun, our tousled hair bleached and stiff with salt, extremely hungry and thirsty. Mrs. Lecouteur knew exactly what Gannie liked and appeared bearing pretty china plates heaped with tiny sandwiches. Gannie poured the tea from a blue and white floral teapot that was kept there for her use alone.

After tea, we dashed back to the sea with Gannie in tow to watch us swim, each showing off something special learnt that day. Then we went to find Pondles who was waiting with Mum and Dad, the flute and the cello.

"I'm longing to hear you play my flute again," he said to me. "What will it be?"

"I'll play my Handel: a slow movement and a fast one. And Jackie can play the cello part. That means I'm the soloist and she's the accompanist! She doesn't really like that, do you, Jack?"

"Now, now, Hilary, none of that. Pondles wants to hear you both," intercepted Mum.

So I played the Handel F major Sonata with Jackie as continuo. Pondles was delighted. "I don't think my old flute has ever enjoyed itself so much. It makes a much better sound for you than it ever did for me! . . . Go on playing, my little Hil, and make sure you have the best of teachers. That's what I want you to do. Now, Jackie, how about something from you?"

Jackie was just thirteen when Bill thought that she was ready to tackle the Elgar Concerto. Elgar was sixty-two and near the end of his composing life when he finished his cello concerto, shortly after the end of the First World War. It is a work of intense nostalgia; a looking-back from the ebb tide at the fading past, reflecting the poignant feeling of exhaustion after the "war to end all wars."

The music is very romantic, with exuberant leaps in the melody and quixotic changes of mood. Quite apart from the technical difficulties of playing the notes, the music requires great depth of emotional understanding. Bill had believed for some time that Jackie, with her instinctive musicality and natural gift, would be able to cope with a work of mature intensity, and felt that stretching her would give him more insight into her potential.

After the Wednesday lesson, he asked Mum to buy a copy of the Elgar, along with the Piatti Caprices.

"Take your time," he had said to Jackie. "Don't rush. Just sketch it slowly and see what you can do with it."

Mum telephoned our local music shop in Purley, and collected the two works on Thursday afternoon.

One and a half days later, at Jackie's Saturday lesson, Bill suggested that they might start by looking at the first Piatti Caprice and then begin to map out the Elgar. Jackie promptly played the entire, fiendishly difficult Caprice brilliantly and from memory. Trying not to show surprise, he asked whether she had had any time to look at the Elgar, whereupon she played the whole of the first movement and half of the second from memory.

Bill was stunned.

Jackie had always found it easy to memorize music. As she played a new piece for the first time, she simultaneously committed it to memory. It was no effort for her.

When Jackie left that day, Bill knew that his first intuitive impression of that little girl was confirmed. She had an inexplicable and unending musical gift. Artistry is unique to the individual. There are no two thumbprints alike. Jackie wasn't a copy of anything or anyone, but a true and untainted original.

In November 1957 the Royal Amateur Orchestral Society held a competition open to any instrumentalists. The prize was a silver medal and a concerto performance with the Royal Amateur Orchestra the following March. I entered, playing the flute, and won. I knew immediately what I wanted to play in the concert: Mozart's Flute Concerto in D, K314.

It would be a momentous occasion, playing in the Duke's Hall at the Royal Academy of Music, a concert hall in which Mum had performed many times. I had a new dress for the occasion, long and pale blue—my favorite color—that Mum had bought in the sales. I felt wonderful in it.

There were plenty of rehearsals, both with Mum and with the orchestra. The more I played, the more I loved it all.

It was my big day and I was ready. Mum sent me to my room for a rest after lunch. But I couldn't sleep. Jackie came in and sat on my bed and we took it in turns to recite poetry.

Everyone was there to hear me: Mum, Dad, Jackie, Piers, Gran, Auntie Em. I couldn't wait to be on the platform, playing. At last my excitement was able to burst into that bubbling and sparkling first movement. The orchestra accompanied superbly and I felt completely at home and comfortable. For me, the slow movement was a divine dream and the last movement a giggling joke. I was borne along by my own enjoyment on a wave that I wanted to ride forever.

The applause was noisy and enthusiastic. When I left the platform for the final time, all I wanted to do was to return and play again—I was still living my big moment.

Backstage, standing alone at the top of the stairs in my own little world, I was aware of someone quietly walking up toward me. He approached with measured step, holding out his hand toward me, and spoke.

"I enjoyed your performance very much—as much as you obviously did. Lovely playing. Thank you, thank you . . ."

We shook hands and I beamed.

". . . I hope we'll meet again one day." He retraced his steps as Mum ran up the stairs and gave me a big hug.

"Hil, that was wonderful, the best you've ever played . . . Do you know who that was ? It was Gareth Morris, the flautist. What did he say to you?"

"He said he liked my playing."

A week later, Jackie performed the Lalo concerto at the Guildhall School of Music with their first orchestra conducted by Norman Del Mar. It was the first time she had played a concerto with an orchestra. The Lalo is an extensive virtuoso piece and suited her particularly well at that time. Born in France, Lalo was of Spanish descent, and loved to use dazzling dance rhythms in his music, making it great fun to play. Jackie captured the vivacious spirit of the music and threw herself headlong into the performance. She appeared to have no difficulties in presenting a full-scale concerto with supreme confidence.

In April, Jackie and I appeared on BBC Television again, this time with Diana and Julian Cummings as the Artemis Quartet, performing a Mozart flute quartet. Prince Charles and Princess Anne were guests of honor in the studio, and we were presented to them afterward.

Prince Charles, who was only eight, asked Jackie if he could try her cello and promptly sat astride it, grasped it tightly and played glissandi, sliding his fingers up and down the strings.

"Don't do that to my cello," she said, taking it firmly from him. "It's not a horse!"

CHAPTER NINE

Piers

From as early as I can remember, Hilary and Jackie were either practicing or performing. Coupled with this was an expectation, from those outside the family, that I, too, would take up a musical instrument. I wouldn't. And nothing was going to cajole me into anything so boring and time-wasting.

After school, I would usually go up to my room and be on my own with my train set, a rather elderly, electric Hornby Double O, laid out on the floor with the tracks going underneath the bed. Often, I would see how fast I could make the express train and its four carriages go round the track without falling off. I would spend hours perfecting the layout to achieve maximum speed. Sometimes a schoolfriend of mine, Jeremy Ard, who was also learning the cello, would be with me. Once, though, and much to my anger, he was "stolen" from me to play duets with Jackie. He didn't reappear for what seemed like hours, and when he did, he was exhausted. This taught me not to have friends round to our house. Instead I went to theirs.

At home, boundaries were clear. I definitely knew what wasn't allowed. The constant instruction to be quiet, well-behaved, and not make any fuss fueled a need in me to be recognized. I began to take risks and do outrageous things. Once Jeremy and I had made a caravan using a discarded pram to tow behind my pedal car. Knowing that Mum would object, I encouraged Jackie to climb into it and we started off down the hill. It was a steep hill, and within moments we were going extremely fast and quickly became out of control. The car hit an uneven paving stone and we were both catapulted into a tree. Jackie and I collapsed on the ground in hysterical laughter, neither of us hurt. We agreed to keep quiet about our escapade. But the caravan needed rebuilding.

I used to walk, cycle or take the bus to Downside Preparatory School. I loathed school. It was difficult to make friends, mainly because our family seemed so different and isolated from others. Although I resented the enormous amount of time that music took, robbing me of my sisters' company, I was still immensely proud of them. When I tried telling the boys at school about Hilary and Jackie, they always thought I was exaggerating and, as a result, I became the target for bullying. One boy began calling me "Slave." I put up with it for ages until one day I just punched him hard and the situation changed overnight. That was the first time I had actually retaliated, and I learnt from it an important lesson of survival.

I also found it difficult that Mum was always so preoccupied by music and seemed not to have time for me. On one occasion, I was in my room doing homework and needed to refill my fountain pen. The inkwell was empty. In filling it from the bottle, I spilt some ink on the floor. I called out to Mum but she wouldn't come. She was too busy teaching. In despair, I spilt more, but this time on purpose. I called her again, but still she didn't come. Finally, I just tipped the whole pot upside-down on the floor. Nothing happened. I felt utterly lonely and wondered what it would take to get her attention. It was only after her pupil had gone that she came to see me—and she was extremely angry.

Meanwhile, I would hardly ever see Dad. He left the house in the morning well before I set off for school, returning after I was asleep. On Tuesday mornings, I would wake to find copies of the *Eagle* and *Knock-Out* at the end of my bed. But the highlight of the week was always Saturday, when Dad and I would go on our "special adventures" together. On these days, Dad belonged just to me.

CHAPTER TEN

Piers

In the spring of 1958, Dad was offered a new position as Secretary to the Institute of Cost and Works Accountants, which brought with it the offer of accommodation above the office. The flat was huge, occupying the top two floors of 63 Portland Place, right in the center of London, which suited all of us. Jackie would be closer to her cello lessons, and Hilary, who had won a double scholarship to study flute and piano, would be closer to the Royal Academy of Music. I was due to leave prep school and had been offered a place at University College School in Hampstead, starting in the autumn.

In the summer holidays, Mum was so busy packing up the house and preparing for our move to London that she took me to my godmother's farm and left me there. Elizabeth Vanderspar, or Big Liz as we call her, and her husband Rufus, had a dairy and arable farm at Enborne near Newbury. It was sheer bliss: open air, fun, and no need to comb my hair. There was no having to be quiet, no stupid school, my hands could become engrained with dirt and it didn't matter. I mastered the tractor, which I was allowed to drive everywhere except along the road.

One morning, a letter arrived from Jackie. I had been suffering really badly from hayfever and had a sore nose. Jackie had heard of this and wrote her version of a "get well" card:

Sorry, can't remember the date . . . 1958

Dear Ba,

Hallo! How are you faring, you upturned fish of Sargasm nose. Fine? I thought so. Probably having the time of ya life being given presents and letters from everybody. What did ya have for your breaking of the fast, boiled toes roasted with potatoes? thought so.

Grandmother Maud wrote a lettre to Mum ce Matin. And at the end she put, "and my best love to you all, Iris, Derek, Hilary, Jackie and of course, Darling Piers" to which Auntie answered, "of course, bless his little heart!!!!!!!!"

I've just had dinner with cold beef, potates and broad beeni-weenies, quite nice. Hope ya have somink nice for yours. I'm finding it most difficult to think of anything to say exept Mum's in the deck chair trying to burn her pretty flowering half-asleep face, her expression cast into a deep frown with her hair casting almost on her brow and a bag of jellie-sshhh hanging down below her chin.

The sun is shining on the overgrown garden with a smile while the washing jumps merrily round the washing line in the breeze. Bill (the budgerigar) is singing quietly to his twin, mourning the temporary loss of his unfortunate aunt.

I'm writing this lettre dans la jardan, scuse, le jardin on Piers's desk. My golden cup in which I held my first cup of tea since you left, is standing solitarily beside the pencil sharpener and the top of my pen with a piece of paper sticking up boldly between the latter with some ideas for this short note (help).

The ants crawling up and down the stems of the rosebush just beside me tell me to pass on to you their kindest regards and they hope that you will be bettre in a second.

Mum has fallen asleep now, her face painted with a smile while her head of gold lies against the wooden post of the deck chair. Now it has moved again and she faces toward the sun in the dark blue sky with white clouds encircling it. Now she awakes, and winks to me, but off to sleep she goes again, facing the other way.

I am in the shade writing this, but my arm is in the somewhat scorching sun and is quite red.

Oh well, you upturned sausage skin of a squashed porpoise, have a descent night.

Flom Jlatsees XXXXXXXXXXXXXXXXXXXXXXXXX

"Sargasm" refers to the green weed which makes up the Sargasso Sea, comparing my nose to green seaweed.

* * *

When Dad started his new job on September 1, we moved to London but there was so much work to do on the flat that it still wasn't ready. Jackie's godmother, Mrs. Holland, came to the rescue and invited us to stay with her at her beautiful home in Kensington.

Within a short time, my excitement at moving to London began to sour. I didn't like my new school and made no effort to work. I made friends but none of them lived in Central London, so I felt isolated and lonely.

Hilary did not find our new life easy, either. At sixteen, she was much younger than most of the other students at the Royal Academy and, like Jackie, shy and unsophisticated. The fact that everyone seemed to have heard of Jackie put Hil under enormous pressure. An added burden was that Mum had been a top student at the Academy, winning all the available prizes. Hilary had much to live up to.

Jackie, still only thirteen, needed most of Mum's attention, including help with carrying the cello, and Mum continued to escort her everywhere, as she had always done. I went to school on the underground like all the other boys, and Hilary walked to the Academy which was just around the corner.

Hilary

Prodigies are always captivating and once we were living in London, people of importance often came to listen to Jackie playing at home. For her, it was another chance to perform, which she loved, but I was becoming acutely aware that I was being bypassed. The greeting was predictable: "Hello Hilary, how's your wonderful sister?" Often, when she was performing, I would stand with my ear to the door in the hope of discovering her special secret. But I couldn't. All I knew was that she had discovered "it" and I had not, and as a consequence, she was leaving me further and further behind. There was something in Jackie's playing which caused the listener to fall in love with her. How I wished that I could find that something too, but in my heart of hearts I knew I never would.

I hoped that the Academy would help me forge my musical

identity. Mum had loved the Academy and had blossomed there: musically, it had given her everything she needed in life.

On the day of my first flute lesson, I waited outside the double doors of Gareth Morris's room at the appointed hour, until the previous student departed. Mr. Morris greeted me and we shook hands. He recalled my performance of the Mozart D major Concerto and I remembered his congratulations at the time. Now I was glowing with the anticipation of the musical life ahead of me. I knew that Jackie was developing very special qualities that everyone loved, but I was confident that now I would find my own place in the musical world too.

Having exchanged lengthy pleasantries, Mr. Morris explained that I needed to alter every aspect of my technique and, in order to do this, would have to go back to the beginning. It would mean giving up concerts until my new technique was established. I was extremely willing: I had always been able to do whatever was asked of me and it didn't occur to me that it might be any different now. Technique had not been taught as a separate issue before, having always been incorporated into our pieces. Mr. Morris told me that the most secure note from which to launch my journey to the new technique was B flat. I was surprised to spend the whole lesson discussing one note, but went home to Mrs. Holland's and practiced it all week. Over the following lessons, he talked about posture, the position of the flute, tonguing, embouchure, sound quality, diaphragm awareness and breath control. These elements had to be altered and relearnt, all based on B flat. Each week I returned to my room with that dreaded note and tried to perfect the new way of standing, breathing and producing the sound.

As I struggled for four hours a day to produce the perfect B flat with exemplary technique, I could hear Jackie flourishing musically. I knew that she loved her lessons and that Bill was extremely pleased with her progress. I was longing for that rare marriage of teaching and freedom. While it was true that my technique needed attention, I felt I was being stifled. This was compounded by being banned from performing: I had to turn down several invitations to play, including a concerto on television, which hurt me deeply. My lifeline had been removed.

While we were staying at Mrs. Holland's, she arranged for a

friend of hers, the pianist and composer, Howard Ferguson, to come to hear Jackie play. We had been told he was important, and were ready for his arrival. I opened the door to him, but Mrs. Holland, Mum and Jackie instantly appeared in the corridor and welcomed him. They swept him past me and up to Mr. Holland's music room. I stayed where I was, in a shattered silence. I felt I didn't exist. I couldn't move. Soon, I could hear Jackie and Mum playing from above. Suddenly, I was overcome with loneliness and panic. I felt as inadequate as I had at the Purley Music Festival. Again, I hid and sobbed.

Piers

On November 28, we moved into our new flat. As Dad's office was underneath, we were never allowed to make any noise. Jackie and Hilary had sound-proofed rooms so their playing wouldn't disturb anyone. But the sound-proofing suppressed the natural resonance of the instruments, deadening the sound. There were no gardens, and no neighbors: the street consisted of offices and embassies.

Dad would go downstairs to work at 5 a.m. and return after I had gone to bed. I would never see him during the day, even though we were in the same building. His job made greater and greater demands on his time because, as a perfectionist, every detail had to be to the highest standard. Mum was always driving off somewhere with Jackie—lessons, performances, interviews, dressmakers. I had to be smartly dressed and on my best behavior all the time because of the constant stream of visitors to the flat to see Jackie. "Hello, Piers, how's Jackie?" I began to rebel. What about *me*?

I would sit on the floor outside Jackie's room and listen to her practicing, waiting for her to pause. The moment she did, I would hammer on the door and shout to her to keep going.

My escape was to climb out on to the roof. It was my secret. All the houses were joined, and my area of rooftop exploration extended from one end of the terrace to the Turkish Embassy at the other. This gave me an idea: I had made a crystal radio set but did not have an aerial. The Turkish Embassy had a huge aerial on its roof, strung from one gable to another. Connecting a wire

To

y dearest Mother
who reighneth like a queen,
Whose tenderness and love
is like a warm sunbeam,
With lots of love
from Jatty.

x x x x x x x x x x x x x x x x x x x

from this to my radio made the reception wonderful. A few days later, though, it just exploded, leaving a charred mess in its small wooden box.

Up on the rooftops, six stories above the road, everything looked small, and rather unreal. Sound was hushed, and no one ever looked up to see me. A perfect place from which to launch water bombs, I thought.

Taking some A3 paper from the office, I made a beautiful bomb, slightly more than half the size of a football. I filled it in the up-stairs bathroom, carried it carefully to the top of the roof and waited for a target to appear. At last a man came wandering along the pavement. I launched it. How graceful it looked as it curved its way toward the pavement below. For an awful moment, I thought I would have a direct hit. But, instead, it landed a few feet away, exploding with a hugely satisfying flash-flood of water, drenching the poor man, who jumped as though struck by lightning. The dull thud of the explosion was quickly followed by his shout. But not knowing where his attacker came from, and with all the of-fices closed on a Saturday, he had to continue soggily on his way, leaving me doubled up with fear and laughter.

Mum and Dad's beige Vauxhall Victor was kept in a garage in

Devonshire Mews, just behind Portland Place. I would offer to clean it and secretly take it out for a drive. I was thirteen when I started doing this but, because of my height, looked older. I would put on one of Dad's old flat hats and set off down New Cavendish Street. On one occasion, while I was waiting to turn into Wimpole Street, a policeman appeared. We looked straight into each other's eyes, and seemed to hold our stare for an age. As he began walking toward me, the lights changed and I put my foot down. I took the car home immediately and ran back to the house. Mum and Dad never found out. But that scare was too close for comfort. Rather than stop me, though, it taught me to be more careful. I planned my routes, keeping to side streets.

One day when I was tidying the garage, I found Dad's clarinet, which he'd bought in Oxford years ago. I took it out of the case, dusted it, put the mouthpiece to my lips and blew hard. Much to my amazement, it made a lovely, sonorous sound.

I took the instrument back to the flat and proudly showed Mum what I could do.

"Darling, that's wonderful. Let's go and play something together."

We went to Hilary's sound-proofed room. Mum showed me how to hold the instrument, and what all the keys did and I was able to play a simple tune by ear. Mum accompanied me. This was great. But all too soon we had to stop.

"Piers, I've got to go now because I must pick up Jackie."

Hilary

My flute lessons had become my weekly nightmare. I practiced my daily four hours without fail, but seemed incapable of achieving satisfactory results. One day in the late autumn, on my way to my lesson, I tried to brainwash myself by recalling the thrill of making my first sound on Pondles's flute and the ease with which I had produced it. I longed to regain that original feeling of effortlessness.

With these thoughts in my head, I arrived in Mr. Morris's room with renewed determination and prepared myself for the perfect B flat. I stood with the finest posture I could muster, my arms at the correct angles, my flute carefully and lightly placed exactly in the center of my lip. I took a huge breath, felt my lungs expanding

back, front and sides, arranged my embouchure, and prepared my
tongue to release the air. Instead, I thought I would burst with the
pressure in my neck, throat and mouth.

Nothing happened. My tongue had jammed completely and
there was awful silence.

"Would you like to try again, Hilary?" he said, in a rather
clipped voice.

I exhaled and took another big breath. Still nothing. My tongue
just refused to function.

I was panic-stricken. I watched as Mr. Morris became increasingly annoyed at my inability to perform such a simple task. I
managed to suppress tears of despair, and tried repeatedly, but unsuccessfully, to produce my note. I am sure he was as relieved as I
was when the dismal hour was over.

Fortunately home was nearby and I knew I could escape and recover alone. Climbing the stairs in our flat I could hear the most
glorious sounds coming from my room: the doors were ajar and
Jackie and Mum were playing Brahms, in full flight. I was instantly
paralyzed and just wept. They were the angels singing from above
and I had been consigned to hell.

By the end of my first term at the Academy I had managed to
achieve one octave of F major, but the sound I was making was
like a stuffy nose. The one thing I had always been able to do now
eluded me, and I felt completely lost.

Jackie was playing the Elgar Concerto with the Ernest Read Senior Orchestra at their Christmas Concert in the Royal Albert
Hall and Mum thought it would be fun for me to play first flute in
the orchestra for the performance. Through her Dalcroze connec-
tions, she knew Ernest Read very well and he agreed that I should
join the orchestra for this occasion. Despite the ban on performing, Mum persuaded me I should take part, feeling sure I would
be able to reach the higher notes. The usual first flute was a young
man named James Galway, but he was willing to play second flute
for this performance.

I was thrilled to be first flute and to be playing with Jackie but,
as the rehearsal began, I felt uncharacteristically nervous. There is
a moment in the second movement when the flute has a short
solo, running upward above the other instruments. Although it is

not particularly difficult, when my moment came, I was unable to play it.

Ernest Read stopped the orchestra and we tried again. I still couldn't play the notes. My confidence was failing me and my heart was pounding. I tried a third time and once more, my fingers tied themselves in knots, which was something that had never happened to me before. Eventually, Ernest Read lost his patience with me:

"Hilary, you can't do it," he said. "James, you play first flute."

I was so overwhelmed with embarrassment and dismay that I couldn't speak. I changed places with James.

That experience confirmed what I knew: I was a total failure.

Mum and Dad had been introduced to the Clwyd family, who were great supporters of the arts, and it was through their influence that our parents decided that Jackie should continue with some form of schooling. In January 1959, just before her fourteenth birthday Jackie started attending classes at Queen's College in Harley Street. Mum used to take her, even though Harley Street was literally just around the corner. Jackie loathed it.

I continued to struggle with my flute lessons but, when the time came to play a piece at the Academy, I knew I could no longer perform. Jackie and I had been trained in colors, shapes and physical movement. My aim had always been to transmit the sheer joy and excitement of telling a story in sounds. Now, faced with a compulsory lunchtime concert before a handful of unwilling students, all I could think about was the position of my flute, the angle of my air stream, and remembering to keep the same embouchure for top B♭ as for top G. I used to love having an audience, but now I loathed it. I felt nervous, looked nervous and played dismally. I felt very alone. I had asked Mum not to come as I knew she would be disappointed.

CHAPTER ELEVEN

Hilary

When Jackie was about fourteen, she met an outstanding young violinist of the same age, Peter Thomas, at the BBC studios. It was decided that he should be invited to the flat to play duos, and Jackie wrote him a courteous letter, complimenting him on his playing, and suggesting a visit.

Jackie was excited, yet terrified. A shy, gallumphing teenager in ankle socks, she refused to greet him without me, so we went downstairs together and I opened the door. She hid behind me while I welcomed him. After an awkward few moments, she turned and ran up the stairs. Peter, without hesitating, followed, leaving me standing by the open door.

Peter had a relaxed, uncomplicated personality and started coming to the flat regularly at weekends, often playing until it was too late for him to go home.

Now the leader of the City of Birmingham Symphony Orchestra, Peter vividly remembers Jackie's impeccable performance of the Saint-Saëns concerto when they first met. It was not the performance of a fourteen-year-old. There was nothing which could be improved upon. She already had supreme mastery and profound understanding of the music and played very much in the Pleeth manner, with a great sense of line. As she played instinctively, Pleeth's style of teaching, which was to penetrate the heart of the music before tackling the intellectual side, was perfect for her.

Peter used to take Jackie up the road to Regent's Park, but was surprised to find that she became exhausted by even a simple game of catch. When walking on Dartmoor as a child, Jackie tired very quickly, often struggling far behind, with Mum keeping her company. Yet she had the stamina to make music for hours on end. Peter was a keen and active sportsman; but his capacity to keep going when playing the violin was exhausted long before Jackie would allow him to stop.

Opportunities for Jackie were presenting themselves thick and fast. Her influential godfather, Lord Harewood, arranged for her to play to the Russian cellist, Mstislav Rostropovich. In his early thirties, Rostropovich was the most exciting cellist at that time. He had grown up in Stalinist Russia, been a student at the Moscow Conservatoire, and had recently married Galina Vishnevskaya, one of Russia's most celebrated divas at the Bolshoi Opera. He was known to be a flamboyant figure—when he met his future wife he sent her not just one bunch of violets, but the entire flower stall. Although he had made his Western début in New York in 1956, he had not yet performed in London.

Lord Harewood, excited by Jackie's ability, was keen to know what Rostropovich thought of her. The meeting took place in 1959, when Jackie was fourteen, at the Harewoods' flat in London. Rostropovich and Jackie sat opposite each other with their cellos. He asked her to copy what he did, taking her through a series of technical exercises which became more and more complex and difficult. Jackie rose to the challenge easily, and he was surprised that at no stage could he flummox her.

The following year, Jackie won two important prizes: the Gold Medal of the Guildhall School of Music and, in July, the coveted Queen's Prize. The participants, who had to be under thirty, were the cream of our British performers. The final round, which took place in the Royal College of Music, was chaired by Yehudi Menuhin, and each competitor had to give a half-hour recital. Jackie played the unaccompanied Suite No. 2 by Bach; *Kol Nidrei* by Max Bruch; *Song without Words* Op. 109 in D major by Mendelssohn; Intermezzo from *Goyescas* by Granados, arranged by Cassado, and *Allegro Appassionata* by Saint-Saëns. She was the youngest performer ever and the four celebrated judges unanimously awarded her the first prize of £150.

The Suggia Trust arranged for Jackie to attend masterclasses with the father of the cello world, Pablo Casals, at a summer school in Zermatt, Switzerland. Casals, at eighty-four, was a legend. Jackie was extremely excited to be going abroad for the first time. At fifteen, she was too young to travel alone so Mum went too.

After one of the classes, someone suggested to Casals that he should stop Jackie's "excessive swaying" while she played, but this made him angry on her behalf. "Don't you dare criticize this girl!" he retorted. "Can't you see that her playing comes from her heart and her movements are part of the whole?"

For the final concert in Zermatt, Mum accompanied Jackie in the Saint-Saëns concerto. Those who heard this performance say that it was breathtaking. Jackie played with such mastery and maturity, there seemed to be nothing left to learn.

Mum and Jackie had been away for eighteen days and we all went to meet them at Victoria Station. Back and forth went the questions, but it was not until later that day that, sitting cross-legged on her bed, I was able to chat to Jackie alone.

"What was he really like, Jack?"

"He's tiny, Hil, and always smoking."

"Yes, but I meant, as a teacher?"

"Well, he didn't really say a great deal, and I didn't want him to, either, but I liked playing to him. But Hil, the mountains . . . I just loved being amongst them and so did Mum. She said they reminded her of Poland."

"But Jack, I want to know about Casals."

"Bill is a much better teacher. He'll always be my cello daddy. I knew what Casals was going to say before he said it. He tried to make everyone play the same way . . ."

She drifted off somewhere else. ". . . There aren't any cars in Zermatt—and there are goats everywhere. They go up the mountain in the morning and come down at night. And there are so many hearty climbers. Not me, though!"

Casals was enthusiastic about Jackie, but she was openly disparaging about him. She complained that it was difficult to approach him since he was constantly surrounded by worshipping women. She didn't think much of his teaching either; in fact, Jackie was critical about anyone who tried to teach her, apart from Bill. She trusted Bill implicitly and couldn't accept what she saw as interference from anyone else. However, contact with other cellists was intriguing for Jackie since she was becoming increasingly concerned about understanding her technique. She was beginning to question what she had always taken for granted.

Piers

By now, I was starting to realize that what had always appeared normal and usual to me, was in fact rare and extraordinary. Music was the heart of the family; anything and everything else was a distraction, and Jackie was the standard by which I was to be judged.

Playing the clarinet was fun but, knowing there was an unnavigable gulf between my ability and Jackie's, all I wanted was just to be involved in music and not to be left out. But when I passed Grade 4, I was told I had to study theory to progress. I couldn't understand why. Surely I could just carry on playing? Jackie didn't learn technique, she just played instinctively. But I wasn't allowed to. Instead, it was decided that I should attend the Guildhall School of Music on Saturday mornings to have lessons in aural, theory and general musicianship, and to play in the orchestra.

My Saturday mornings with Dad disappeared.

Eventually, after a morning of intense boredom, I would have my clarinet lesson. Having not enjoyed the hours of studying, I was not in the best frame of mind for playing. Being at the Guildhall also introduced me to a different pressure. "Do we have another du Pré?" How I wanted to say, "I'm Piers, not Jackie."

One day Mum informed us that we had been asked to give a family concert at the headquarters of the China Inland Mission, now known as the OMF, where "Aunt" Muriel worked. Muriel Walker and her sister Pat (Jackie's godmother) came from Irish stock, and had been friends of Mum since their student days. Both were devout Christians and missionaries. Muriel was tall and rather shapeless with a stentorian voice. She knew "what was what" and had a no-nonsense attitude to life. Her imposing stature and strictness rather scared us when we were children, although she was the gentlest person at heart. Pat spent most of her time in Africa as a missionary and would visit us when on leave; we always found her rather abrupt and equally terrifying.

In the weeks leading up to the concert I couldn't see how I

could be good enough. I practiced hard and went on and on at Mum to rehearse with me. Mum knew exactly how to encourage and, as my confidence grew, I even started telling her how she was to play the accompaniment for me.

At last my great day came. The piano was an old upright and, unbeknownst to me, it had been tuned a quarter-tone too sharp. I walked proudly on to the stage. It was the first time I had performed and didn't really know what to do but, having watched my sisters so often, I just copied them.

There seemed to be so many people in the audience and all looking at me. Since I had always seen soloists tune their instruments before playing, I did the same. I blew an A and Mum played an A on the piano but they didn't sound the same. At first I thought I was playing the wrong note, so I played a C. Mum played the A again. Then I realized with a feeling of dread that the piano was out of tune. But, I knew what to do: I had seen clarinetists pull out the sections of their instruments to alter the pitch. I did this as casually as possible to make it look natural, but when I played the A again, it was even worse. It was lower still. I had flattened the note, whereas it needed sharpening. Suddenly I felt out of my depth. I looked at Mum, searching for help and she said, quietly, "There is nothing we can do. I'm sorry, we won't be able to play."

To my mind, not playing was simply not an option. My big moment couldn't be canceled just because of a feeble out-of-tune piano. I went over to her.

"We must play," I whispered. And so we began.

I shut myself into a world of my own and played my heart out. As I played the last note, I held the clarinet high and waited for the sound to fade into the distance. Then came the applause. My moment of glory. I bowed low and walked off stage. That was enough. I never wanted to play the clarinet again.

And I never did.

CHAPTER TWELVE

Hilary

In 1961, when she was sixteen, Jackie made her professional début. It was Bill Pleeth's idea that she was ready to play at the Wigmore Hall, which was, and still is, the traditional showcase for musicians facing the national press for the first time. It was agreed that Ernest Lush should accompany her rather than Mum, since this was the start of her career.

Mum trusted Bill and took his advice but she knew that Jackie would be unleashed into the professional music world if the Wigmore was a success, and would probably be catapulted out of her protective environment at home. It was obvious that Jackie was impatient for new challenges, so Mum, although anxious, did not disagree with Bill's suggestion.

Bill asked his agents, Ibbs and Tillett, to handle the arrangements for the concert. Terence Palmer, who was put in charge of Jackie, wrote to Mum on January 4, 1961:

Dear Mrs. du Pré,

Thank you very much for your letter of 1st January and for returning our agreement form duly completed, together with your cheque for £18.18s. being the first deposit on your daughter's recital on March 1. You will be pleased to hear that we have booked the services of Ernest Lush at a fee of 35 guineas, and he always gives three very generous rehearsals. I will be contacting you within a week or two regarding the program details.

With kind regards,
Terence Palmer

With her Wigmore recital in sight, it was time for Jackie to have an instrument which could produce the best possible quality of sound. So far, her secret benefactor had provided suitable cellos to match her progress: these included a seven-eighths Guarnarius, a Ruggieri and a full-size Tecchler.

Mum now received instructions to take Jackie to try a selection of cellos. There was no explanation about any of them. Jackie was simply told to play them all and choose the best. She knew immediately which one she wanted: the beautiful deep brown one. It was a 1673 Stradivarius, which had been found in America and cost £6,000, a high price for a cello at that time.

I was in my room when they returned that evening.

"Hil, come and see what I've got," Jackie called. "I've fallen in love!"

I dashed downstairs. There in the sitting room was the new whopping creature.

"Listen to this, Hil. I haven't been able to make sounds like this before. And it'll get even better!"

The powerful, rich tone enveloped us and we all became as excited as Jackie, while she played her heart out in a world of her own.

That evening the cello was in the kitchen while we had supper.

"Why did you choose that one, Jeetz?" Dad asked.

"Daddy, there was no comparison. It was the only one that sang." She went over to the cello and turned it round. "Who can guess what this is?"

She pointed to a small circle in its back.

"Was it broken?" asked Piers.

"No, silly! It used to be a hole for a strap, so a monk could play it while he was processing. It was strapped to his front!"

That night the cello was beside her bed. No one was allowed to touch it.

The preparation for the Wigmore had been carefully organized. Jackie's lessons continued as normal, and she rehearsed several times with Ernest Lush, also recording with him the Sicilienne by Maria Theresia von Paradis for her radio début on *Rising Generation*, an appropriately titled program, to be broadcast on March 22.

Jackie had a new dress for the Wigmore, and a new haircut. The dress, a long one of pale blue material, was specially made for the occasion. Jackie's dresses had to accommodate her energetic style of playing.

Almost before we knew it, it was *the* day, March 1. I awoke to the sound of the bathroom door banging.

"Sshh, Piers," said Gran, in her loudest whisper. "Jackie's asleep. I don't want her to wake yet."

I leapt out of bed and tiptoed downstairs as quickly as I could: Mum was running the bath for Dad, who planted a kiss on my forehead as he hurried along the corridor. He whispered to Mum: "I haven't time now; you have the bath instead. I'll have mine this evening before we go."

He pottered off to find the cup of tea that Gran had already made for him and Mum disappeared into the bathroom. In the kitchen we were all talking in lowered voices. Gran was frying bacon and eggs for Piers, who was crunching cornflakes. Even this sounded too noisy.

"What time's the concert, Dad? Can I have the afternoon off school?"

"Bad luck, old chap, it's at seven-thirty. . . . And I want you to be smart tonight. It's a big do and there will be important people there. Come home promptly for a bath and hair wash, and I'll have one after you."

Mum came into the kitchen in her dressing-gown and Gran poured a cup of tea for her. It was obvious her mind was spinning with all the things she had to remember. "Now, Jackie's dress will need to be ironed this morning so I can take it to the hall and leave it hanging there. We'll leave Jackie asleep for as long as possible. Her rehearsal isn't until eleven. If the phone rings, answer it quickly, so it doesn't wake her up."

The post arrived with several cards for Jackie. The telephone rang, and Gran lurched forward to grab the receiver.

"Speaking?" She always answered the phone in that way.

It was for Jackie, but Gran explained that she was asleep.

It was now 8:30 a.m. and I had an early lesson at the Academy, and had to go. "I'll be back at ten-thirty. Will you be here, Gran?"

"Oh, yes, dear. I shall be getting lunch ready."

Hoping to see Jackie before her rehearsal, I ran home and found

a florist on the doorstep with a magnificent bouquet. I took it and
rushed up to the flat. Jackie was just leaving and, with a low
sweeping curtsey, I presented the flowers to her.

"Look, Hil, I'll show you how to bow properly." Jackie raised
her right hand in the air, swung it across her body, and flopped
clumsily forward.

Several demonstrations later, Mum was becoming agitated.

"Come on, Jackables. We must go. See you at lunch, Hil. I think
we'll have a walk this afternoon, so do your practice this morning."

And they left.

Gran had made me a hot drink and together we looked at the
greetings telegrams and good-luck cards that Jackie had received.
There were dozens of them. I couldn't practice, I was much too
excited.

At half-past one, Jackie reappeared. "I'm starving."

"I'm starving too, and I'm hungrier than you."

"Well, I've been working with Slush, so I'm hungrier."

"Blessed are the peacemakers," sang Mum firmly, in her stop-
quarreling-at-once voice.

We all sat down to one of Gran's marvelous lunches before setting off for Regent's Park and a brisk walk. But it was cold, so half
an hour's fresh air was enough. When we returned Jackie plunged
into a hot bath, singing at the top of her voice while she had a
long soak. It wasn't long before Piers came home from school,
having had, as usual, a miserable day. He was hungry and cold but
Gran produced a large plate of home-made scones and cakes. As
his tummy filled, his spirits rose.

Dad arrived, clutching a copy of the *London Evening Standard*.
There was a picture of Jackie, surrounded by flowers. The article
described her as a tall, calm girl of sixteen with a Christine Truman hairstyle. Dad was glowing with pride.

Jackie did not feel nervous in the conventional sense before
concerts, and certainly showed no signs on that day. We had performed in public so often that it was second nature to us. She
needed adrenaline to play, and Mum had always trained us to control our excitement so that we saved it for the performance.

The historic 500-seat hall was packed, and as many people again
had been turned away. The manager was quoted as saying that he
could have filled the house twice over. Bill Pleeth and Jackie had

chosen a very challenging program, including an unaccompanied Bach suite, sonatas by Handel, Brahms and Debussy, and some dances by de Falla.

Despite my pounding heart, I felt immensely proud when Jackie strode on to the platform. She tuned, slipped into her extraordinarily concentrated world and began the first work: the Sonata in G minor by Handel. Then, to my utter astonishment, she began playing out of tune. My heart missed a beat. What had happened? Jackie so rarely played out of tune. Her fingers were climbing further and further up the fingerboard. Soon it became clear that there was something seriously wrong with one of the strings. Suddenly she stopped, and rose to her feet.

"Ladies and gentlemen. My string has broken and I'll have to go and change it. Please excuse me."

She left the platform, changed the string, swept back and started again, as though nothing had happened. The audience was captivated.

I will never forget how deeply moved I was by her that day. She played as she had always played but somehow, in that environment, and with her beautiful rich "brown Strad," seemed more impressive than ever. The music flowed as if she and the cello were one being. There were no emotional or technical barriers and she communicated without inhibition. She and her cello were revealing her true nature through music.

For Bill Pleeth, her performance was more than he had ever dreamed possible. He said: "The perfect marriage between real passion and an innocent reverence. It was a spiritual not just a physical thing. She let each piece live so completely. People were practically crying."

Dad had arranged for all the newspapers to be delivered the next morning. The reviews confirmed what we had all known for so long.

The Times headline announced: "Astonishing mastery of cello at sixteen," and went on:

> To speak of promise when reviewing her performance would seem almost insulting, for she has attained a mastery of her instrument that is astonishing in one so young.

Percy Cater of the *Daily Mail* went further:

> In Jacqueline du Pré, England has a cellist bound in my opinion
> to become a world-beater. It was astonishing to listen to the
> sounds that issued from her nut-brown Strad, enchanting, spon-
> taneous and marvelously organized, thrilling in its emotional
> range. The maturity of this child's performance was indeed in-
> credible. Jacqueline was born to play the cello. She thoroughly
> understands its genius and so instinctive is her reaction to the
> music that one feels the subtlest ideas of the composer to be
> embraced. She is in love with her cello . . . What we saw and
> heard from a schoolgirl artist was cello mastery.

Martin Cooper wrote in the *Daily Telegraph*:

> This country has produced very few string players of first rank,
> but it may well be that last night's concert at the Wigmore Hall
> revealed a cellist who will reach international rank. We are ac-
> customed to British artists who seem instinctively to divorce
> themselves from their music, but here is a young player whose
> technical accomplishments have not prevented her from being
> wholly committed to whatever she plays—and this is one of the
> first essentials of a great player.

Jackie had become a star overnight. Offers of recitals and concerts
came pouring in. She could have done anything she wanted, but
strangely, the critical confirmation of her genius gradually started
to worry her. The idea of "making a name" for herself had never
really occurred to her. She just loved playing the cello. The word
prodigy meant nothing to her. "There are lots of prodigies," she
would say. "It's nothing rare."

Nowadays, music students are taught how to handle their careers, deal with agents, the press, travel arrangements, and finances. But, at that time, none of this support was available.

In the cold light of day, Mum's greatest fear, that Jackie would
be extricated from the bonds of the family, was now a reality, and
the excitement of Jackie's success was tinged by anxiety for the
changes which lay ahead.

Out in the world

CHAPTER THIRTEEN

Hilary

One of the first concerts in which I was allowed to play was with an Academy orchestra, performing the Bach Magnificat at the Corn Exchange in Newbury. It was incredibly cold, so we ran from the train to the café opposite the Corn Exchange for a cup of tea. I was just about to take my first sip when a tall, dark figure in a black greatcoat appeared at the door.

"For God's sake, hurry up, you're late!"

It was Christopher Finzi, who was conducting the Newbury String Players in the same concert. The panic caused me to gulp my tea so quickly, I burnt my tongue. It made playing extremely uncomfortable. Afterward he took my telephone number.

I was seventeen, very shy and felt awkward because I had no faith in my playing. I was impressed by his confidence. He was practical and energetic, and his string players were obviously fond of him. Son of Gerald Finzi, the composer, he was always known as Kiffer. He said there was another concert he would like me to play in.

He telephoned a few days later to arrange a rehearsal of Bach's Brandenburg Concerto No. 4, which I was to perform with Sebastian Bell and Peter Thomas. The concert was on November 27, 1960 with the Richmond Community String Orchestra, and it was sold out. The audience enjoyed the Brandenburg so much we played the whole work a second time.

In April 1961, shortly after Jackie's Wigmore Hall début, I was performing with Kiffer again. This time it was a Vivaldi flute concerto with the Newbury String Players in St. John's Church, Stockcross. It was arranged that I would stay the night at Kiffer's

home in Ashmansworth, and because Kiffer's mother, Joy, was
there and would look after me, Mum and Dad cautiously agreed.

Kiffer collected me from Portland Place in his green Morris Minor. I was tongue-tied, but he chattered away, asking me about
the family. As we drove nearer to Ashmansworth, the Hampshire
Downs lay before us, the narrow country lanes, reminding me of
Jersey, and I was bowled over by the beauty of the countryside.

"It's just up here," said Kiffer, turning right off the main road by
a country inn. We drove slowly up the twisting, single-track road,
to the top of the hill, and there was the sign "Ashmansworth."
The village was pretty, with wildflowers in the banks and late daf-
fodils in the gardens. We turned right by a flint wall, through the
gateway and along the drive into the cobbled yard of Church Farm
where the gardener was filling a watering can by the potting-shed
door. Kiffer stopped and jumped out.

"Hello, Jack, how are the chickens? All alive?"

I looked at what seemed to me an enormous house. The front
door was covered with a huge overgrown jasmine already in full
flower and its scent was wafting into the car. I waited. Kiffer and
Jack were so involved in their conversation that I didn't dare get
out without an invitation. On the front doostep appeared a tall,
elegant woman, her soft, dark hair swept up into piles of curls on
top of her head.

"Hello, dearie. You must be Hilary. I'm Joy, Kiffer's mother."

I opened the car door and went to shake hands with her.

"Hello, Mrs. Finzi."

"What a magical day it is for your first time here. The daffs have
stayed in bloom in your honor!"

We went inside. Joy had cake and biscuits ready on a tray.

"I thought we would have our tea outside, dearie, on the terrace. It's too lovely to stay indoors. Kiffy needs some fresh air and I
should think you do, too. Here he is!"

We walked through the house on to the terrace and there ahead
of us were rolling hills and valleys as far as the eye could see. I had
been welcomed warmly and was relaxing quickly in what I
thought must be the most beautiful place in the world. At last I
found the courage to say, "What a wonderful view!"

"Oh it is, isn't it! On clear days we can see the Isle of Wight.

Now, do tell me, Kiffer says you come from Jersey. It's very tiny, isn't it?"

That was my invitation and the family history flooded out. Joy brought the conversation to a halt.

"Now, dearie, I think Kiffer should show you the well. I'm going in to do a bit more work before supper. Kiffy, I've put Hilary in the spare room, overlooking the view."

Kiffer showed me everything: the well, the garden, the chickens, the house and, as there was at least an hour until supper, we walked across the fields to Cowslip Dell. He became very excited explaining the background.

". . . we decided to have chickens after Dad died. It was a way to use the land and give Mum a little extra income. We didn't expect to have so many though—there are hundreds of them now!

". . . and that's the cottage where Jack and Olive live. They've been with us since I was young. He looks after the outside and she does the inside, and cooks. They're great characters.

". . . and this is our land, from Jack's cottage, right over to the oak tree . . ."

For me, it was a new world.

Supper was in the dining room, with Joy as a magnificent hostess.

"Vegetarian of course, dearie. You know that Kiffer doesn't eat any meat or fish."

I looked in amazement as I had never heard the term vegetarian before.

Kiffer had told me about his mother on the way down in the car. Joy had met Gerald Finzi in March 1933, when Gerald was staying in a cottage in Lye Green, Sussex. The cottage belonged to her family, and she lived nearby with her sister. Joy's interests were in sculpture and pottery, drawing, playing the violin and literature.

Gerald Finzi left school at eleven—he hated it so much he staged increasingly alarming fainting fits until he was allowed to leave and follow his passion for composing. He became part of the flowering of twentieth-century English composers, and his close group of friends included Ralph Vaughan Williams, Edmund

Rubbra and Howard Ferguson. They shared their new works with one another, playing, discussing and criticizing.

No one was surprised when Gerald and Joy announced their engagement a month after their first meeting, and, six months later, were married in Dorking register office. The only witnesses were Ralph Vaughan Williams and his first wife, Adeline. After their honeymoon, Gerald and Joy searched for their perfect house. Eventually they found this beautiful spot in Ashmansworth. There was already a farmhouse on the site, but was in such a bad state of repair that it had to be demolished. An architect friend, Peter Harland, designed a house for them, which was eventually finished in 1939, just as war broke out. During the war Joy ran the house, looked after evacuees and helped organize the Newbury String Players, an orchestra which Gerald and Joy had formed. Many musicians moved out of London during the war, giving Gerald an ideal opportunity to research and perform unknown music, particularly English works.

Now, here I was, surrounded by Joy's portraits. Although she had no training, she was able to capture the essence of character in her art. I was stunned by her capabilities, as I looked at her drawings of Gerald Finzi, and their sons, Kiffer and Nigel.

After supper, Kiffer asked if I had ever heard a nightingale. I hadn't.

"Good," he replied. "I know where we can hear one. We're off for a treat, to Happy Valley. Jump in the car."

And off we trundled in his Mom's Minor. It was a sublime, balmy evening. The light had just gone; we left the parked car and walked to the edge of the woods and waited. It was so still and quiet, I hardly dared to breathe. Suddenly, and unexpectedly, a stream of the most glorious, clear and effortless song burst from right above us. I was transfixed. The passion, the volume of sound and the ease with which it was delivered were unbelievable. I was in heaven. The performance was just for us. I could have stayed there all night.

The next morning I was woken by Kiffer dashing into my room. "Quick, there's a cuckoo. Listen."

He flung open the window and from far away the cuckoo was

calling over the valley. "Watch carefully, we may see it. It looks like an arrow when it flies."

I was still in seventh heaven and the prospect of spending the whole day here was blissful. For the first time in years I was excited about performing that night.

The concert went extremely well. I poured all my intense feelings for Kiffer into my playing. The huge applause at the end swept through me and I felt my old confidence returning again. A few days later, the enthusiastic reviews were another boost: "Hilary du Pré, a young flautist of remarkable technique, obviously has a great future ahead of her."

With Kiffer in my life, everything had a new meaning again and I felt safe in his strength and confidence.

The first time Kiffer came to visit us in Portland Place, he took the lift to the top floor and Piers opened the door. He was twelve and was alone in the flat. Within a few minutes of Kiffer's arrival, he had told him everything about Jackie, including the closely guarded secret about her cello benefactor.

One of the things I loved about Kiffer was his unpredictability. He would just turn up at our flat unannounced. On one occasion, he arrived at ten in the morning to learn that Jackie was still in bed. She was depressed and lethargic, often staying in bed all morning. Mum certainly never disturbed her, feeling that the rest must be necessary.

Kiffer found us all tiptoeing about, trying not to make any noise. "Why's everyone whispering? What's going on?"

I took him to one side. "Jackie's sleeping. We mustn't wake her."

"What's wrong with her?"

"Nothing. She often sleeps late in the mornings."

Kiffer was astonished. "Really!" he said, heading for the staircase.

He strode upstairs into Jackie's room, ripped off her blankets, and flung her over his shoulder.

"Good morning, Jackie. Wakey, wakey!" he shouted, laughing heartily as he carried her downstairs and plonked her in the kitchen.

Mum was stunned, her face a picture of horrified bewilderment,

as she awaited an outburst from Jackie. Much to everyone's surprise, Jackie didn't protest at all but started laughing.

At that moment Jackie recognized that Kiffer was not overawed
by her, and she never forgot.

One evening, Kiffer and I were sitting in the car near Portland
Place saying our goodbyes.

"I shall love it when we are both living in Ashmansworth," he
said. "I need to spend more time there."

"I could always come by train," I said. "If it's easier for you?"

"Don't be silly. I mean, once we're married."

"Married!"

"Yes! You do take it for granted, don't you?"

"Well . . ."

"I shall write to your parents. They'd like that . . ."

The following weekend I returned with the letter for Mum and
Dad. We sat in the kitchen. I was on Dad's knee as he read it, out
loud at first, and then to himself, with Mum reading over his
shoulder. Very soon, they were both in tears.

I knew they would support my engagement, but when I
announced my wish to stay with Kiffer rather than go on the
family summer holiday, Mum told me I was being very unfair to
Dad. He wasn't coping easily with the sudden realization that the
family might soon be scattered. He couldn't understand why I
was in such a rush to get married. I overheard him talking on the
phone to Lalla, saying that I was "going," as if I were leaving
forever.

In the end, Mum, Dad, Piers and Jackie went to northern
France without me. Kiffer and I went to stay first with Gran and
Auntie Em in Plymouth, and then to Jersey, to visit Gannie and
Pondles. I was proud of Kiffer and loved showing him off to all
our relatives, introducing him to my world, and revisiting childhood haunts. How lucky I was that he enjoyed it all just as much
as I did.

The opportunity for Joy to meet the whole family presented itself
in late August, when we all returned from our holidays. Mum,

Dad, Jackie, Piers, Gran, Lalla and I crammed into the Dormobile and set off for Church Farm.

After elevenses, we went to look at the well, collecting flints to drop through the grid. One by one we pitched the jagged stones over the edge and waited for them to splash in the water far, far below.

Piers was thrilled. "How deep is it, Kiffer?"

"Three hundred and sixty-five feet, Piers. It's as deep as St. Paul's Cathedral is tall."

"Wow!"

Lunch was jovial and friendly. Mum and Joy discovered they both loved Dalcroze Eurhythmics and had worked with Dalcroze himself. As a child, Joy was at Moira House, the Sussex school which Dalcroze had used for some of his demonstrations in England. Very soon Mum and Joy were comparing notes about their many experiences.

"What shall we do after lunch?" asked Kiffer. Everyone looked at him expectantly. "I know, we'll go up to the Gibbet!"

"The what?" asked Jackie, which surprised everyone because she had hardly uttered a word since we arrived.

"The top of the world!" said Kiffer.

Joy interrupted. "Did you ever see *The Black Legend*? It's all about the Gibbet. It was our little foray into the film world—both the boys were in it. Nigel played a leading role, Kiffer was in the crowd and I was the continuity lady."

"So, they're old gallows?"

"Yes. In the seventeenth century there was a double hanging and, as neither county wanted to take responsibility, the gallows were put on the boundary between Hampshire and Berkshire. The old gallows still stand there, high on the windy hill and on clear days you can see seven counties. It's a wonderful spot."

"Dad, Dad, can we go, please?" said Piers eagerly. "I could fly my kite up there. Fantastic!"

We needed two cars and Joy came to keep Gran company in case we wanted to rush ahead. Lalla took his rucksack and geological hammer; Piers carried his kite and Joy took a bag of sweeties for us all.

Kiffer and Piers found the highest spot to fly the kite and it instantly caught a gust and soared up and up into the blue, its tail swishing from side to side. Very soon Lalla was crouching over a large flint and tapping it with his hammer. Jackie and I raced ahead, along the crest of the hill, to the Gibbet, leaving the others behind us. Jackie had never been a runner, but the freedom of this wide open space compelled her forward. She was much bigger than me, with broad shoulders and heavy limbs, and almost seemed to be bursting out of herself as she thundered along. On the peak, we collapsed in an exhausted heap, lying flat on our backs, gazing at the sky.

"Jacks," I whispered. "Frogs in bed . . ."

She joined in, as we yelled at the top of our voices over and over again, banging our legs on the turf:

"FROGS IN BED, FROGS IN BED. ALL THE WAY TO RASPBERRY JAM. FROGS IN BED . . ." Our voices trailed off into the silence.

"Penny for them, Jack?"

"Oh, nothing . . . It's lovely here, isn't it?"

"It's *wonderful*."

"Did they really hang those men here, Hil?"

"It was a man and a woman, actually. Spooky, eh? They were swinging just above us . . . We could walk all the way back to Ashmansworth from here, you know. It would only take about two hours. Would you like to?"

"No fear. I couldn't do it. I'm worn out . . ."

We lay there, unmoving, listening to the warm wind rustling the grasses.

"I'm going to miss you, Jack." We smiled at each other. "You will come and stay with us when we're married, won't you?"

"Of course I will. I'll come all the time . . . if I can . . . Oh look, look."

Gran and Joy were heading in our direction. We both burst out laughing at the comical sight of the two women: Joy, tall and straight, gliding rather than walking, Gran, short and angular, trotting to keep up.

Mum and Dad were strolling quietly, holding hands and admiring the view. Piers was still racing about, holding tightly on to his tugging kite.

"Come on, Hil, Jackie, I'll race you back." Kiffer appeared and set off at a gallop.

"Oh, no, I can't run anymore," protested Jackie. "You go, Hil. I'll walk with Mum."

Kiffer and I ran for sheer joy down the hillside into the valley, egging each other on as we went, and sank into the soft grass.

"Jackie seems very quiet today," remarked Kiffer.

"She's worried about being lonely when we're married."

Arm in arm, we ambled back to the car.

Piers

Although I was only thirteen, I remember how anxious Mum and Dad were about Kiffer when he started seeing Hilary. At twenty-six, he was quite a bit older and certainly more worldly. Dad was worried that Kiffer would make Hilary pregnant, and, for this reason, whenever Kiffer came to stay at the flat, Dad would wait up until Hilary and Kiffer were soundly asleep in separate rooms.

By the time he met Hilary, Kiffer was working as a freelance, professional cellist. When his father died suddenly in 1956, Kiffer took over the conducting of his orchestra, the Newbury String Players. He loved this and the Saturday rehearsals and twelve concerts a year quickly became the focal point of his life.

Although Kiffer had trained at the Royal Academy of Music, he had never seen Hil there. During his third year there, he went to prison as a conscientious objector. When Mum discovered this, she was horrified.

Kiffer was quick to notice that the du Pré family was very different from his own, finding us enclosed and unsophisticated. Fearlessly, he would challenge every value our family stood by. Dad, the eternal gentleman for whom these values were incredibly important, couldn't find it in himself to fight back. Kiffer didn't give up—indeed, he seemed to enjoy this endless teasing.

When Kiffer announced that he was taking Hilary to see *Cat on a Hot Tin Roof* at a cinema in Soho, Dad was quietly horrified. He was appalled at the idea of Hilary being in Soho, and warned her that white-slave traffickers were known to be operating in that part of London and that she might be abducted. Hilary had no idea what Dad was talking about!

In his childhood, Dad had been fearless—indeed adventurous almost to the point of recklessness. He was the one who would challenge the world. Something must have happened, perhaps during the war, that made him so fearful.

Dad was changing. While he presented a friendly yet rather formal front to the world, in private he seemed to be shrinking away from life, becoming more and more distant and consumed in his work.

CHAPTER FOURTEEN

Hilary

If I was on a wave, Jackie was often in a trough, and vice versa. As Kiffer and I were falling in love, Jackie became increasingly depressed.

During the months following the Wigmore she was battling with a terrible inner conflict. The shattering realization for her was that the world had declared her a cellist. So far she had simply been herself, making music. But now, the apparent elevation imposed a demand and an expectation that alarmed her. For the first time, she was questioning how she played, but could find no answers. She began to doubt the very root of her ability.

Her depression manifested itself in a lack of energy. She would stay in bed all morning and had little inclination to play her cello. It was difficult to find anything which gave her any pleasure.

Mum knew that Jackie's gifts would soon lead her far away from the warm protection of the family nest. She was anxious and afraid, and she and Jackie were unable to communicate over the problems of growing up. Mum had led a sheltered life and was very shy herself. Jackie, big, blond, beautiful and increasingly in demand, was becoming aware of Mum's naivety. Jackie was gauche and clumsy, and longed to have social graces, which neither Mum nor Dad had been able to teach her. Dad was immensely proud of her, but privately resentful of the amount of Mum's time that she still absorbed.

In her lessons with Bill, Jackie talked about the difficulties she was having with Mum. He listened, as he always did, but assumed that her complaints were just the usual tussling that goes on between any adolescent girl and her mother.

Her lack of motivation prompted advice from all directions: she should do yoga, she should learn about the basics of music. Teachers came to the flat, and Jackie attended the lessons but was bored by them.

Jackie hated school, and had lasted only two months at Queen's College. Fortunately, a friend, Joan Clwyd undertook private coaching at her home, and Jackie was duly taken to her for English and History lessons. The Clwyds were very involved in the arts and loved entertaining. Joan's daughter, Alison, had just been through the teenage years. Four years older than Jackie, she was astonished to learn, for example, that Jackie had never been on the tube by herself.

Joan, however, discovered that Jackie had the most remarkable intellect, and found her clear-headed, unselfconscious, a good judge of character and disarmingly honest. She became Jackie's closest confidant. Jackie told her that she was unhappy about the changes that would be inflicted on her if she followed the emerging path. She was confused and depressed and wasn't at all sure that being a cellist in the professional world was for her.

Dad needed more support than Mum was now able to give. He felt alienated by the tremendous affinity between Mum and Jackie—a bond which had driven Mum to put Dad in second place from twelve days after Jackie was born. Over the years, he had tried to penetrate this attachment and had been unsuccessful. Now he was resorting to childish behavior. His own private language, which had been so much a part of our family fun, had developed into an annoying babytalk. The seesaw effect, of Dad's whining and Jackie's powerful temperament, became a great strain on Mum. She was pulled between them like a worm between two blackbirds.

Dad had organized yet another huge function for the Institute at which he was to deliver an important speech.

I was sitting in the kitchen writing a letter to Kiffer, as he was preparing his speech.

"Would you like a kerzuppateseesles, Dad?"

"Mmmmm. Yes please, Hibs."

"Dad? How do you make a speech," I asked. "What do you have to do exactly?"

"Well," he replied. "It's very easy really, Hibs. First you explain what you're going to talk about . . . then you talk about it . . . then you say what you've talked about! And you've done it!"

We laughed. At that moment, Mum and Gran appeared in the kitchen. Jackie was still in bed.

"You are coming with me to this dinner, aren't you, Mubs? The president and his wife will be there."

"Remind me. When is it, Dobs?" Mum seemed distracted.

"It's on Friday evening, and it's tails."

"I'll have to see how Jackie is: she's been very tired recently, and she's playing in Bath next week. I think I should really be here in case she feels like practicing."

"Please come. It's just one evening. Gran will be here to look after Jackie. Please? *Maam?*"

He was beginning to plead using the kind of voice that always made Gran furious. She sniped at him. "Derek, it's her job. Of course Iris should stay with Jackie. Don't you dare try and stop her. She's quite right."

Dad went to the dinner on his own.

Kiffer and I married in September 1961 and we lived in Ashmansworth, sharing the family home with Joy. I was riding a delirious wave of love, that delicious form of madness which overwhelms all wisdom and good sense, and offers a hitherto unexperienced freedom. My opportunities seemed limitless and I knew that, in Kiffer, I had found everything I could possibly want.

No longer need I be afraid of anything. His inner strength and lack of boundaries gave me new-found confidence. His enthusiasms overflowed and bore me along in tremendous excitement. His love of reading and knowledge of fiction and poetry opened new pathways for me. His sense of humor gave me hours of mirth. He made me feel like a queen.

He was from an unusual background and was different from anyone I had met before. He was determined and fought for his principles. As a young man, he refused to be conscripted into National Service against his will in peacetime. Consequently, he was sentenced to six months in prison. There were no allowances for vegetarians and the combination of lack of food and hard labor in a quarry caused him to lose four stone. He was astonished to discover that many of the inmates could neither read nor write, so he wrote numerous dictated letters on their behalf. He was starved of books, but read both the Bible and the entire works of Shakespeare repeatedly. He told me that although the months spent inside were terrible, he nevertheless appreciated the experiences and the insight they had given him. It was the first time he had been among people who had no background or security. It was a shock, but one for which he was grateful.

Kiffer had already decided that a freelancing life was not for him: he wanted to base himself at Ashmansworth and develop the chicken business. Within the next few months, the chicken capacity increased from hundreds to thousands. A van arrived laden with boxes of baby chicks which were unloaded on to the wood shavings under the infra-red lamps in the old chicken shed. And it was not long before Prima Pullets was up and running.

My life was changing fast. I loved my new home, learning to cook, to garden and to be involved with life in the country. Our days were full and, carefully trained by Joy and Olive, I was increasingly absorbed into the running of the household. We ate an early breakfast of home-made yogurt with runny honey and toast. Jack and Olive arrived at eight o'clock; Joy disappeared into the book room; Kiffer and I did the chickens with Jack, and Olive sorted out the house. At eleven everyone congregated in the kitchen around the big table. It was always a merry time with steaming mugs of coffee or Milo.

One day in the winter, I asked Jack why his shirt was rustling.

"It's the newspaper, Hilary."

"What newspaper, Jack?"

"I always wear it when it's cold, all country people do. Under my shirt, it is, and it's the warmest thing out. Not expensive neither."

Shan, Jack's large dog, a cross between an alsatian and a labrador, was there too. Everyone knew I was afraid of him, and inevitably someone would make him bark. I became brilliant at emergency exits. But that was the only blot on my new idyllic life. New horizons had been opened for me and I was as happy as a lark.

I adored the openness of the household, where people came and went as they pleased. Joy had befriended many artists and writers, and seemed to collect creative people, who loved visiting

Ashmansworth and were inspired by her company. Consequently, there was a constant stream of visitors. Piers used to come regularly, often staying for weeks during the holidays, but it was more difficult for Jackie to leave London.

I tackled my final year at the Academy with renewed enthusiasm and confidence, traveling up to London with Kiffer for my lessons. I was enjoying my flute lessons again, and playing regularly with the Newbury String Players was gradually restoring my old enjoyment of performing. One day there was a telephone call from the Director of Music at Downe House, a school near Newbury. Their flute teacher had been taken ill and I was asked if I would be willing to help. Although I had never taught before, I agreed, and stayed for many years.

Three months after our wedding, gentle Auntie Em died. Mum and Gran were devastated and Gran began to spend more and more time at Portland Place. Poor Gran—she had no friends in London and must have been lonely. Her presence often made the atmosphere strained: she and Dad continued to irritate each other but her life had always been devoted to her daughter—and so it continued.

Mum, Jackie and I were to give a recital at Blackheath High School. As the concert approached, Joy, who knew it would be an important occasion for me, took me under her wing. "Hilly, dear, I really think the time has come to find something else for you to wear in this concert—something other than that dress with those large green spots!"

I knew that I had no dress sense at all. She, with her artistic eye, was imaginative with clothes.

"I have a length of black velvet which we will take to Josephine, my little Spanish dressmaker. I'm sure she will be able to make something lovely for you. And we'll have to find some little concert slippers, too. Those sandals just won't be suitable."

I was swept along by Joy's authority and enthusiasm.

We arrived at Josephine's house one afternoon, bearing several lengths of material: black velvet for me, printed corduroy and a Scottish tweed for Joy.

"Josephine, dearie, this is Hilly, Kiffy's wife. I've found some lovely black velvet for her. She needs a simple concert dress."

So I was measured and designed. There were little sleeves, a round neckline, a shaped waist and flared skirt, plenty of room for breathing, and lots of little buttons down the back.

"So pretty, dearie."

And I was dismissed, while Joy discussed her new garments with Josephine.

On the day itself, December 5, 1961, we met to rehearse. I was excited about seeing Mum and Jackie. I was also thrilled that they would witness how extremely happy I was. Kiffer was there, and the welcomes were warm and jovial.

"Let me carry your cello, Jacks." Kiffer laughed. "I'll swing it around my head: it needs a breath of fresh air!"

Jackie clutched her cello. "No fear—you should carry Hil's flute. And cuddle it tightly or she'll have a fit!"

Mum, the peacemaker, intervened. "Take care, Jackables, and do look where you're going. It's this way, I think . . . Jacks, we'd better rehearse first, and then you can look out for Bill while Hil and I play. Come on."

The fooling over, Jackie launched into the Adagio of the Beethoven Sonata in D and I was instantly overcome by the intensity of her sound. Her playing was becoming even more powerful and confident. As always, she gave everything, and there she was, pulling me emotionally to pieces again, when suddenly she stopped.

"Your turn, Hil. I've done enough. I'll wait for Bill."

I began to feel as if I was going to the gallows. I knew I should not be playing in the same concert as her and that I would not be able to perform.

Mum was urging me to hurry.

"Come on, Hil, we haven't too much time. I'm sure your flute is warm enough now."

We started with the Handel Flute Sonata in G and I tried so hard, but where Jackie soared effortlessly, I struggled and puffed.

"Mum, it sounds ghastly. I don't want to play."

"Yes, you do, Hil, and it's only a rehearsal. We'll just try the Poulenc for speed."

Exactly the same happened.

People were arriving to prepare the hall.

We bundled into our Green Room where there was much admiring of my new black dress, and all those little buttons. Joy had given me a beautiful gold brooch too, another source of amazement, and for a while I felt reasonably pretty. We plunged our hands into hot water, gave them a good soak, and were ready. Dad and Piers arrived just in time to find their seats next to Bill and Kiffer.

The concert was announced and we were welcomed. I was playing first.

"Good luck, Hil," whispered Jackie as I left the comfort of the Green Room.

And there I was, bowing, smiling and responding to the applause. Mum was beaming at me and waiting for me to play. I had to concentrate on concentrating, as I wrestled with my lack of confidence. It was not an easy performance and not one that I loved, but Mum was totally supportive in her accompanying and winked approvingly at me as we bowed together at the end.

Now it was Jackie's turn and, wanting to hear her, I slipped into the back of the hall. The atmosphere was afire with expectation. Everyone had heard about this phenomenon and her cello, and of her huge success at the Wigmore Hall, and now here she was, ready to play just for them.

The moment her bow touched the strings, the shy girl vanished. Her command, freedom and total involvement transported the audience out of their everyday lives. They loved it, and showed it too. She had given a superb performance.

I had to play in the second half but didn't know how I could face everyone again.

Kiffer found me in the interval. "That was the best you've ever played the Handel, Hil. Lovely sound, lovely shapes. And we've still got the Poulenc to come. I'm loving it."

"Kiffer, I can't. They want Jackie, not me. And Bill's here too."

"Forget all that, Hil. Just play your Poulenc for *me*. I'm longing for it. Concentrate on me, on us; forget everyone else and we'll enjoy it together."

He gave me a huge hug.

"Look at me in the audience before you play. I'll wink!"

Jackie and I waited in the Green Room. Mum gave us both a kiss and went to join the audience. Jackie was called for the unaccompanied Bach Suite in G.

"Good luck, Jack. I shall be listening from here. Who are you going to play to?"

"You, Hil. It's all for you."

She did play for me and I knew it and treasured it. Every person in the audience knew she was playing just for them. That was her strength: she gave to every individual, and how we all loved and absorbed it.

Then it was my turn for the Poulenc Sonata. I found Kiffer and his wink, and playing for him carried me through the whole sonata. The audience was generous and I was relieved. Jackie's Bartók Rhapsody was a stunning end to the concert.

After her bows, we all bowed together and pushed Mum in front of us. The audience responded to her and rose in recognition. It was a fitting end to an emotional evening.

Mum knew it was possibly the last time the three of us would play together. Her feelings were in a jumble: elated by the playing; happy for my happiness; proud of Jackie; but sad that her family life was changing, and upset by the hard realization that, having held us together for so long, we were now going our own ways.

CHAPTER FIFTEEN

Hilary

After the Wigmore, the agents Ibbs and Tillett were assigned to look after Jackie and organize her concert diary. Emmie Tillett was one of the most powerful agents in the business. She booked Jackie's concerto début: the Elgar at the Royal Festival Hall in London, with the BBC Symphony Orchestra conducted by Rudolf Schwarz. As bookings were usually fixed well in advance, the earliest date that could be arranged was March 21, 1962, a year after the Wigmore.

This concert marked the beginning of Jackie's special relationship with the Elgar concerto, which she would play many times throughout her career. Her unique interpretation of the music was fresh and exciting, and eclipsed everything that had gone before. Jackie's ability to portray the emotions of a man in the autumn of his life was one of her extraordinary and inexplicable capacities. We cannot imagine or rehearse untried emotions, but with Jackie and her cello they erupted: she loved them, played with them openly and was fearless of them. Nothing stopped her going as far as she wanted and further than anyone had ever been before. She had infinite imagination, total freedom: there was nothing in her way. She found the heart of the music and expressed it with such penetrating directness her audiences were enraptured.

In some ways, her astonishing emotional maturity had been a huge dilemma for her. As a little girl, these adult insights lifted her out of her childhood on to another plane. It is not surprising that she was unable to be part of her own age group. She *was* different and therefore a target. Her salvation was her cello voice, enabling her to release these colossal feelings in a way that would not only be understood, but hugely appreciated and enjoyed.

Jackie used to say, "Once the composer has written the music on the page, it doesn't belong to him anymore, it belongs to me." The reviews for this performance were ecstatic, and from that moment the Elgar unquestionably belonged to her.

Jacqueline du Pré, a brilliant cellist now, at 17, made her "adult" début at the Royal Festival Hall last night in the Elgar Concerto. Her playing united technical command with a maturity of feeling remarkable for her age. The Elgar Concerto with its serious beauties, its frequent changes of mood and tempo, poses some formidable interpretative problems. The tall, fair girl in an evening dress of pale blue, hair bobbed, with a fringe, was a picture of self-possession throughout its 29-minute course. She reacted instinctively to its emotions, profound and serene. The tone of her walnut-colored 1673 Strad, which might have been larger had the player been more familiar with the acoustics, was heartfelt. The soloist gave us smooth and sympathetic phrasing, a moving range of nuance. She swayed to the rhythm, in fast figuration her head tossed, her fingers raced confidently bridgeward and down. The occasional fault of intonation, unusual for her, I attribute to the tension of the occasion. But a calmer platform figure could hardly be imagined. To me it was affecting that this later Elgar work, with its hints of autumn, should be presented to us by a girl in her springtime.

Percy Cater
Daily Mail,
March 22, 1962

The *Guardian* called her "The first cellist of potential greatness to be born in England."

1962 was a big year for Jackie. She gave her first TV recital with Mum accompanying her; attended Dartington Summer School in Devon for masterclasses with the French cellist, Paul Tortelier; and stunned the musical world at the Edinburgh Festival with a performance of the Brahms F major Sonata, accompanied by Ernest Lush. Later, in August, she played the Elgar at her first Prom Concert, this time with Sir Malcolm Sargent conducting. *The Times*

called her performance that of a "thinking adult and not an intuitive musical child."

Working with Tortelier at Dartington had been such a success,
it was decided that Jackie would study with him in Paris for six
months. As usual, the Suggia provided the necessary finances. She
left in October. It was the first time she had been away from home
on her own.

October 1962

You'd bedder write to me while I'm in France
If you don't
WATCH IT! *Maan*
If you write when you're too tired
WATCH IT! *Maan*
But whether you do or you don't
You'd bedder
WATCH IT, *MAAN*

Much love, Jzeeeet

Jackie lodged with Madame Bernard at 20 rue de Lyvette, Paris 16
and wrote home almost daily:

Dear Folks,

Thank you for being so frightfully forward with your letter
writing (hum). Every morning I awake with the gloomy
knowledge that I have been left to starve on this barren and
hostile coast, unloved, uncherished under-fed—reason ?

Two days ago I had a frightful attack of an embarrassing illness called diareah—LAUKS. You should have been there to
witness the velocity of that rare liquid's short journey. Niagara
Falls isn't in it! I never experienced such a flutter of anxious
French ladies as on that day when I was packed to bed with a
hot water bottle on my tum which made me feel embarrassingly
pregnant! No doubt it was all a sympathetic pregnancy for Hil!

However, I was kindly left to starve until the tummy "de-
rangement" rectumified itself. Oh, another embarrassing thing—
when the French take your temperature they stick the blooming

thing dans le bloomin rectum! Madame Bernard patiently explained the proceeding but I still don't know whether it means "*up* the doodah" or just "between the doodah."

Madame B is very keen to know when you two will come to Paris and she's very keen to meet the old man (can't think why) about whom she has heard so much.

If you come, mind you live up to what I have said about you, fat man. (I have stressed your gaiety, wit and natural charm) and it would do me good to have the old Gothic Pillar (you Mum!) round for a while—moral support and all that lark.

I'm wishing you luck old girl with your interview with Emmie T.[Ibbs and Tillett] I'm glad you took the initiative.

A tout à l'heure

tell everyone to write to me!

much love Jeeeeeeeeeeeeeeeks

PS read this letter out with discretion. You may agree that certain parts aren't suitable for younger and older ears.

PPS Bar, where is your letter ?

Jackie was unhappy and disorganized, but gradually made friends with other students and started exploring Paris. She posted her washing to Mum at home where it was duly laundered and sent back. Mum in turn would send her lists of questions to answer and return:

Did the thick shirt arrive?	Yes
Did the red twin-set arrive?	No
Which dress shall Mrs. Holland bring out for you to wear?	Le rose
Which dress will you wear for Paris concert?	Blanche
Can you last until March 6th for money, when I come to Paris?	Yes, but bring lots to pay for cello repairs.

Jackie was under the impression that she was to have private lessons with Tortelier but this was not the case. She was in a group with several other students who had only three sessions of three-quarters of an hour each with him per week. At first she complained that he used her to demonstrate technique to the other students and had nothing new to show her. Jackie knew he was trying to find out how she did things, so she purposely confused him. After a month she wrote home to Mum and Dad:

Bad news, I phoned Tortelier after the class today to see if he could give me one or two private lessons but he says he is unable to as it is against the Conservatoire rules. I feel unhappy in the masterclass because there is a barrier between us and had I known that private lessons were impossible at the Conservatoire, I certainly would not have joined. At the moment I feel utterly depressed and miserable as what had seemed to be my salvation now turns out to be the opposite. I had to tell you because it's too much to keep to myself. His wife would probably give me weekly lessons, but it's not the same and I am ill at ease with her although she is absolutely charming and utterly sincere.

I am utterly worn out having had very little sleep so everything is probably considerably magnified but it is the personal contact which had helped me more than anything else in the private lesson.

Tortelier also wants to have something done to the A string because he is convinced that it is not my fault when I force. If nothing can be done having tried this, one can conclude that the cello will never be more open.

Saw Marilyn Monroe for the first time in *Some Like it Hot*. She is certainly a very great actress. Please don't be too alarmed and upset by this letter. I'm sure I'll feel better when I've had some rest.

Love, Jackie

The change of environment was making a deep impression on Jackie. With Tortelier she was coming up against a different work

ethic and, by the time of her next letter to Mum, was feeling
more positive.

I feel a great difference between the musical life I led in London
and the musical life here. In London I was a carefree, abandoned
country girl. Now I am with an aristocratic family who are
judging me much more strictly and mercilessly. I love it, by the
way! Tortelier wants to integrate the two sides—the abandoned
with the disciplined, polished and dedicated. At the moment I
am going through a difficult initiation ceremony.
    Write soon please, Old Girl, a few consolatory lines. And
please send new pairs of stockings.
    Absolutely OUT.
    Much love, Jacks

Tortelier made two immediate and fundamental decisions for
Jackie, confirming what others had been saying for months. First,
that she should slow down and not play in any concerts for at least
six months. This had been Bill Pleeth's advice as well. Secondly,
that her cello, the 1673 Strad, was inadequate for her style of playing and would need substantial alterations in order to produce the
sound required of a world-class virtuoso.
    Jackie was very attached to the big brown Strad. It was her first
serious cello, and she had achieved her early triumphs with it. But
Tortelier told her that since it had been made nearly three hundred
years ago, at a time when the cello was not a solo or virtuoso instrument and its main function was to play the bass line, Stradivari
had concentrated on making the bass of his instrument strong.
Hence the choice of wood and the thick build would not produce
the resonance required by a soloist to fill a large concert hall. Later,
as the cello was becoming a solo instrument, Stradivari made the
treble equally powerful.
    Tortelier's advice rang true for Jackie because several people in
London, including Sir John Barbirolli, whose opinion she trusted,
had told her that her cello was unbalanced and the tone required
of it was not big enough.
    However, it was typical of Tortelier to want to make changes
to everyone's cello. He had designed a special endpin which he
said was to help the sound: by lifting the cello to a higher angle,

where player's bowing arm could benefit from the force of gravity, in a similar way to a violinist's. The other alterations he made to Jackie's cello were to change the bridge, and fit a hollow sound-post and metal strings. Jackie thought these innovations had definitely improved the sound, but the message she sent home to Mum and Dad was that Tortelier still considered the instrument inappropriate.

Despite Tortelier's advice that she shouldn't play in any concerts, Jackie came home at Christmas to perform the Schumann Cello Concerto in the Royal Festival Hall. The *Daily Express* announced "We have a world class winner here," and *The Times* said: "She has an instinctive feeling for the true significance of every phrase as if she had a lifetime of experience behind her."

Jackie was amused to find that Tortelier was performing at the Royal Festival Hall five days before her, but couldn't stay to hear her. She wrote home to Mum.

. . . I have not yet had a private lesson and I am shy about asking for one, although I want them so much. He has so much to say, but his character always makes me feel more light-hearted and yet purposeful when needed! Because I have had to prepare the Schumann, I haven't had much time to concentrate on technique, which I want to study "cold" for a while sometimes. At the moment I think it is partly due to the weakness of my 3rd and 4th fingers which is hampering me so much. They are weak because I previously held my hand sloped (therefore the strength and weight was on the 1st and 2nd fingers) and I never had to press because of the gut strings. Now, after practicing a scale, my fingers ache with strain! It's a bit lonely sometimes, as I don't see anyone during the day and, although I'm in Paris, I can't think what to do if I'm not practicing (the old lack of initiative). I can't hang around the Conservatoire because Tortelier likes us to go off and work after we've played. That's why I like books, so please send three at a time. By the way, I need a black posh bag, a posh pair of walking shoes, posh shoes for going to concerts or the theater and a black cocktail dress.

Mum decided to take the matter of private lessons into her own hands and wrote to Tortelier on December 31, 1962:

Dear Mr. Tortelier,

The Christmas holidays have given my husband and me the opportunity of discussing Jacqueline's progress with her and we are delighted to hear that she is so happy with you.

As you know, there are probably no more than two years in which her studies can take precedence over her professional engagements. We are all therefore anxious that she should benefit to the maximum during this short period.

Will you accept Jacqueline as a private pupil so that she may derive the greatest possible benefit from your teaching ? If you will, as we all greatly hope—she would resign from the Conservatoire as soon as that can be arranged.

Thank you for your kind letter of December 27 and for inviting Jacqueline to give a broadcast on March 5 in Berlin and a concert on 7th March.

Jacqueline, my husband and I deeply appreciate your kind suggestions, and Jacqueline has asked me to say how sorry she is that she is not able to accept either of them because she has already canceled concerto engagements in March and April, giving the reason that she wishes to be free to study.

My husband and I would much like to talk things over with you. Could you spare us a few moments if we come to Paris to see you? We could call on you at any time on Saturday 5th or Sunday January 6. Please send us a telegram or telephone London, Langham 5832 "en pcv"—which Jacqueline tells me means "reversed charges." We all join in sending our warmest greetings to you and to Madame Tortelier.

Yours most sincerely

Iris and Derek du Pré

Tortelier's response was to telephone Jackie.

Dear Folks,

Since speaking to the old gargoyle on the phone, I had a call from Tortelier. He apologized for making me play Schelomo to the pupils in his class. He realized that the moment he gives me an emotional piece to play I start forcing again and revert to bad habits. He said that I must do no concerts for at least six months and says I must cancel the Schumann and the West of England tour. He wants me to work on Bach, Haydn and scales *only*, allowing me to play no louder than mezzo forte. I did say that I find it difficult not to force at the Conservatoire because with other people listening, I always feel as if I've got to give a performance. He understood this. He is, however, very frightened about private lessons, especially as he cannot trust himself to keep secrets however much he wants to keep them. I'm having one on Saturday, though. Tell *nobody* about this . . .

Jackie managed, in the end, to have seven private lessons with Tortelier. He lost count and thought there had only been two or three, but Jackie knew the exact number. She wrote home:

It is interesting that after Uncle Bill's [Pleeth's] lessons I felt physically exhausted and that after Tortelier's I feel mentally exhausted. I have never seen such merciless driving after a point on which he is convinced and I have never tried so hard to *try* and fulfil what anybody says. His quickly passing flashes of humour are an immense and longed for relief! But this is only because I am not used to pitching concentration at such a high and consistent level. I cannot think how he can stand this mental pressure and as I know him better and better, I admire his wife beyond bounds. There is *no mercy* in his convictions. I am not saying that I find him hard. As you know, he is the most lovable person.

CHAPTER SIXTEEN

Piers

With Hilary married and Jackie away much of the time, it became unusually quiet at Portland Place. Disliking London, I found every opportunity to escape, splitting my time between Big Liz's Street Farm and Hilary and Kiffer's Church Farm. Only four miles separated them.

I missed Jackie enormously when she was away. There was so much to tell her about the farm. I was an appalling letter-writer, but whenever Jackie complained to Mum that she hadn't heard from me, I would try and put pen to paper, usually scribbling down my latest set of terrible jokes. Jackie's letters, though, were always the highlight of my week.

Dear Bar,
Thanks for your maaarvellous letter which made me laugh until the cows came home! I have obeyed your orders and torn it up.

Congrats on your science doodah Old Boy—You'll make it yet. Vous faites mal pour bien faire. This means, believe it or not, You work hard to do well. "Faire mal" is "hard work." I am so cross because I have just shoved the tooth of a comb down my thumb nail and I can hardly write for pain (Oh, La, La).

This business about Cuba I cannot understand in the French papers, so could you tell me what is happening by now? It didn't turn out so bad, I believe but I don't know. Eh bien. Au revoir. Much doodah to all.

P.S. Sorry for the French lesson.

When Jackie came home from Paris in February 1963, I couldn't wait to have one of our special chats. I wanted to know all about her time there: what she had done, who she'd met, the food she had eaten; and, by far the most important, to catch up on the latest round of jokes. I knew she hadn't told me everything in her letters and when I asked her if she'd liked Tortelier, she glanced sideways at me, blew a loud raspberry and said: "I didn't like him at all!"

"Why not, what was the matter with him?"

"All he wanted was to learn how *I* did things," she said crossly. "He had nothing to teach me."

"Really! How awful!"

"Yeah! It was. So I deliberately misled him. Ha!"

She paused, suddenly serious. "Bar, I have learnt something, though. There are two ways to make music: one is to play technically well, playing exactly what is written, perfectly. The other is simply to make music, which is what I can do . . . That's *all* I can do. The problem is, I don't know *how* I do it."

Jackie wasn't at home for long. She was booked for a West of England tour with Tortelier's daughter, Maria de la Pau, an accomplished pianist the same age as Jackie. And so, by early March, she was back on the road again.

Hilary

On April 2, 1963, Theresa, our first child, was born. I had her at home, following the Finzi family tradition; it was the most joyous thing that had ever happened to me.

When Theresa was a day old, Mum and Dad arrived with Jackie and Maria, who were in the middle of their West of England tour. I was in the pink room, and besotted by my tiny baby. Maria stayed downstairs with Joy.

Mum was moved to tears as she cradled her first grandchild.

Jackie was entranced. "Can I hold her, Hil?"

Mum eventually passed the little Theresa to her.

"She's so *tiny* . . . what does she weigh?"

"Eight pounds, Jackie! But look at her hands . . ." We marveled at the exquisiteness of the newborn Theresa. It was the first time for both of us that we had been closely involved with a baby.

Two weeks later, Jackie arrived to stay and the Newbury String Players were to give another concert in Stockcross Church. Jackie was in ebullient spirits, having finished her tour, and now had some free time. She adored the baby, as everyone did, so the atmosphere in the house was one of celebration and happiness.

When Kiffer discovered that he was short of a cellist for the concert, the remedy was obvious and simple. Although Jackie needed a little persuasion, she agreed that it might be fun.

Little did the orchestra know what it was in for. The first problem was that Jackie always played as a soloist. The second was that she was used to having space around *her*, and in the cello section there was no space. She seemed to fill the whole area, so there was a lot of kerfuffle as everyone tried to fit about her.

I was excited about Jackie playing with the String Players and was sitting in the audience with a sleeping Theresa in my arms— her first concert.

Kiffer lifted his baton and began the first piece—the Stanley Concerto No. 1. I could see Jackie looking slightly surprised by the restrictions of baroque performing, and she was certainly not having any of that. Off she sailed, playing the music her own way, as if it were a romantic concerto, and loving every moment of it. Here was new ground to explore, and she did. No one stood a chance.

I could see Kiffer fighting to keep the tempo and style, but the orchestra was being swept along on a powerful wave and his desperate gestures had no response. He tried to encourage the violins to project their sound, but the more they did, the more Jackie did too. She had never been in a position where she couldn't hear herself, and had a much greater capacity to soar and sing than anyone else. The cello part rose and swelled, and filled the whole church. Kiffer and the entire orchestra were her flock—they had no option but to follow wherever she went.

When the audience applauded, it was Jackie who, without thinking, stood and bowed. She played with the lead cellist all through the solo parts, and told me afterward that when it said "solo" she didn't understand why "that girl sitting next to me was playing as well!"

The next morning, Jackie and I were chatting while I was breast-feeding Theresa.

"Hil, that looks so cozy."

"It is! It's wonderful."

"Oh, Hil. I wish I could have a baby . . ."

"You will, one day. Just wait a bit."

"I suppose so . . . But I'm not sure I want to be a cellist. Everyone's always telling me what I should be doing and Mum's driving me mad."

"Why?"

"She's always fussing about everything. And Dad just sits there and doesn't say anything. He seems to work all the time."

"Well, you know you're always welcome here, don't you?"

"Yes, I know," she said, with a resigned smile. "The latest thing is that everyone thinks my general education is lacking, so I'm going to have math lessons. I hate math!"

"Is that with Joan?"

"No, I'm going to a colleague of hers—George Debenham. He's really nice."

Soon it was time for Jackie to go home to prepare for another broadcast, Granada's *The Art of Music*, performing the Beethoven A major Sonata, accompanied by Anthony Hopkins.

In late May, she left for Italy where she had been invited for the second time to perform in the Accademia Internazionale di Musica which took place in Castello di Sermonetta. The castle was owned by Princess Caetani, who enjoyed inviting young musicians to perform there, and it was an honor to be invited.

Piers

One of the most wonderful journeys I ever made with Mum and Dad was in the summer of 1963, when I was fifteen years old and we went to visit Jackie in Sermonetta. We could easily have flown, but Dad decided to drive through France and turned the trip into one of his great adventures. When I was checking Dad's diary recently, I found he had even made a note of the odometer readings, the time of day, and the main towns we passed through, with jottings such as "camped by the road, couldn't sleep" or "Indian, eagle, cable car." Looking at the map of France, I retraced the journey and found I could recall every detail with clarity. I will never forget how the scenery changed from rolling hills to dramatic mountains as we crossed into Switzerland at Vallorbe.

After several days of traveling, we were in a disheveled state. With one day left before seeing Jackie, we stayed in a hotel in Buonconvento, near Florence, to have a comfortable night and a good wash. The next afternoon, having passed through Rome, we wound our way up a seemingly endless mountain road, arriving at the top in the village of Sermonetta, dominated by the huge ancient castle in which Jackie was staying. Dad announced that we had driven 1,334 miles since leaving Portland Place.

There was no one about as we walked up the steep village road, over the drawbridge and under the portcullis into the castle courtyard. Everything was still, as though suspended in the heat.

"Must be siesta time," whispered Mum. "Shall we come back later?" With that, Jackie appeared in the doorway to the main castle and stood looking at us, with her head slightly to one side. For a few moments, none of us moved.

"Mum!" she shrieked, and ran toward us.

Jackie introduced us to our hostess, Princess Caetani, and later we drove to her home in Ninfa. Enormous stone pillars guarded the entrance. Someone appeared from the lodge house and opened the gates. It was like staying at Buckingham Palace. We had dinner together that night, and for the next few days we lived like royalty. I had such a crush on Princess Caetani—she was so elegant. Dad wrote in his diary, "The most glorious time! Incredible gardens, streams, huge plants, cypresses, cacti, dragonflies in profusion. Six baths! Sun Sun Sun."

On the last day of our stay, there was a concert in the evening in the vast open-air castle courtyard. There had been warm rain during the afternoon, but everything was now dry, and the skies were clear. Chairs were arranged and music-stands were festooned with candles. Just after the sun set, flaming torches were lit around the courtyard and the guests began to arrive, dressed in all their finery. When everyone was seated, out came the instrumentalists. I clapped enthusiastically for Jackie. I was proud of her and wanted everyone to know that she was *my* sister. The stars were bright and sparkling against the dark night sky. The only light was from the glow of the candles, flickering on the music-stands. The music began and the castle walls seemed to encapsulate and concentrate every note. All I could see were the silhouettes of the audience against the candle-lit movement of the players and the occasional flash of Jackie's blond hair.

Suddenly thousands upon thousands of fireflies appeared from nowhere and began dancing to the music, their tiny flashing lights floating, jumping and pirouetting just above the ensemble. As the music ended, they vanished as quickly as they had appeared, almost as though they too had finished their performance. But for them, there were no curtain calls.

That night we stayed at the castle. I shared a room with Jackie and some of the other musicians. As I lay in bed, Jackie shone a torch up to the high ceiling.

"What can you see?" she asked, in a half-whisper.

The torchlight settled on some naked figures.

"Wow!" I said. "Don't show Mum and Dad, they wouldn't understand."

"In that case, I will," said Jackie, with a naughty laugh. The torch went out. " 'Night, Bar."

" 'Night, Jacks."

By now I was becoming used to the extraordinary things that revolved around Jackie. She led us into exalted circles and every encounter seemed to be yet another almost unbelievable experience for me. I longed to share these moments with my friends when I returned home, but I knew in my heart that they probably would not believe me and it would only lead to ridicule. I was learning it was far better to keep these moments secret.

Jackie returned to Sermonetta the following year:

Castello, Italy, 1964

Dearest Mobs and Dobs,

Firstly, a happy birthday to Old Bean with much love from me. The journey was uneventful until I arrived at Sermonetta where I was greeted by two scruffy village boys who remembered me—that was nice.

Then came the throat-gripping reunion with all the Argentinians and since then nothing has happened. There will be twenty at this course from the 15th. I have asked Alberto if I can leave on July 10th: I am just so fed up with everybody here.

Since having seen quite a lot of people I really like recently, the people here just feel so false I can't stand it. (Sorry this isn't exactly a cheerful letter.)

Let me see, yes, the food has been good, and have managed to meet insincerity with insincerity which is quite fun as a game!

When I arrived last night I set out to woo everyone with my sparkling humor and spontaneity (English inferiority complex!) and judge my pleasure when I heard one Argentinian (married) say "quelle cretine." However, that impression slightly deteriorated when I suddenly got bored and couldn't be bothered to act. The trouble with these guys is, you've gotta be vivacious to be accepted. Blast em!!!

There have been some moments of light entertainment. The other night I dressed up as an Indian Chief with toothpaste smeared all over my face as war paint. I then started shouting Apache sounds and strode into the dining room. I went up to Alberto at the head of the table and with the excuse of my disguise, poured contempt on him in proud and unpardoning Indian fashion.

I have made two good friends here: Sonia and Ruden Gonzales. Argentinians, of course. We communicate in French and they call me "Jackie la Cocotte" for some reason. Oh well, I'm gonna practice now. Do hope you can change my ticket without too much trouble.

See you soon, rotters.

Much love as always, J.

CHAPTER SEVENTEEN

Hilary

George Debenham had fallen in love with Jackie. To her, he was a stable father-figure, providing a supporting arm outside the family at a time when she was striking out for her own independence. I know she appreciated his wisdom and faith in her, yet felt guilty about their relationship, knowing she couldn't return his deeper feelings. He was her first boyfriend and she used him mercilessly as a taxi service, or for whatever she required. Despite this, George was devoted to her and constant in his love and help. An able pianist and extremely good sight-reader, he often accompanied Jackie, although they never played together professionally.

Jackie brought him to Church Farm, and immediately suggested they should go for a walk to the Gibbet—the initiation ground for all new visitors.

When they returned and George was out of earshot, Jackie and I found a private moment together.

"What do you think of him, Hil?"

"He's extremely kind, Jack, and very shy."

"I know. Guess what happened on the Gibbet?"

"What? What?"

"I was charging up the hill, racing him to the top, when my bra strap snapped . . . Oh Hil!"

"Jackie! What did you do?"

"I just said, at the top of my voice, 'Swing low, sweet chariots'."

"What did George say?"

"He didn't get it!"

We collapsed laughing.

★ ★ ★

Jackie so wanted to have a normal life, and would be high with excitement at Church Farm, where she felt free to be silly and lark about. But her beloved cello always called her back, and she had to go. Tortelier's comments about the brown Strad were very much on her mind, so when she was introduced to Charles Beare, the renowned specialist in stringed instruments, at a party on New Year's Eve, she wasted no time in telling him that she needed a new cello. Charles had returned to England from America in 1961, and having heard much about Jackie, was delighted to meet her. Knowing all about the brown Strad, he offered to look after it for her and to search for a new one. But the kind of cello Jackie wanted comes at a price, and it wasn't clear who would pay for it.

Pondles died suddenly on January 27, 1964 and Dad, who had been feeling for some time that he had reached a crossroad in his career, realized it was time to reassess everything. His contract was due for renewal and his strategy was to request a further five-year term and a suitably larger salary. If accepted, he had won. If rejected, he would be offered a golden handshake and still win.

The golden handshake was agreed and a new chapter began. As the news leaked, offers of jobs arrived. But first, house-hunting would have to begin in earnest since the Institute owned the flat in Portland Place.

Dad accepted a new position as Secretary to the Chartered Accountants Students' Society in the City and, not long afterward, found a 1930s three-bedroomed detached house with an acre of land in Gerrards Cross. This was an ideal location. It brought the family nearer to the country again, and was within commuting distance for Dad and for Piers, who was still at school in Hampstead. Mum could continue to give private tuition at home while teaching also at Apsley Grammar School in Hemel Hempstead. The decision made, they planned to move in August, during the summer holidays.

This gave Jackie her chance to make her break. When she announced to Mum that she was leaving home, Mum was devastated. Around that time, Mum was interviewed for a magazine article and said she was happy for Jackie to explore her independence. But this was not entirely true. In reality she knew that

Jackie wasn't capable of looking after herself and she was worried that she would not cope well enough.

Soon after her nineteenth birthday, Jackie moved by herself into a flat in Kensington Park Road, owned by Kiffer's younger brother Nigel. But it wasn't long before she felt lonely, so, when Alison Clwyd, who was by now a good friend, asked her to share her flat, Jackie accepted eagerly and moved to the basement flat in Ladbroke Grove.

Piers

Jackie really enjoyed her new freedom, but still depended on Mum to sort out her clothes and her washing, to tidy up and help with her arrangements. Mum would go to Jackie's flat in every spare moment, leaving Gran to look after Dad and me.

As she became more confident living away from home, Jackie started to take charge of her own life, and had special concert dresses made by a friend, Madeleine Dinkel. Madeleine had been appalled by the old-fashioned skirt and blouse Jackie had worn at one concert, and immediately set about creating dresses to match Jackie's increasingly flamboyant personality. Madeleine used silk and lace in strong, vibrant colors, always with skirts full enough to accomodate the cello. For the first time ever, Jackie felt glamorous.

One Saturday, Mum and I went to visit Jackie in her flat. As usual, she needed some groceries, and while Mum went off to shop, I stayed behind with Jackie. At last there was an opportunity for one of our secret chats. We always had these when we hadn't seen each other for a while and there was personal news to catch up on. Jackie brought the coffee over to the table and sat down next to me.

"How's school?" she asked.

"Ghastly," I replied.

"Gran all right?"

"Yes, tetchy as ever. Still snorting."

"Poor Gran."

"Poor Dad," I said. There was silence.

"Bar, have you ever heard of Helena Wright?"

"No."

"Well, she's a gynecologist."

"What's that?"

"It's someone who knows about women's parts."

Wow. Bombshell. What am I getting into? I thought.

"I went to see her and she fitted me with the cap."

"What's wrong with you?" I asked hesitantly.

She laughed and looked at me sideways.

"Nothing, silly. It's just to stop me getting pregnant. It's horribly messy, but it's safe."

I waited a few moments before admitting my ignorance.

"Jacks, what's the cap?"

She laughed again and said: "I knew you didn't know, Bar. I'll go and get it."

She disappeared to the bedroom and reappeared clutching a round white container, which she opened.

"That's the cap," she said. "It's called a Dutch cap. If the cap fits, wear it!" Then she started drawing a diagram of where it fitted and how it worked. I stared in amazement, feeling very uncomfortable.

Mum arrived back at that moment, so Jackie scooped up the little box and fled to the bedroom.

"Your *drawing!*" I whispered loudly. Jackie ran back, crumpled it up and threw it in the bin.

The incident had a strange effect on me. I felt Jackie needed protecting. I was frightened because she seemed to have moved into new territory which I didn't understand and which felt wrong.

I was totally out of my depth. I was a schoolboy and Jackie was a star.

In June, Jackie went to Rome to do a series of concerts. Later she told me that while on the aircraft she remembered she had left the cap floating in the sink and that Mum was in the flat clearing up at that very moment. It was too late. Mum would know. But when Jackie telephoned Mum later that evening, Mum did not mention it. When Jackie returned to the flat, she found Mum had put the cap neatly away. I suspect Mum was deeply shocked by many of the things that Jackie was doing at that time but was unable to confront her about anything.

★ ★ ★

On August 25, we began the move from Portland Place. The removal firm had set up a gantry outside the flat so the two boudoir grand pianos could be removed through the window and lowered four floors to the street. The Blüthner descended unscathed, but as Mum's beloved Bechstein, which she had won in a competition in Plymouth when she was a child, was suspended and maneuverd through the window, the rope snapped and the piano fell silently before impaling itself on the railings below with an ear-shattering crash. Bits of piano ricocheted in every direction. Fortunately, Mum hadn't witnessed this disaster. She had gone out for the morning because she was worried about the pianos. She returned to find one of them being shoveled into the back of a lorry.

Mum and Dad named the house in Gerrards Cross *Na Hali*, Polish for "On the Hillside." At last we had real neighbors again, a huge garden and fresh air. Mum and Dad bought me a motorbike, a Triumph Sports Cub. How I loved it and the independence it gave me.

I was outside cleaning my motorcycle when I saw our next-door neighbors coming out of their house obviously dressed for church. Over lunch, I mentioned this to Mum and Dad and the following Sunday we set off for St. James, a low-Anglican church— no bells and smells. The choir was superb. As we were driving out of the car park, a lady with a big blue hat appeared out of nowhere right in front of the car, forcing Mum to stop. She introduced herself as the vicar's wife and, after a few brief words, fixed me with her eyes and stated, "You must join the choir. Fridays, in the vestry, eight o'clock sharp for practice."

The choirmaster, Lesley Norrish, placed me with the basses. This was really fun. But there was more. There were girls there, as well. And I was just waking up to girls. That sealed it: choir was for me.

It was also a youth club. There were parties every weekend and, after the Sunday morning services, we would all go down the road to The Bull for a drink. We called this "thirst after righteousness."

One Saturday morning Mum came to the church with me to play the organ while I sang. I had the whole echoey church in which to indulge my voice. This was the first time Mum had played the organ there and, to ensure a full sound, I had pulled out every stop. I walked to the front of the church and nodded to her to begin. She did. What a superb sound! And I sang with everything I had.

But Mum's tempo became slower and slower. I, in turn, sang slower and slower until I began to run out of breath. I had to stop.

"What's wrong?" I asked.

Unfortunately, neither Mum nor I knew that the St. James organ worked on a tracker action principle which caused a delay between depressing a key and sounding the pipe. The more stops out, the greater the delay.

Hilary

Jackie's bid for independence was a time of exciting exploration for her and she challenged life with explosive energy. The full power of her womanhood speedily emerged. Great company, a brilliant mimic, with a huge repertoire of crude jokes, she was by now electrifyingly sexy. It appeared that every man she met fell in love with her. She had irresistible magnetism.

As duo works were such an important part of Jackie's concert repertoire, Emmie Tillett thought it would be a good idea for her to form a regular partnership with a pianist. She recommended one of her American clients, Stephen Kovacevich (also known as Stephen Bishop Kovacevich). Like Jackie, Stephen had been a child prodigy: born in Los Angeles in 1940, he was five years older than her. He made his début when he was eleven, and performed the Schumann Piano Concerto with the San Francisco Symphony Orchestra when he was only thirteen. In 1959 he came to England to study with the legendary Myra Hess, and made his British début at the Wigmore Hall in November 1961, seven months after Jackie.

Ibbs and Tillett arranged for Jackie to meet Stephen at his flat. Stephen was nervous. He had been present at her début and knew she was a girl with an exceptional talent. He was startled by her appearance: she had changed dramatically since the Wigmore. The Christine Truman haircut had grown into corn-colored tresses, and she was no longer a little girl in ankle socks, but a maturing and seemingly confident young woman. She appeared at his door wearing an outrageous bright-red mini-skirt and strode into his living room, looking like a typical modern twenty-year-old. On the coffee table was a book by Freud which she picked up.

"Oh, Freud," she said. "He's the one who invented the atomic bomb!"

The ice was broken.

Jackie and Stephen made their début at Goldsmith's Hall on October 15, 1964, performing the Bach G minor Sonata, the Beethoven G minor Sonata, the Brahms E minor Sonata and the Britten Sonata. *The Times* review the following morning commented that the partnership "still had some way to go before it achieves an ideal identity of purpose." Desmond Shawe-Taylor reviewed the concert in the *Sunday Times*:

> This cellist and pianist make a well matched pair, whose playing was consistently musical, if still occasionally tentative. Just now mutual consideration is more noticeable than the strong corporate character that should develop in time.

Stephen knew that Jackie didn't worry about performing and was envious of her attitude. She believed she had a God-given gift and was privileged to share it with friends. When they rehearsed together Jackie knew what she wanted from the piano part and sometimes pushed for this beyond Stephen's good humor.

If they disagreed about the speed of a particular movement, they would just flip a coin and say, "That movement's yours, honey, you choose the speed."

It was not long before they became romantically involved. This time it was reciprocated. Jackie was in love. She tried unsuccessfully to conceal her feelings from George, but he was brokenhearted and extremely angry, seeking solace and explanation at Ashmansworth. But there was no hope.

Meanwhile, Stephen and Jackie had been booked eighteen months ahead to tour the country together, giving concerts.

Mum rang up one day in June suggesting a visit to Ashmansworth. I knew it would be a fun day, since she loved playing with Theresa and reading to her. I was expecting our second child, and was very large and heavy. It was the perfect day for a picnic, so off we went in Mum's car to the Gibbet, where Theresa could run and run. Mum loved it up there too, and we had a lovely afternoon, playing hide-and-seek.

On the way home, Theresa soon fell asleep on the back seat of the car, and I noticed that Mum seemed rather distracted.

"How's Jackie, Mum?"

She instantly stopped the car and put the handbrake on.

"Oh, Hil, I'm so worried about her. I don't know what to think."

"Why, what's happened, Mum?"

"It's Jackie and Stephen. They're together all the time and people will guess what's going on and start talking. What if it gets into the newspapers?"

She was a picture of concern.

"And Dad would be so upset if he knew . . . Stephen's married, you know." Tears were running down her cheeks.

This doleful moment was broken by a hoot from behind: we were blocking the road. Mum, in her panic to start the car, stalled it, and Theresa was jolted off the back seat on to the floor. There were instant loud wailings from a shocked Theresa, and confusion from Mum.

"Don't worry too much, Mum. I'm sure it will sort itself out." I was trying to be as comforting as possible, but there was little I could say. "They're both sensible people and Stephen's very kind."

"Jackie thinks that I don't know about Stephen and she certainly wouldn't talk to me about it. Will you try to talk to her?"

I said I would try but I'd have to wait for the right moment. That moment never actually came and Mum didn't mention it again.

In the autumn of 1964 Jackie informed Charles Beare that her secret benefactor had offered to buy her another cello. Charles knew the Davidoff Stradivarius, one of the top five instruments in the world, was on the market in New York. It had belonged originally to an Italian nobleman, but disappeared for several years, only to reappear in Russia in the hands of Count Wilhorsky. In 1863, he presented it to Carl Davidoff, one of the greatest Russian cellists at that time. When Davidoff died in 1889, his name was given to the cello, which was taken out of Russia during the Revolution. It

ended up in America, the property of the businessman and amateur cellist, Herbert N. Strauss, who had collected Strads as a
hobby. His widow now wished to sell it.

The instrument was duly brought to England for Jackie to try. It
was just before Christmas 1964 and Bill Pleeth was with her. Jackie
played it and was totally captivated.

Bill then played it for five long minutes, his face expressionless
with concentration. "It's absolutely superb, there is nothing wrong
with it. The only question is, will it suit you? And the only way to
find out is to play it."

So Jackie played it again, falling hopelessly and desperately in
love with it. It was purchased for $84,000 (approximately £32,500)
which was a world record for any instrument at that time.

Although the Davidoff had a lovely tone, it was difficult to look
after. At that time no one fully understood the importance of
constant humidity for old instruments, although it was known that
exposing them to the cold was not good. Charles Beare explained
to me that if Jackie played in New York, for example, on a June
afternoon with ninety-eight percent humidity, and then went
back to her air-conditioned hotel room where the humidity was
in the thirties, there would be trouble with the Davidoff, which is
a lightly built cello and therefore even more susceptible to climatic
changes than other instruments.

The other problem with the Davidoff was the force with which
Jackie played fortissimo passages. If too much pressure is used on
this instrument, rather than producing a louder sound, it tends to
close up. Jackie was careless about looking after her cellos, and
every so often the Davidoff would collapse under her demands,
cease to be able to sing, and have to be returned to Charles Beare's
workshop in Soho for a rest.

CHAPTER EIGHTEEN

Hilary

1965 marked the beginning of Jackie's international career. The year started with two performances of the Elgar in Liverpool and Leeds, followed by recitals with Stephen Kovacevich, and a television program, *In Rehearsal*. In the middle of her tour with Stephen, she agreed at short notice to perform the Dvořák Concerto at London's Royal Festival Hall. Some critics wrote that her playing was too aggressive and wayward, that she played wrong notes and that her tone was thin.

The conductor, Sir Malcolm Sargent, was so upset by the reviews that he wrote to the *Evening Standard* to complain.

I am told that headlines to musical criticism are arbitrarily chosen by sub-editors. These can be misleading as they obviously depend either upon chance, or the kindly disposition (or otherwise) of the sub-editor concerned. I suggest that these gentlemen should be encouraged to be as magnanimous as possible. The heading "TOO AGGRESSIVE MISS DU PRE" could with equal truth be quoted from the criticism—"MASTERLY STYLE MISS DU PRE."

The *Daily Mail* review was slightly more complimentary:

Girlish musical manners are not for Miss du Pré. She attacked her first entry with furious energy, her shoulder-length golden hair tossing as the bow carved purposefully into the strings of her Stradivarius. The orchestra's contribution was often coarse and insensitive.

Things were very different when, on April 7, she performed the Elgar with Sir John Barbirolli and the Hallé Orchestra at the Royal Festival Hall. She was in tremendous form and had already enjoyed success with the Elgar both in London and abroad. This performance was to become legendary. Barbirolli had a mission to restore Elgar to his rightful position as the greatest English composer since Purcell. Barbirolli, himself a fine cellist, had been the soloist for the second performance of the concerto when he was a young man. He was also a fan and supporter of Jackie and had wanted to work with her from the moment he first met her at the Suggia audition, when she was eleven. But it had taken nine years for the opportunity to present itself, and now the combination—of Barbirolli, Jackie and the glorious sounds of the Davidoff—produced a performance of unique power and haunting beauty.

The headline in one newspaper summed it up as "The music that wept."

The concert stunned the musical world. Jackie was given the ultimate accolade: according to *The Times*, she had "realized an ideal which the composer himself would have blessed."

Piers

Jackie was playing the Elgar at the Royal Festival Hall in one of Ernest Read's Young Persons' Concerts and Mum decided that it would be a good experience for me to earn my ticket by selling programs before the performance. At the final bell, I took the money and left-over programs to the information desk, after which I could choose any spare seat in the hall. I knew exactly where I wanted to sit. Thankfully, the seat was still available. It was in the middle of the front row, exactly opposite where Jackie would be playing. She would be only a few feet away from me.

She swept on to the platform and took her place but didn't notice me. After she began playing, I tried thinking of ways I could distract her. I coughed: no reaction. I moved my legs: no reaction. I dropped my program: no reaction. I waited. "Look at me," I thought. Eventually, she did. Immediately, I poked my tongue out as far as I could. Instead of the reaction I wanted, she simply smiled sweetly and carried on.

After the concert, I went backstage. The Green Room was crowded, and I struggled to find her. But she had already seen me. She laughed loudly and shouted above the noise: "Come here, shit face. I have something to say to you!"

Everyone turned to look at me. I looked around as though Jackie was speaking to someone behind me—and left.

Later we laughed, but I had to promise Mum not to do it again.

Hilary

Jackie was invited by the BBC Symphony Orchestra and their conductor, Antal Dorati, to join the orchestra on its first tour of the United States. It was scheduled to open in Boston, Massachusetts on April 25 and end in New York a month later. Pierre Boulez was the guest conductor, and the three British soloists were the soprano, Heather Harper, the pianist, John Ogdon and Jackie. The repertoire was almost exclusively twentieth-century music, including Webern, Copland, Boulez, Stravinsky, Shostakovich, Gerhard, Britten, Bartók and Elgar. The orchestra gave fifteen concerts in a three-week tour of the eastern states. Six of these concerts were at Carnegie Hall, in New York.

On May 14, Jackie made her début at the Carnegie Hall, playing the Elgar with Antal Dorati conducting. She was described as a tall, slim blonde who looked like a cross between Lewis Carroll's Alice and one of those angelic instrumentalists in a renaissance painting. Jackie used her brown Strad, not the Davidoff, which had gone to Charles Beare's workshop for a rest. From the moment she struck the opening notes of the Elgar, the audience was enraptured.

The *New York Times* critic, Raymond Ericson, was ecstatic:

> . . . Miss du Pré and the concerto seemed made for each other because her playing was so completely imbued with the romantic spirit. Astonishing was the color she brought to the concerto's dominant lyricism, the constant play of light and delicacy of emotion in a fresh, spontaneous, yet perfectly poised way.

John Gruen in the *New York Herald Tribune* was even more bewitched:

. . . She attacks her instrument like an impassioned lover and extracts from it the deepest, most stirring responses. To say that her technique is flawless would be an understatement—it is dazzling.

Robert Lyon in his review in the *Corning*:

This is the way to play. We have all seen too many modern performers who present their pieces with dry-as-dust detachment, who refuse to involve themselves in the music for fear of being considered naive. Now we have a youthful genius from a country noted for its musical restraint, who is leading us back to a richer tradition which admitted that music is the expression of emotion.

During the American tour, Jackie became friends with the leader of the BBC Symphony Orchestra, Hugh Maguire, and once back in London was quickly drawn into his circle of musical friends, playing chamber music at his home. Jackie adored these evenings of spontaneous music-making and her insatiable appetite and energy for performing meant that she would often drag Stephen Kovacevich round to Hugh's house to play through the night.

The Newbury String Players were giving an afternoon concert conducted by Kiffer on Sunday June 27 in a pretty little church in Great Bedwyn, near Marlborough. Celia Nicklin, the oboist, was playing a Vivaldi Concerto, while Jackie was to perform the Rubbra *Soliloquy*. Together they were to play *Veris Gratia* by Kenneth Leighton.

It was some time since I'd seen Jackie.

"Hil, you're enormous, and I'm starving—where's the cake tin?" Jackie headed for the larder, while I made a pot of tea.

"Come on, Jackie, what was it like in America?"

"Well, fatty puff, I'm an angel—the papers said so—and I had a standing ovulation for ten minutes! Just imagine, delicate little me in front of all those people and having to beam for all that time. My mouth got stuck, and I couldn't un-smile at the end."

We ate an early lunch and left for Great Bedwyn. It was a hot, shining day and soon Jackie was in full flight playing the Rubbra, her long golden hair tossing about her. I was almost nine months pregnant and had a very wriggly two-year-old Theresa on my lap, but when Jackie played, the poignancy of her sound stilled my little girl. There was no movement from her, or anyone in the audience.

During the interval Theresa and I were joined outside by Jackie and Celia, where we played a lively game of hide-and-seek among the gravestones. The audience and the orchestra had spilled outside into the June afternoon to enjoy the peace of that lovely day, but when the interval came to an end I stayed outside with Theresa. We played about to the strains of the Elgar Serenade seeping through the walls, until the time came to creep inside to hear Jackie and Celia in the Leighton.

Theresa was full of fresh air and energy and as soon as she saw "her" Jackie in front of the orchestra, she struggled to leave my lap. I contained her, but again it was the sound of Jackie and her Davidoff that caused Theresa to relax completely, dissolving in my arms to the performance. As the orchestra was packing up, Jackie and Celia came outside.

"That was truly lovely, Jacks and Celia. Probably the most moving performance of that work that will ever be heard. I wish you could play it again."

"I'd love to, Hil. But I don't think I'll have a chance."

Suddenly Jackie noticed a girl of about ten standing by a gravestone.

"Hello—I saw you in the audience. Did you like the concert?"

"I loved it. Please will you sign my program?"

"Of course I will. Do you play anything?"

"I play the cello."

"You do! Would you like to try mine? It's in the church. Come on."

The astonished child disappeared into the empty church with Jackie where she and the Strad gave an impromptu lesson to that little cellist. They reappeared, glowing, ten minutes later.

When Clare was born on July 23, Jackie was away at the Spoleto Festival. She returned at the beginning of August, and came immediately to Ashmansworth to see us. After much cooing over the new baby, and while she was still holding Clare, I asked her about Italy.

"Some of it was wonderful and some of it was ghastly."

"So what was wonderful about it?"

"Richard Goode!"

"Who's he—not *another* one!"

"No, Hil," she chastised me. "He's just a brilliant American pianist."

"I thought Stephen was a brilliant American pianist."

"He is, but this is another one!"

"Jackie!"

"No, Hil, it's not like that."

"Jackie!"

"Well . . . he's going to be in London, so I'll probably play with him . . ."

At this, we both laughed.

"Does he know Stephen? What will happen to Stephen?"

She shrugged. "We'll see . . . Come on, Hil, I'm hungry! You take Clare."

Piers

In London, on August 19, 1965, Jackie recorded the Elgar Concerto with Sir John Barbirolli and the London Symphony Orchestra for EMI at Kingsway Hall.

Attempts to record Jackie's interpretation were first discussed within EMI Records in May 1964, when John Whittle and Brian Culverhouse proposed a recording with Sir Adrian Boult as conductor. Unfortunately, there was no interest outside Britain and, because of the shortfall in the estimated sales return, the proposal was rejected. In September 1964, Sir John Barbirolli and his recording producer, Ronald Kinloch Anderson, were at Abbey Road Studios to assess a recording of Elgar's *The Dream of Gerontius*. John Whittle and Malcolm Walker seized the opportunity to suggest to Sir John that he should record the Elgar cello concerto with Jackie. He was very positive about the idea, but the earliest available date in his hectic schedule was August of the following year.

Three sessions had been booked for the recording. When Jackie came home that evening she was full of it.

"How did it go?" I asked, as she flew in the door.

"Amazing. Well, that's what the producer said. He couldn't understand why it had taken only thirty minutes. He kept thanking me. 'But I booked the orchestra for two days,' he said."

"What went wrong, then?" I asked.

"Nothing, silly. The concerto *is* only thirty minutes."

The impression Jackie gave of the recording was that she had played the concerto straight through. In fact, I later found out that it was recorded over two sessions, the first two movements in the morning and the last two in the afternoon. Each movement was played in its entirety. There were thirty-seven takes altogether: seven of the first movement, six of the second, four of the third and seven of the fourth. There were five false starts and the remaining takes were patches of the individual movements.

Hilary

Jackie disliked the fact that her concert life had to be mapped out for anything up to three years ahead. It was hard for her to adjust to long-term commitments since she had always been such a spontaneous person, living in, and for, the moment. Consequently, she was inclined to cancel concerts at the last moment if there was something else she wanted to do. This was extremely annoying for her agents and concert promoters, and caused bad feeling. She also hated traveling abroad, a prerequisite for an international artist. She couldn't bear the loneliness in foreign cities, or being in hotel rooms with nothing to do. Frequently she would telephone Mum and say, "Can I come home please? I don't want to do this concert." Often she sounded confused, sometimes barely knowing where she was, so Mum would just drop everything and join her.

It was hardly surprising that Jackie found her new lifestyle difficult to organize: the girl who couldn't find her way from Portland Place to Harley Street, which was literally round the corner, was now faced with navigating international airports and foreign cities on her own. She had been catapulted from a protected environment, where everything had been done for her, into unfamiliar surroundings, where she had to organize her meals, her clothes and her time. There was very little support either practically or emotionally for a solo artist traveling alone. Jackie talked of her feelings when she appeared on the BBC radio program, *Artist of the Month,* with Stephen Kovacevich.

> An artist spends a great deal of his time working alone. He is therefore very happy to work with other people, with an orchestra and conductor, for example. This is extremely exciting. There is seldom enough rehearsal time to develop a really satisfactory musical relationship. For this reason, I have always found it extremely rewarding playing chamber music—music for small groups of players. Here companionship and hard work are combined, as long as the other players aren't feeling lazy. Recently I have been doing duo work with Stephen Bishop. A combination of two artists is a thought-provoking one, for here there are two different ways of looking at music which simply have to be reconciled, but it is enormously rewarding when they are finally fused.

Mostly, though, Jackie managed to keep a good sense of humor about the demands of her professional life. The unfamiliar circumstances, and the many different people she met, became ammunition for her mimicry. She had a natural ability to soak up the atmosphere around her. Whenever she came home from abroad, she had a strong accent, having picked up the local inflections. In describing her traveling life, she would impersonate characters she'd met, making even the most awful event sound funny.

In September, she was quoted in the press saying that she wanted to study again and the long awaited invitation to study with Rostropovich was confirmed, subject to a second meeting and an audition. Jackie arranged for Richard Goode to accompany her at the audition and they played Beethoven.

One day she lifted the phone to speak to Richard Goode and dialed Stephen Kovacevich's number by mistake. As Stephen and Richard both have American accents, and one hello sounds very much like another, Jackie didn't notice her error and launched into a tirade about Stephen, thinking that she was talking to Richard.

Stephen said nothing and just listened. When she stopped for breath, he interrupted:

"Jackie, do you realize who you are talking to?"

She was mortified and Mum, who was with her, immediately drove her round to Stephen's flat to apologize.

Fortunately Stephen found the whole event rather amusing, especially as they were soon to embark on a long recital tour together, giving fifteen concerts in two months.

Richard Goode returned to America.

During the tour, Jackie managed to fit in two more concerts, playing the Haydn C major Concerto with Barbirolli and the Hallé Orchestra in Manchester, and the same concerto two days later in London at the Royal Festival Hall, with Harry Blech and the London Mozart Players.

The Elgar recording was released in December and became an instant best-seller. It remains a best-selling classical disc to this day.

CHAPTER NINETEEN

Hilary

In February 1966, just after her twenty-first birthday, Jackie left for Russia to study with Mstislav Rostropovich who, at thirty-eight, was a dynamic force. He was once asked what he taught his students and answered: "I teach my students to truly love music. I have no favorites among the works I'm playing. Each work I play must be my favorite at that moment. If I care for it less, the public will feel it."

Jackie's trip had been arranged as part of a new Anglo-Soviet cultural agreement which allowed an advanced arts student to be accepted in Moscow in return for a Soviet student of industrial design coming to Britain. Jackie had been told that it would be dangerous to take the Davidoff to Moscow because, as it had originally belonged to the Russians, they would undoubtedly want it back. It was the middle of the Cold War, and, fearful of trouble, Dad decided there should be a secret code as a warning of any problems. They agreed that "Dying to see you" should signal "Trouble, come at once."

The Soviet Union, despite remarkable strides in intellectual tolerance, was still a totalitarian state, where the KGB enforced the regime with constant vigilance. Jackie arrived in Russia during the more enlightened days of Brezhnev, and true to character, soon made friends, and quickly entered into the spirit of things:

May 24, 1966

Dearest Family,

I'm *pissed* drunk in the "Aragon," one of Moscow's most marvelous restaurants and I'm just waiting to devour a large hunk of hot Georgian bread about one foot long.

Have just had a lesson on the third Bach Suite followed by half a bottle of neat Vodka in the company of my beloved teacher and his wife, and Lisa [Elizabeth Wilson]. We are at the same table as some devastatingly ugly men (on heat!) to whom we are giving glances of royal indifference.

Where *is* the damn food! We're going to eat cold chicken in delectable gray sauce, a stunning Russian soup, and, in fact, as much as we can to dispel the drunken stupor. Then we shall retire, tails between legs to our determined study. What a life!!!!!!!

My appetite rumbles on. By the way, I definitely arrive in London on June 20th, or around that date. As I am flying home with R [Rostropovich] it is likely that my appearance depends on his arrangements.

HERE IS THE FOOOOOOD . . .

(P.S. have enclosed a bit of onion from the meal)

Jackie was unusually in awe of Rostropovich. When she played for him at the age of fourteen, he had challenged her to the limits of her technique and she had not forgotten it. Now, at the age of twenty-one, she respected him because she knew he had something special to offer her.

Russia was a real eye-opener for Jackie. The Russian students were extremely disciplined, and she was flabbergasted to discover she was required to practice for six hours a day, prepare written work and learn to speak Russian, all of which she found very difficult. Her first letters home talk of her astonishment at the amount of practice the other students did:

. . . Professionalism is the key word and everybody goes about their work in a way which makes me feel that I have never done any in my life. R has been away for two weeks and I cannot live without the stimulation of his lessons and concerts and I long for his return so that I can charge ahead. Rococo Variations, Schumann, Prokofiev Symphony Concertante and a little Bach have so far taken up all the lessons. There are thirty more lessons to come and I have drawn out a program of what I want to learn with him in that time. God! (the Russian for that delightful chap, by the way, is "BOG") . . .

Rostropovich gave her confidence. It is possible that their successful liaison was because of their similar working methods. Despite the insistence on practice, he didn't talk about technique but about the feeling and shaping of the music, which was consistent with Bill's teaching. She found confidence in Rostropovich's strength. "He's so terribly dramatic, he's like Cinerama," she told me. At last here was someone whose philosophy was the same as hers. She could relax and stop trying to analyze her technique.

Moscow

Dearest Kiffer,

I certainly did get a lump in my throat and of considerable size when I read your description of Spring bursting around you all at Ashmansworth. I promptly had to go down to the hostel buffet and drink *black* coffee where I managed to drop a raw egg on the floor and look generally so pitiful that I had to be escorted back to room 229 by a considerate Brazilian, who happened to be suffering from the same throat swelling. Looking at my fiendish concert program for next year, I find your description particularly tough to take as I realize I shall not see next year's English Spring either. I had not realized until now how very much the country means to me. Here, there is still quite a lot of snow and it will be a long time, I imagine, before the great heaps at the roadside will be cleared or just melted into great streams of brown water. Summer ought to be marvelous tho, as there are long, beautiful boulevards full of trees which will be covered with green and blossoms.

A few days ago a big festival was celebrated here—in fact, all over the Soviet Union. It was "Woman's Day." Everybody took a holiday from work, and the women were given presents, had music played for them on the radio and were generally honored by all the men-folk. I was given two marvelous little icons, worn with age and fondling, a Mexican necklace and a Chinese ring (all from my girlfriends!) and in the evening we was toasted with countless cups of vodka (which I now adore and drink with professional style).

Apart from that, I heard Beethoven's 2nd Symphony which

I've never heard before! Stepped on someone's toe and had to address R in front of a distinguished collection of Russian Musicians (I was plastered at the time!).

I have no news about my work to tell you. I think of the approaching concert work with horror and fright. I forget so easily what other people drum into me—that I have a big talent and if I lived with you in the country, I think I'd almost forget about it completely. Here, however, word has spread around about this miracle from England and students crowd into the lessons (where I'm dying of nerves) to hear me. I get some really wonderful musical tuition from R whom I love very much. He turns out to be a supremely sensitive man and I can't get over his kindness to me. I find it a great consolation that he not only cares about my playing but about me too. I could not *conceivably* be his successor—not possessing his capacity and not being a man!

All the reports one hears about the standard are completely correct. It is an amazing star-splitting collection of students— everyone of them *at least* a very reasonable and competent performer. Their norm is about 8 hours work a day (on their principal subject alone) and to inform them that 2 hours is my maximum is like speaking to them in Greek. There are some very sweet Natashas and Tamasins in the class who somehow manage to look marvelous as well as play marvelously.

There is a bird outside my window who is singing away. It makes me feel quite near home! There are a couple of crows which keep almost continual guard outside the window too. Rather a threatening presence!

Your diet sounds infinitely preferable to the one my sweet chubby room-mate enjoys. I wonder if you have ever been offered four boiled potatoes for breakfast? The discovery of the varying beauties of bread I'm sure you have not yet experienced, and if you'll be a sensible man, you'll realize that fruit and veg are boring to the palate and tedious to peel and prepare. Long live pasta dough and potato.

I'm going to buy some prints now to stick on my walls, so I'll say goodbye for the moment. Thanks more than I can say for sending your letter. I send you all much love and long to see

you in three months. I have a vivid memory of you and
T[Theresa] disappearing on Newbury railway station.
      JACKIE

Piers

One Saturday morning, as we were having breakfast, a letter arrived from Jackie. Dad put it to one side until we had finished.
Jackie's letters were important and not to be shared with anything,
not even eating. We had to concentrate. Once the table had been
cleared and Dad had his cup of tea, he ceremoniously slit open the
envelope. The letter was in green biro, on a page torn from an exercise book.

He passed the letter to Mum to read, and she scanned the opening lines before beginning. As tears filled her eyes, she passed it
back to Dad, who started reading it out loud.

Dearest Mum,
      This is just a tiny private note to tell you that I have, finally, at
last! decided to be a cellist.
      As you know, I have been battling in the unconscious for
years against becoming one and against not becoming one, and
one way and another, quite a lot of dust has been kicked up in
my noggin.
      It was R who finally made this more obvious to me. He has
been a really good friend and has been a great help in many
things.
      Whether I can stand up to such an arduous life is another
thing and my technical limitations worry me a lot. I now have
the dubious business of sitting back more or less and seeing if I
can finally make it. I shall be very sorry if I can't. R believes so
totally in my talent. I can't tell you what a relief it is to finally
decide on what I want so much. It is largely due to your ambition for me and your belief in my playing that has kept me at it
all, despite everything. So here is a life-long "Thanks" to you,
old girl.
      I'm giving a concert here on June 18th and will arrive
back in London June 20th, with R! It's sort of twilight at the

moment and a lot of kids are playing outside the window. Must practice.

Sending you lots of love, JACKIE.

As Dad finished reading, Mum was drying her face on her apron, and I blurted out, "What a silly letter to write. Of course she's a cellist. Silly old moo."

Mum and Dad just looked at each other, and said nothing.

Hilary

It was five months since Jackie had departed for Russia and during that time we had written frequently to each other. I had become pregnant again and the four-month-old embryo was already kicking minutely. Theresa was a very lively three-year-old, Clare, at eleven months, was crawling, and I was longing for Jackie to see them again. I wondered if Clare would remember her; a five-month gap is a long time in an infant's life.

Theresa had picked many little bunches of flowers to welcome Jackie. She had also collected special treasures, which had been stored in matchboxes and paper bags, and, like a little squirrel, had hidden them in safe places, all over the garden.

I heard a car drive into the yard, followed by a shriek from Gran. Sweeping Clare into my arms, I dashed across the lawn and up the steps. Gran ran out of the kitchen door, Joy sailed out of the front door, and there was a medley of people squawking, jumping and hugging our longed-for Jackie. She was back at last.

But I noticed straight away that she didn't look well, nor did she seem her usual bouncy self. Gran went to put the kettle on and said she would bring tea down to the paddling pool. Theresa was already in Jackie's arms, clamoring excitedly.

"Jackie, come with me, please come *now*. I've got a surprise for just you and me. No one else must come."

Clare looked on in silence, staring with her big blue eyes as though she was struggling with a distant memory. Jackie and I continued chattering, which made Theresa more and more impatient.

"*Stop talking.* You've said hello. Mummy can talk to *Clare.* Come *on*." She wriggled to be released from Jackie's arms and started tugging on her sleeve in the direction of the garden. The treasure hunt was imperative: the cow parsley in the nuttery was the first domain to be searched and it didn't take long to find the treasures because Theresa, in her excitement, led Jackie straight to them. Soon they returned to the paddling pool, laden with pretty stones, shells and tiny drawings.

Joy appeared bearing biscuits and, although it was close to lunch, I was too excited to mind. Eventually, Joy and Gran went indoors to put lunch on the table. This was the moment Jackie and I had been waiting for. The children were still absorbed in their water games, and as soon as Joy and Gran were out of sight, Jackie clutched my hand, and tears began to stream down her face. I put my arm round her.

"Jack, what's the matter?"

She was too consumed with tears to speak.

"Come on, Jack, come on."

There was no response.

"It's much better to say than to hold."

Still no response.

"There's no one else about, it's quite safe, I promise."

She was now sobbing inconsolably, the tears dripping off the end of her nose. I gave her a hanky and she blew her nose noisily.

"Hil," she whispered between sobs. "I've been raped."

"What?" I caught my breath.

She looked around anxiously to be sure that everyone was out of earshot before continuing.

"I was taken to the hospital in Moscow because I was frightened I might be pregnant. The doctor was horrible to me. I was so frightened that everyone would find out. *Please* don't tell Mum."

She tried to dry her puffy red face with the sodden hanky. "Anyway, I'm not pregnant."

She told me that she had been operated on to terminate any possible pregnancy and that the doctor had been rough and unsympathetic.

"Who on earth could have done that to you, Jack?"

She paused before whispering, inaudibly.

I asked if she would like to talk to our family doctor, whom she knew, but she was adamant that she didn't want to see anyone.

I hugged her. "Thank you for telling me, Jack. Don't worry, I promise I won't tell Mum."

We were interrupted by Gran's singing call from the house: "Cooeee. Hil-a-ry . . . Ja-ckie . . . Lunch is rea-dy."

Lunch became a noisy gathering. Gran was bustling around attending to everyone's needs, and Joy wanted to hear every detail about Russia. Jackie cheered up and started to mimic the people she had met, showing off her apparent command of the Russian language: she was so convincing, we were completely taken in. How were we to know that she was speaking gibberish with a Russian accent and intonation?

After lunch Jackie went upstairs for a rest while Gran and I took the children for a walk. It was obvious to Gran that Jackie wasn't well. I did my best to persuade her that Jackie was just exhausted from traveling and that Moscow had been very hard work for her. Gran knew she would not be able to winkle anything out of me, and gave me one of her knowing looks. Seeing a new role for herself over the coming days, she announced confidently:

"Well! We'll make sure that she has plenty of rest. We'll build her up with lots of good home cooking, and I'm sure she'll feel better in no time."

Jackie didn't mention the rape incident again, so I simply acknowledged her sadness by giving her the occasional supportive hug.

CHAPTER TWENTY

Hilary

When Jackie left for Italy, Kiffer and I set off for France to stay with an old friend, Janet Tessier du Cros, in her Cévenole house in Valleraugue. With our third child due in four months, we were glad to accept the suggestion of a few days' holiday while Joy and Gran, with the support of Olive, held the fort.

France was another world for me, new and exciting. Every day we walked, or visited Janet's colorful and aristocratic cousins in their ancient houses. We watched the shepherds, in their blue *casquettes*, tending their sheep and goats, moving with them through the mountains. One day Janet decided we should explore further afield, so off we launched in her little whining Deux Chevaux into the heart of the Cévannes. Eventually, we arrived at a little town called Sumène, parked by the bridge, left the car and explored the tiny roads and alleyways. The houses were tall and the road narrow and there was a strong smell of goats. The local people were short and brown and wrinkled like walnuts, and some were sitting outside their front doors, chatting and preparing vegetables. There was a grocer's with fruit and vegetables in boxes outside on the road. No one seemed to be in any hurry: it was quiet and the pace of life was slow. They watched us as we passed— some nodded, some just stared. In the square was a huge plane tree and underneath a donkey, harnessed to a high-sided rubbish cart. Many times we would encounter that cart at the top of the only road through Sumène. With no room to pass, we just had to be patient, following it on its slow, interrupted journey, while the dustmen tossed the rubbish into the cart. Not even pedestrians could squeeze past and no one would dream of hurrying.

We walked behind the square and found the Hotel à la Rose.

"Perfect!" Janet said, and in she went to ask if monsieur le patron could produce some lunch. He asked us to give him twenty minutes. Janet explained that Kiffer could not eat any meat or fish. "Pas de problème."

More time to explore. The little alleys now smelt of *potages*, garlic and hot French bread. We could hear the clanking of pans and French chatter through the partially closed shutters.

On our return a table had been simply laid. We marveled at the flavors Monsieur Priet had composed, and drank the perfect wine to complement his meal. Conversation flowed, we were light-hearted, and without a care in the world.

After much hand-shaking and promises to return, we departed. Janet was still chattering and such was our exuberance we missed the signpost for Valleraugue and happily followed the winding road along wide valleys and round mountains. The hot air was blowing in the open car and we soaked up the warmth and the scents, as we bowled along the narrow pot-holed road which was just wide enough for one car. There were no other vehicles.

In the valley a river bounced over rocks and boulders. Sometimes it was visible and sometimes it wasn't. A little clutch of Cévenole houses with their pretty pink and wiggly tiles came into view and an ancient sign saying Sanissac. On we went and there, just around the bend, over the valley, on top of its own little mountain stood a beautiful and distinguished house with two huge arched vaults. Janet slowly stopped the car. We sat in silence and gazed.

"I'd love to buy that house," Kiffer whispered.

"No hope," said Janet. "Those houses are owned by several members of a family and they'll want it and, even if it's uninhabited, French inheritance law makes it impossibly complicated."

Kiffer tossed and turned all night and, the next morning, immediately after croissants and coffee, he and I retraced our journey in our own car until we found the hamlet with its one or two houses dotted among the mountains.

There didn't seem to be any road up to the house.

"Come on, Hil," said Kiffer. "We'll wade over the river and climb the terraces. I'll push you up if it's too steep."

We walked through a grassy orchard of peach trees, toward the river. The air was warm and balmy and still. The only sounds were creaking cicadas, twitching grasshoppers, and our breathing. The intense perfumes of the wild herbs as we trod them underfoot made us feel almost drunk. We removed our shoes, paddled over the river to the bank where we waited a moment while our feet dried, then, beshoed again, started the scrambling climb over the terraces. It was very hot, the terraces were crumbling and I was pregnant.

"How much further, Kiffer? I can't see the house at all."

Frequently Kiffer had to heave me over the tricky bits, disturbing lizards and creatures unseen as they scuttled away in the prickly undergrowth. It was a long puff and pant for me and we couldn't see the house because we were climbing up right underneath it.

Suddenly, there was a wall. We skirted it, to find ourselves standing on a terrace in the presence of a house that had been planted hundreds of years ago and seemed to have grown out of its own ground. We felt in a time warp and knew we were meant to be there. There was silence. It was as though this house had been waiting for us and, at last, we had arrived.

"Let's explore," Kiffer whispered. "We'll try that ancient door."

The house was boarded up, so instead we explored the extensive vaults underneath. There were *caves* too, but they were completely dark.

"Come on, Hil. Let's go back to the terrace and soak up the view."

We emerged into the brilliant sunshine and stood still, absorbing the silence, the heat, the view, the scents, and centuries of history. After a while I noticed someone scything grass in the valley.

"Look, Kif, there's someone near the river."

"Good, just what we need. We can ask him who owns the house."

Down we went, over the terraces, slithering over rattling slates until we came to the little river. The man was short, dressed in blue overalls and cap, and leaning on his scythe watching us.

"Excusez-moi, Monsieur," I began, in my stumbling and embarrassed French. I asked him who owned the house and to our astonishment, he said it was his.

That was our first meeting with Monsieur Portales. There followed daily negotiations on the terrace of his family home in the welcome shade of a huge plane tree, with Janet as translator. The price started at five thousand francs and rocketed to five *hundred* thousand before descending to five thousand again. Finally, it was a deal and it was ours. Five thousand old francs, which at the time was about three hundred pounds. As it had been completely boarded up we had been unable to explore the house itself, but Kiffer took some photographs of the outside and of the view. All the way home we talked of nothing else.

When Jackie returned from Spoleto at the end of July, she still looked exhausted, and I wasn't surprised when she told me that she had glandular fever. She took to her bed, canceling all her engagements for a month.

There had been friction between Mum and Jackie, caused by Jackie choosing to stay with the Maguires in London, rather than remaining at home where Mum could look after her. Jackie wrote to Mum apologizing for her tantrums and told Mum to ignore them. By mid–September, Mum and Dad were so worried about Jackie's health, they arranged for her to spend ten days in hospital in Fulham. In the midst of all this, Gannie died, and Dad went to Jersey for her funeral, leaving Mum to organize Jackie.

Mum felt Jackie needed peace and quiet to convalesce and arranged for her to stay with her old friend, Mary May, at her house in the South of France. Jackie amused herself by swimming in the sea even though it was freezing. Soon, though, she was bored, a sure sign that she was recovering. She returned on October 13.

In November she traveled to Northampton with Hugh Maguire and Anthony Hopkins to give a trio concert. It was her first public appearance in England for ten months.

Daniel Barenboim was staying in London at the Westbury Hotel, and, by coincidence, was also suffering from glandular fever. He was complaining miserably and his friends teased him: "If you think you have it badly, you should see Jacqueline du Pré." He was so fed up with hearing about Jackie that he telephoned her agent to ask for her phone number. They had met briefly once, backstage at a concert the year before, and he had booked her to perform in a concert with him the following year. He phoned on the pretext of discussing the concert but quickly changed the subject to glandular fever. He was eager to compare notes.

When Jackie came to see our new baby daughter, Nico, she didn't mention her conversation with Daniel, and seemed non-committal about her relationship with Stephen, giving the impression that it was all over.

Just before Christmas, Hugh Maguire announced that he was leaving the BBC Symphony Orchestra with the intention of forming a piano trio with Jackie and the pianist Fou Ts'ong. Jackie was invited to a Christmas party at Fou Ts'ong's house to play chamber music. Daniel had also been invited, but arrived late. Everyone was drinking coffee when a small dynamo burst into the room. Jackie was so thrown by meeting him, she reached for her cello.

They played the Brahms F major Sonata with unusual musical communion, a thread so strong that discussion was superfluous. The music had its own life and force, flowing naturally and spontaneously. There was an immediate electricity between them and as the evening progressed it was clear to them both that something extraordinary was happening.

Jackie rang me the next morning at the crack of dawn.

"Hil, I'm in love, I'm in love."

Before I could say "hello" or ask her how she was, she had told me the whole story. I knew who Daniel was, of course, and that he was one of the most exciting young musicians around at that time. It was wonderful to hear her sounding so bouncy and happy. We both squealed and giggled as she described their meeting in minute detail.

Daniel was two years older than Jackie. Born in Argentina, the son of Russian Jews, he too had been a child prodigy. Both his parents were pianists. His mother, Aida, had grown up in a Zionist household, and his father, Enrique, was torn between making a career as a concert pianist and being at home for his family. Enrique Barenboim's real passion was teaching and his philosophy had remarkable similarities to Bill Pleeth's. Daniel was never made to practice scales and arpeggios, but developed his ability through playing the music itself. As a result, he was not taught to play mechanically.

He once described learning the piano as being "as natural as learning to walk." He gave his first public concert in Buenos Aires in August 1950 when he was seven, and performed with an orchestra for the first time when he was eight, playing Mozart's Piano Concerto No. 23.

After the State of Israel was created in 1948, the Barenboims decided to emigrate there. They left Argentina when Daniel was nine. Having grown up speaking Spanish, he now had to learn English and Hebrew. The entire family, including his grandparents, lived together in one flat. In 1954, his parents decided to send him to Salzburg to study conducting. When he was twelve, he went to study in Paris with the celebrated composer and teacher, Nadia Boulanger who had also trained Paul Tortelier. On his travels he had the opportunity to meet and work with many musicians of the time, particularly Arthur Rubinstein, who was a great inspiration and encouraged him both as a conductor and pianist.

By the time he met Jackie when he was twenty-four, Daniel was already an experienced and highly successful international soloist and conductor. At sixteen he played in over forty concerts in Australia and, a year later, performed all thirty-two Beethoven Piano Sonatas from memory in a cycle of eight concerts in Tel Aviv. In 1965, when he was twenty-two, he conducted the English Chamber Orchestra for the first time, taking over at short notice when their usual conductor became ill. He was such a success with both audience and players that the orchestra insisted he should continue his association with them. Now he was based in London working with them, making recordings, and giving concerts in Europe.

When Jackie met Danny they quickly became inseparable and she no longer had time for her usual circle of friends. She dropped her former boyfriends.

On January 3, 1967, she set off on a tour of Eastern Europe with the BBC Symphony Orchestra. She was to give twelve concerts: two in Prague, two in Warsaw, four in Moscow and four in Leningrad. The tour had been made possible by an exchange agreement between the British and the Russians. Under the agreement, the Moscow Radio Symphony Orchestra would be invited to Britain the following summer. This was the first time radio orchestras had been exchanged between the two countries. The program for the BBC tour included several twentieth-century works, with music by Britten, Arnold, Bliss, Stravinsky, Bartók, and even more radical works by Schoenberg, Webern and Boulez. No foreign orchestra visiting Moscow and Leningrad had ventured this far into the twentieth-century repertoire. There had been a growing curiosity in the Soviet Union about modern music which few Russians had been lucky enough to hear, and the visit created excitement in the musical community.

In Russia, the soloists and the 130-strong BBC Symphony Orchestra traversed thousands of miles by train, warding off the freezing winter by enjoying the world-famous Russian hospitality.

Jackie was to play the Elgar in Moscow on January 7. That night the Moscow Conservatoire was packed with over two thousand people. The concert was televised by the city's second-largest TV channel, which had a peak audience of fifteen million people. With Sir John Barbirolli conducting, Jackie once again gave an historic performance and received a ten-minute standing ovation. Russian cellists had tackled the Elgar in the past, but its English-ness and emotional range was, and still is, difficult for non–English instrumentalists to portray. To hear this magnificent music expressed by Jackie with such originality was astonishing for the Russians.

Jackie came home on January 16, performed the Schumann Concerto in early February at the Royal Festival Hall with the Royal Philharmonic Orchestra, conducted by Christopher Robinson, and left immediately afterward to make her Canadian début with Seiji Ozawa and the Toronto Symphony performing the Saint-Saëns concerto.

It was rumored that Jackie and Danny met in America, and had secretly become engaged.

Piers

Jackie would often call me if she was in London and at a loose end. One Saturday morning she rang. "Piers, I'm at the Westbury.

Come and meet me. We can go shopping and have something to eat."

When I arrived in her room, Danny wasn't around.

"Look, Bar, I've got something to show you," she said. Producing a huge, light-brown suitcase she put it on the bed.

"Look."

As she opened it, I couldn't believe what I saw. It was jam-packed with banknotes of different denominations—concert fees from her tour.

"I've been dying to do this," she said, and plunging her hands into the case, threw the notes in the air, laughing with joy. Within seconds the room was completely full of floating money. I had never seen anything like it. She danced around, laughing, swirling and turning in the cloud of banknotes.

It took ages to cram it all back into the suitcase. "Come on, Bar, let's go shopping," she said, and off we went, leaving the suitcase unattended on the bed.

I remember how happy she was that day. We laughed and joked as we trotted down Bond Street, Jackie being greeted by name by the doormen in the magnificent shops. I was so proud of her.

In March, she was off again, this time to New York to play the Schumann Concerto with Leonard Bernstein and the New York Philharmonic and to give what were to be her last recitals with Stephen Kovacevich. Within days of leaving, she was on the phone.

"Hello, Bar."

"Jacks! Where are you?"

"New York," she replied, mimicking the accent as usual. "I need to speak to Mum. I want her to send the cap over. What do you think she'll say?"

"No idea—here's Mum."

I was relieved to hand the phone over. In the same way that Mum couldn't confront the problem, nor could I. Not wanting Mum to be embarrassed by me being within earshot, I disappeared into the garden.

A week later, she was on the phone again. She wanted to move out of the Ladbroke Grove flat and could Mum find her somewhere to live? Mum asked everyone and eventually a colleague suggested a flat in Upper Montagu Street.

Hilary

Harold Schonberg's review in the *New York Times* carried the headline: "Upstaging Lenny." *Time* magazine said that she looked in one instant like a puckish milkmaid and the next like Ophelia going mad.

She couldn't sit still for a minute. Swathed in acres of floor-length red chiffon, she attacked her cello in an ungainly frenzy, reaching forward to take a massive chop with her bow, arching her back, tossing her head, closing in on the cello again and again.

Jackie's spontaneity was leading her to extremes of musical expression, and her exaggerated movements were beginning to upset some critics.

When Jackie returned from America in the middle of March, she and Danny moved together into the flat in Upper Montagu Street.

CHAPTER TWENTY-ONE

Piers

At the end of March, Jackie arranged to bring Danny for supper with Mum and Dad. The entire week was spent scrubbing and polishing, until the whole house was sparkling. We were all excited. It was rare now for Jackie to come to Gerrards Cross, let alone bring someone. And this someone was really *someone*. Mum had telephoned Jackie to find out what Danny would like to eat and Jackie had told her he liked all the things she liked.

Mum had worked hard to make everything perfect. Jackie and Danny arrived in the early evening, with a large bottle of vodka. Jackie was wearing one of the mini-dresses which marked the 1960s and which did absolutely nothing for her. She was much taller than Danny, who looked dapper and immaculate. To me, it was as if Jackie was the big sister proudly holding hands with her little brother.

After somewhat nervous introductions, Danny found Mum's Blüthner grand piano and music was soon filling the house. Mum was in her element. She flowed everywhere, singing. When the food was ready, we went into the dining room where she had lit the candles. After the hors-d'oeuvre, Mum proudly carried in the meat on a huge plate which she placed with ceremony on the table. To coos of anticipation she picked up the carving knife.

"Now," she said. "Who would like some . . ." Her voice trailed off and her face changed from serenity to horror.

"Oh no!" she gasped. "I've just realized. You don't eat pork, do you?" She looked at Danny and then in disbelief at what she had spent all day preparing.

"Of course I don't eat pork, Iris," said Daniel, with a twinkle in his eye. "What do you think you're doing? Trying to make me commit a terrible sin?"

Mum didn't know what to say. Daniel held her stare, frowning. No one spoke or moved. The silence was deafening. Then, very slowly, a smile crept over his face.

"Iris, of course I eat pork. I always have. And I'm hungry, so don't serve me short."

We all burst out laughing and the tension was dispelled.

After supper there was more music-making and a vodka-drinking contest between Dad and Danny.

At one stage I went into the kitchen to refill the coffee jug. Jackie followed me.

"I love him, Bar."

"Really?" I said. "I would never have guessed."

She blew a wet raspberry at me. "And hurry up with the coffee, shit face."

The original concert booking that Daniel had planned for Jackie before they knew each other had arrived at last. On April 5, Jackie performed the Haydn C major Cello Concerto, conducted by Daniel with the English Chamber Orchestra at the Royal Festival Hall. Jackie had hinted at an engagement as I, the nosy younger brother, probed for "juicy" information. When the audience burst into its customary enthusiastic applause, I turned to Gran, who was sitting next to me and said:

"I think Danny should announce his engagement to Jackie when the clapping stops." I really hoped he would. Gran gave me one of her withering looks that said, "That's none of your business."

When the applause ended and they left the stage with no announcement, Gran gave me a smug glance and made one of her favorite pronouncements.

"Well, there you are, you don't know where you are."

Within a week Jackie's and Danny's engagement was made public and the newspapers were full of excitement about the union of this golden couple. Concert tours were arranged; parties were organized; glorious meals were eaten.

But among this happiness, a storm of intense ferocity suddenly blew up out of nowhere. It was fueled by people who, because of Jackie's greatness, felt they had a right to offer unsolicited advice, and the family was caught right in the middle of the cross-fire. The cause of the storm was Jackie's proposed conversion to Judaism.

Mum and Dad began receiving awful letters from complete strangers and, worse, from well-meaning but misguided close friends. They made statements such as, "Jackie will be eternally damned because she will have to renounce Jesus Christ," and, "If you don't stop it, you will have to answer to God."

For the first time Mum and Dad were involving me in what was happening to Jackie, and needing my support. Some letters were so cruel they destroyed them straight away. I watched as all this fed fear and unhappiness into Mum and Dad. They couldn't cope. Dad described it as "a hundred bowlers bowling simultaneously while you, as the only batsman, try to defend a one-hundred-yard-wide wicket. If you missed even one ball, you would be out." Many of the letters were sent to them to forward to Jackie, but of course they never passed them on. They wanted, above all else, to protect Jackie and Danny.

They needed to find answers. What is Judaism? Is it a cult? Is it occult? Dad announced at supper time: "Only one thing to do when in doubt. Call in the vicar."

The Reverend Gordon Harrison, vicar of St. James, Gerrards Cross duly came round for tea one Sunday to talk to us. When he was shown some of the letters, he sighed. Dad had his notepad ready to take down what was said. The tall, gentle minister explained that Judaism certainly was not a cult, but that the Jews are the chosen race, chosen by God and set apart from all others. If Jackie converted, she would be part of that chosen race and so would her children. He also pointed out that Jesus, of course, was a Jew. That was all it took to put Dad's mind at rest.

One day toward the end of May I was finishing some homework when the telephone rang. Mum answered it.

"It's Jackie!"

I called Dad who came to join us and we huddled round the phone. At first everything was fine: lots of the usual questions and laughter. Then there was a pause and Mum's eyes became glazed and she stared anxiously out of the window. I knew this look. As the conversation became more stilted, I began to realize what was happening.

The Middle East conflict had come to a head. The enemies of Israel were determined to "thrust them into the sea." It was a time of intense danger and Danny wanted to be with his parents and friends. Jackie was phoning to say they were both leaving for Israel immediately. They wanted to give concerts to the troops on the front lines, and help boost morale. Jackie, living in the moment as usual, and totally in love with Danny, had canceled all her concert engagements without a moment's hesitation to go with him and take part. Yehudi Menuhin, with whom Jackie was booked to do one of the concerts, was livid.

Mum tried to listen to Jackie's plans without persuading her to change them, but was deeply troubled that her beloved daughter should be flying straight into a war zone. After a difficult goodbye, Mum replaced the receiver and just looked at Dad. Then they both went upstairs and shut the bedroom door. I listened from the foot of the stairs and heard them talking and Mum crying.

Even though the prospect of war was frightening, I thought it exciting and romantic.

After Jackie and Danny left on May 31, Mum and Dad listened to every possible news broadcast. When war was finally declared, Dad was on the telephone immediately, but calls to Jackie's agents and to the Israeli Embassy didn't yield anything. An Israeli news blackout meant there was nothing in the papers of any substance at all, and news programs had very little information.

Then on June 7, a telegram arrived:

> Situation completely under control. Feeling very relaxed and happy. Please don't worry much love, Jackie

It took a moment to realize that "much" was on the wrong line!

Miraculously, only six days after it had begun, the war was over.

Then another telegram arrived from Jackie announcing that she and Danny were to be married at the Western Wall in Jerusalem and we were all invited to join them.

* * *

Normally, to convert to Judaism, it is necessary to study for at least a year in order to experience all the festivals and holy days in the Jewish calendar. Some rabbis even require five years' study and for the pupil to live with a Jewish family for the period. It is then necessary to go before a rabbinate court to establish the desire for conversion is genuine. Even after conversion, it is usually six months before a wedding can take place. But in the case of Jackie and Danny, special dispensation was made. Maybe it was the mood of joyful optimism in Israel immediately after the war that allowed the usual caution to be cast aside. David Ben Gurion didn't particularly care for music, but he was a great admirer of Jackie, and there was the special significance of an English girl coming to Israel when the country was again fighting for its very life. Jackie had become a symbol in Israel, and Ben Gurion was very aware of this.

Jackie and Danny discussed their desire to marry with him and he arranged for Jackie to be converted by the orthodox rabbinate within twenty-four hours. Jackie told me later that conversion involved walking into a pool, immersing herself under the water, and climbing out the other side—totally naked. Usually, this would be witnessed by one or two rabbis. But, as Jackie said, "This time, there were *dozens* there!"

The wedding was arranged for a few days later. As usual with Jackie, everything was happening quickly. She chose Shulamith as her Jewish name. Shulamith is the loved one in the *Song of Songs*. The word means "peaceful mind."

It was difficult for us to get a flight since all the airlines had stopped flying into the war zone, except for El Al, the Israeli airline. But El Al was not flying from Heathrow direct to Tel Aviv Lod Airport. We had to go via Amsterdam and Munich.

We left early on Wednesday, June 14. I wondered what it would be like with Jackie married. Although it was three years since she had lived at home, we all knew in our hearts that her marriage to Danny would whisk her away into an exotic world far from our own. The romantic nature of their wedding forewarned us of this.

We stayed at the Ramataviv Hotel. Because of the war, we had the whole place to ourselves. The rooms were lovely, bungalow-style, on the ground floor. We left our luggage there and went immediately to the Music Guest House to see Jackie and Danny. Danny's best friend, the Indian conductor and double bass player, Zubin Mehta, was there too.

Jackie and I greeted each other with huge hugs. She was a great hugger.

"Bar . . . great to see you."

"How are you, Jeets? I've missed you."

"Me too . . ."

She told me that they had been giving concerts in Tel Aviv and Haifa every night since their arrival. Their last concert had been in Beersheba, which is about halfway between Tel Aviv and what was then the Egyptian border.

"It was amazing, Bar. We were driving back to Tel Aviv last night, when suddenly these huge tanks came thundering past us, going in the opposite direction. We hadn't realized that the war was so close. It was so exciting."

There was little time to talk before we had to go back to the hotel to change for the evening concert.

The Mann Auditorium was packed, with standing room only. Jackie played Saint-Saëns's youthful concerto with all the exuberance of a young woman in love. Even before the final bars, the audience was on its feet, clapping and cheering: another one of Jackie's "standing ovulations," I thought. Everyone was surging forward to the stage, and the clapping changed to a slow beat. It hit me that this was a completely different appreciation of classical music: to the Israelis, Jackie and Danny were pop stars.

The following morning, Aida and Enrique Barenboim arrived to drive us to the wedding in Jerusalem. We arrived at the King David Hotel shortly before midday. Many friends of the Barenboims were there, and we walked together to the Rabbi's house next to the Wailing Wall. On the back of my head I had a small Russian yarmulkah which Jackie had brought back from Moscow. The streets were narrow with high sandstone walls, and there were soldiers everywhere.

When we arrived at the Wailing Wall, crowds of Jews were praying, swaying backward and forward, singing and weeping with joy. There was so much happiness and so many tears. The Israelis had taken back their city, Jerusalem, during the war. The Western Wall of Solomon's Temple was theirs again.

In the Rabbi's house, only the men were allowed to sit at the table. The women had to sit against the walls, either on chairs or on the floor. Even Mum was on the floor. The Rabbi came in and sat down at the table. How magnificent he looked with his huge beard and smiling eyes. We men were each given a drink, and a small amount of food was placed on the table. But the women were given nothing: they just sat still, without speaking. Eventually more rabbis arrived, with Jackie and Danny.

The ceremony began with an excited bargaining for the price of the bride. Once agreed, the marriage certificate was read with great seriousness. Lighted candles were handed out and we all filed through the door into the courtyard. A canopy was produced and held over Jackie and Danny. The wind was so strong the candles kept blowing out. A number of Israeli children, intrigued by what was going on, joined us and sat on the wall.

The Rabbi read the marriage service and chanted. Finally the marriage certificate was signed and pinned to the wall and Jackie and Danny were pushed into a room on their own, while we went back to the house to sit around the table. Suddenly, there was silence. The Rabbi looked up and started singing, his gray beard waving in front of him. As he continued, the other men gradually joined in. Then Zubin Mehta began, copying the Rabbi, sound for sound. Without stopping, the Rabbi opened his eyes and smiled at Zubin in appreciation. By now I found myself caught up in this wonderful polyphony of deep, sonorous voices although I had no idea what I was doing. Dad also joined in the singing, harmonizing with all his heart. Zubin started conducting, and the sounds seemed to reverberate and fill the room. There was much smiling, laughing and competition between the men. But the women kept quiet, sitting cross-legged against the wall.

After an age, the intensity began to wane, the last notes drifting away while the Rabbi finished the singing on his own. Another period of silence and then, slowly and with purpose, the rabbis stood and left the room. Laughter again burst out as Jackie and Danny suddenly appeared from their room holding a bedsheet. Everyone cheered, although I didn't understand the significance until Dad explained it to me privately, later that day.

As we began walking to the King David Hotel, many people joined in the fun of the procession. It felt as though the whole town was with us, to share in this wedding. At the hotel, Moshe Dayan and Ben Gurion came out to greet us. I was impressed. I stood back out of the way and watched as, one after another, the exalted guests arrived. I was conscious that Jackie and Danny were celebrities now, and that their wedding, coming so soon after the end of the war, symbolized a spirit of hope in Israel. Many dishes of exquisite food arrived and everyone sat down to a magnificent feast. The conversation was fast and multilingual.

That evening there was another concert in honor of Jackie and Danny. Danny played and conducted the Mozart Piano Concerto in D and Jackie played the Schumann. At the dinner afterward, Sir John Barbirolli made a speech in his deep, gruff voice, extolling Jackie for ages. But when he started to talk about the groom, his gaze went beyond Danny and settled on Zubin Mehta. Someone tried to correct him, but he didn't take any notice. Eventually, everyone was laughing so much that he realized his mistake.

The next day we waved Jackie and Danny off on their honeymoon to Marbella, where they stayed with the Rubinsteins.

At the hotel, Barbirolli caught me singing in the corridor, and put his hand on my shoulders, saying, "Now, that's a voice. Come and sing to me in London." I told Mum, who was excited for me. That night I wrote in my diary, "I've been talent-spotted." But I never did sing for him. Music was Jackie's world, not mine. There was no place in it for me.

We flew back to England the next day with KLM, taking the Davidoff with us. The airport staff were upset when Mum refused to put the cello in the hold, insisting it should be in the cabin with us. When she told the airline how much the cello was worth, the captain at first refused to have it on the plane at all. Eventually, however, he allowed Mum to carry it on board.

The whirlwind adventure of the last few days was coming to a close. As we took off and Israel slowly receded beneath us, the feelings of sadness returned. A new chapter was beginning in our lives, a chapter where Jackie was with Danny, and I was the only one left in the nest. I wondered what would happen to me now. Where was I going in the great scheme of things? One thing I knew for certain was that my life could never be as exciting as Jackie's.

Retreat from the world

CHAPTER TWENTY-TWO

Hilary

Kiffer and I would have loved to have been with Jackie at her wedding, but we couldn't leave the children. When Jackie and Danny returned from their honeymoon, they immediately started their travels.

Jackie was completely absorbed with Danny and their new life, so inevitably we saw less of her. She wrote and telephoned regularly from all over the world. Her life always sounded exciting but her letters were full of how much she missed us and wished she could be at home.

Under Danny's supervision, Jackie's career soared. Recently, I looked at her concert schedule from 1967 onward and noticed her engagements had more than doubled. The name Barenboim appeared with du Pré in many concerts, together with Mehta, Zukerman, Perlman, Ashkenazy, Boult, Barbirolli, Abbado, Bernstein.

Danny lived at the cutting-edge of the music world, and swept Jackie along with him. Their romantic marriage and fairy-tale lives attracted a great deal of publicity: they were tailor-made for the changing style of the media which craved personal insight and revelation. Everyone wanted a glimpse into the life of this golden couple, to know which spices Jackie used for her curries, and what their plans were for managing two busy careers when they had children. Although she detested being interviewed, Jackie usually sounded confident. She was able to present a public persona which was very different from the Jackie I knew.

I was due to play Vivaldi's Piccolo Concerto in C with the Newbury String Players and had been lent a wooden instrument for the purpose. As it had not been played for years, I needed to take it to my flute repairer, Mr. Morley, in London. It would be a good opportunity to see Jackie too. I managed to gather enough mothers, mothers-in-law and grandmothers to look after the children, allowing me to have a day in London. I caught an early train and sat among the commuters. Not a word was spoken.

Jackie was waiting for me and we burst into each other's arms, with much giggling and fast chatter. The coffee was ready and we tucked into a huge breakfast, talking non-stop between mouthfuls. She wanted to know all about the children and I wanted to know all about her. As usual, she mimicked everyone she mentioned and tore them to shreds, reducing me to helpless laughter.

We decided that a shopping spree would be fun, so headed for Harrods. But when the taxi came to a halt, Jackie spied a little clothes shop which looked unusual. Inside, was a demure lady who was only too pleased to help, but Jackie swept past her, heading for the dresses. There were ridiculous creations in loud and obvious colors and no garment escaped our trials. Between us, we tried on everything in the shop. I was a real country bumpkin, and seeing me squeezed into the newest fashions brought hysterical giggles from both of us. The little lady followed, picking up the rejects.

The dresses exhausted, we turned to the skirts—even more preposterous, as many of them were extremely skimpy. Jackie put on a mini and I climbed into a long tight skirt. We shrieked. Jackie's legs were not suited to too much exposure, and I couldn't walk with my legs bound together. What was worse, I couldn't get out of it.

Fortunately there was no one else in the shop, for we must have caused chaos. We bought three pretty blouses and departed, leaving a still smiling, only-too-pleased-to-help lady, who hoped we would come back. Exhausted by our antics, we collapsed into a café.

"How's Danny?" I asked, although it was obvious she was deliciously happy.

"He's wonderful! But he never stops, Hil. I don't know how he keeps going. He works all the time and then goes out for dinner all night. He knows everyone."

"What's the next concert?"

"It's the Schumann, with Danny, in the Queen Elizabeth Hall. Can't wait!"

"When is it? Perhaps Kiffer and I could come?"

"Oh, do come. I can't remember when it is, though. Sometime soon. Danny will know."

"I'll phone you when I get home. Remember to ask him."

It was time to say goodbye. We hugged each other, Jackie hailed a cab and disappeared into the London traffic. I took the tube to King's Cross, to Mr. Morley.

I hadn't seen him for some years. Once again, I climbed the seemingly endless concrete stairs to his flat and knocked. I heard his footsteps approaching along the corridor. The door opened. For a moment he hesitated before breaking into a smile.

"Oh, Hilary. How are you?" There was a pause. "Well," he continued. "Your sister made it—but you didn't."

In the autumn of 1967, Christopher (Kitty) Nupen, who was then working with the BBC, decided to make a "behind-the-scenes" documentary about Jackie and Daniel. Kitty's film coincided with the invention of the 16mm camera, which was ideally suited to the new fashion for a relaxed and more revealing style of film-making. Previously, musicians were presented on television in the formal setting of the concert platform. But Kitty's film was different and ground-breaking in its format. It gave the audience an intimate portrait of the real people behind the talent, showing Jackie and Daniel in unguarded moments, laughing and joking with fellow musicians and simply having enormous fun with music.

The film captured Jackie at a very special time in her life. She was madly in love with Daniel, incredibly successful and winning the hearts of audiences all over the world. She was flying on the crest of a wave. Most people who have seen the film will never forget the scene at the end where Jackie and Danny are running and laughing together by the Serpentine.

The film, broadcast by the BBC for the *Omnibus* program on November 30, ended with Jackie performing the Elgar with the New Philharmonia Orchestra conducted by Danny. The television reviewers were very impressed with the program. Henry Raymor said in *The Times* on December 16:

This program may come to have some influence on future television music programs. With Miss du Pré placed with the orchestra and cameras moving obliquely across the players instead of approaching them head on, Christopher Nupen's program gave the most thoroughly detailed account we have yet seen of the actual work of an orchestra; the players were seen to work together and were not isolated when they carried the melodic line.

It was in the depths of the winter of 1967-8 when Jackie telephoned to say she wanted to bring Danny and Zubin to Ashmansworth for the day. I told the children they were coming and explained that Zubin was Indian.

On the great day, the weather was terrible, blowing a gale and extremely cold. They arrived wearing their town clothes, looking as though they belonged to another world.

Theresa, who was only four, was first at the front door to greet them, but looked disappointedly puzzled.

"Where are your feathers?" she asked.

"Oh, I've left them at home. I thought they would blow away in the wind," Zubin replied quickly. "And I would be so sad never to see them again."

Theresa took him by the hand and led him to the sitting room. "Come on, Dustbin and Danny, I want to show you something."

Jackie, Kiffer and I went into the kitchen where Jackie entertained us with stories of their travels. She was in tremendous form.

"You know, Hil, I'm fascinated by American mouths," she suddenly announced, changing the subject completely. "Rows of perfect teeth, set in a hideous grin and a gushing 'aren't-we-pals' expression."

Her mouth stretched to reveal a mass of grinning teeth, as she pranced round the kitchen.

Soon the sounds of Danny's piano-playing were coming from the sitting room and Zubin reappeared, with Theresa and Clare.

"Come on, Hilary, Danny wants you and Jackie to play."

"Oh yes, let's," shrieked Jackie, as she ran off to find Danny.

My heart sank. I desperately wanted to play but was afraid I simply would not be good enough.

Danny chose something for us to sightread together.

He romped off, playing brilliantly, and all too soon it was my turn to come in. I took a deep breath, but within seconds was fumbling.

"Sorry, Hilary, too fast. Let's try again."

He repeated the introduction more deliberately and I managed slightly better the second time, but it was not good. My confidence was failing me. It was all bound up with Jackie, knowing that whatever I tried to do she always did much better. Joy inadvertently baled me out. She was in her element. She had mixed with musicians all her life, with performers and composers, and was genuinely pleased to see Jackie so happy.

"Hilly, dear, would you like some help with lunch? I'm sure everyone must be starving."

"Yes, please. I'll come." It was such a relief to escape.

"I know what," said Jackie. "Let's go to the Gibbet!"

"The what?" asked Danny.

"The top of the world! Come on, we'll work up an appetite."

The children quickly chorused, "Can I come, can I come?"

"No, darlings," I replied. "It's too wet and cold today and they'll need to run fast up there. We'll go another time."

We found warm coats, hats, gloves and wellington boots and Kiffer ferried them up to the Gibbet. He told me that Jackie jumped out of the car and ran, her long golden hair streaming behind her, as the four chased one another over the top of the world.

On their return, Jackie told me Danny had loathed it.

"You know, Hil, when I walk in a very beautiful place I have the same feeling as when I'm playing and everything's going right. Playing lifts you out of yourself into a delirious plane where you feel abandoned and very happy—like being drunk. That's how I felt up there."

Lunch seemed to go on forever and was a jolly affair, with stories of concerts, musicians and traveling. Joy loved it, and Danny and Zubin enjoyed the children and were charming with them.

After lunch, Jackie and I at last found ourselves alone, washing up.

"It's so lovely to see you, Hil! . . . and Kiffer . . . and the children are adorable."

"It's wonderful to see you too." We embraced. Jackie seemed a little doleful.

"I so want to have children one day but I just can't see how we could ever make it work. Danny wants them too, I know, but our lives are so hectic. We're never in one place for long enough. And I just can't see how we could travel with babies as well. It would be too much."

They were both committed to an ongoing schedule of concerts planned at least three years ahead.

"It'll happen when the time is right, Jack. I'm sure it will."

It was an extremely happy day. Everyone was relaxed and the atmosphere was easy. It was the only time, though, that Danny came to Ashmansworth.

CHAPTER TWENTY-THREE

Hilary

In many relationships, the strongest element is also the weakest, just as it was in Jackie's and Danny's marriage—they were opposites in so many ways.

Jackie was at heart an English country girl, gauche and unworldly. She loved nature and walking in the rain, and was at her happiest with simple things. Despite her larger-than-life personality, she was shy: she loathed publicity and the necessity to promote herself. She was absentminded and often had no idea what day it was, rarely putting the date on her letters. Frequently, when telephoning from abroad, she forgot the time difference and rang in the middle of the night. She was extremely generous, and loved sending parcels with presents for the family. When her foreign fees were paid in cash, she would go shopping, blissfully unaware of exchange rates.

Daniel was completely at ease with their high-speed, jet-setting life, enjoying good living, Havana cigars and stylish clothes in their comfortable world of luxury hotels. A great socialite, he often invited twenty or thirty people out to dinner after a concert. When I asked Jackie about this, she replied: "That's nothing. Zubin takes the whole symphony orchestra out for dinner, and that's a hundred people." Daniel was brilliant with the press, and highly organized. His memory was phenomenal: he knew not only the date of any concert in their diaries for the next three years but also details of the programs.

Jackie and Danny had the most remarkable bond in music. It was their life-blood. During the first three years of their marriage, they traveled the world together: America, Australia, Israel, Europe. They were rarely at home.

In their music-making, they complemented each other perfectly. Technique was taken utterly for granted, and Jackie's uninhibited emotional exploration was offset by Danny's responsive control. Their unique performances had a vital spontaneity that made them memorable.

Jackie loved the playing and performing, and did her utmost to adjust to the lifestyle, but found it harder and harder to keep up with Danny's dynamic energy. That very energy and drive made it almost impossible for him to adapt to Jackie's essential being. The wide open spaces of her personality had little chance for expression except through their music-making. She had to be the Jackie the circumstances demanded.

After a long tour, Jackie would often arrive home in London with the Davidoff worn out and her bow with about three hairs left on it. Charles Beare would go to Upper Montagu Street to eat scrambled eggs and to collect the tired cello and the thinning bow. By the next day, careful treatment had restored both cello and bow.

In 1968, a year after her marriage, the Davidoff was in such bad condition that it was not immediately reparable, so Charles lent her a Francesco Gofriller cello which had been stored in the basement of his workshop. He told me he felt the ideal cello for Jackie would have been a Montagnana; these usually have a tremendous sound and do not collapse under heavy use. But Jackie adored the Goffriller, and eventually purchased it from Charles for £4,500. She used it for many of her recordings.

Daniel was not particularly fond of Jackie's Strad, often finding it difficult to hear the Davidoff clearly when they were playing sonatas. Although a Strad's voice projects easily to the back of a concert hall, it does not fill the immediate vicinity of the conductor or accompanist. Daniel had heard his friend, the violinist Pinchas Zukerman, playing a modern violin made by the American Sergio Peresson, and in 1971 decided to commission a cello from him for Jackie. She loved the Peresson, and didn't have to be careful with it, describing it as raw, very healthy and strong as a tank, and used it for many of her performances. Daniel also preferred it although some people felt that it didn't have the richness or variety of colors of the Strad.

Not long after their visit to Ashmansworth, I happened to hear Jackie and Danny being interviewed on the BBC World Service.

"How do you cope with the stress of both a personal relationship and a professional relationship?"

"Well, I can only say that it doesn't feel like stress. I find myself a very happy person. I love my music and I love my husband and there seems to be ample time for both."

"How do you manage practicing when you're traveling?"

"Well, it's actually very hard because there is only the bathroom to practice in. On the other hand, I can't stand practicing—I only practice if I really have to. Daniel is the same."

"Do you find that being married to each other is a help professionally or perhaps a hindrance at times?"

Danny answered this time. "I think it makes no difference because we play different instruments therefore there are no similarities in that respect. I think things would be different if we were both pianists or both cellists. We can spend a lot of time together because we can be in the same city at the same time and in the same week and play different concerts, and we certainly couldn't do that if we played the same instrument. Most people think it's very much related to the personal relationship, but I don't believe in that at all. It sounds romantic to say that two people are in love and they get married and they play concerts together. But it's nothing more than old ladies' chatter. I know a lot of people who are very much in love and happily married and don't play together at all, and I know people that play extremely well together and don't love each other at all."

In July 1968, when I was seven months pregnant, the Newbury String Players, conducted by Kiffer, gave a performance of Bach's St. Matthew Passion in St. George's Church, Wash Common. Wilfred (Bill) Brown was the Evangelist and I was spellbound by his singing and his complete absorption in the music. I became so inspired, I forgot all the complications of playing the flute and for that performance was able to play uninhibitedly and from my heart.

A few days later I received a letter from Bill Brown:

Dear Hilary,

I have resisted writing this letter, but the strain is too great. So, you'd better know, in my unworthy opinion, among the many exciting and felicitous and moving things that went to make up Saturday's St. Matthew Passion at St. George's nothing matched your playing of the obligato in No. 58. Your total absorption in the piece, the nuances, the timing of every minutest detail, and the sheer beauty of the sound you and your pipe produced, were unforgettably lovely.

I think I am one of those rare folks who have actually *seen* a nightingale in full song. It was in daytime of course and I had him under binocular observation for three utterly fascinated minutes. He not only sang from his ankles (as Jean de Reszke said a man should) but the whole tone, the earth from which it sprang, indeed the whole riotous late-April Spring were all concentrated into the bird's throat. You achieved this same effect on Saturday.

Thank you.

My love to all at Ashmansworth.

During the early years of Jackie's marriage she and I had to snatch time together whenever we could. We lived in different worlds, my life being completely absorbed by the children and Kiffer. Letters and telephone calls became our main forms of communication: Jackie had always been a marvelous correspondent and when a letter arrived, it would be passed round the whole family. Her vivid descriptions of wherever she was; her perceptive and extremely funny portrayals of friends and people she met; her honesty about herself and her concern for us all, were always a source of excitement and joy.

One night, just after Kiffer and I had gone to bed, Jackie rang.

"Hil?—Jacks."

"Where are you?"

"Guess?"

"Can't."

"Listen. I'm in the *lavatory*! There's a telephone in here."

"In where?"

"Actually I'm in a castle. The Bel Air Hotel. We're surrounded by wildflowers and trees and bomb-patch smells, and yet we're in the middle of Los Angeles."

She chatted about her loathing of New York and the heat, and how the cello had collapsed the moment she arrived.

"Hil, it was *vile*. But now the big decision is, do I practice or swim?"

"Practice, of course."

"Oh, bugger off!"

"When will you be home?"

"In about two weeks—I'm dying to see you all. But we're only home for two days . . ."

I knew we wouldn't see her.

"Did Gran get the blouse?"

"Yes, she loves it and it fits perfectly."

She sounded on top of the world.

Jackie and Danny were touring America, leaving crowds of excited fans in their wake. A week later, she was on the phone again. She said that her last call had come from paradise and now she was in a high-rise concrete hell: Philadelphia. But the orchestra was stunning, which made up for the horrors.

She was longing to come home to the England she loved. She loathed the hysteria, the heat, the dust and the constant invasion of light music played everywhere.

"Have you been shopping, Jack?" I asked, knowing she would if she had the chance.

"You bet I have. But so has Danny. We've bought each other armfuls of clothes, so we're both very happy."

In August, we returned to France with eight friends. The fact that the house was extremely basic did not concern us. We had enough beds for the adults, and the children slept on lilos on the floor. I was hugely pregnant, expecting Orlando in less than a month. Our three babies had all been born at home, and it didn't worry me that this one might arrive in France.

The children's days were spent picnicking, swimming and running all over the mountain. Occasionally, I managed to have a rest, lying like a beached whale on a rug on the terrace, soaking up the sunshine and the view. In the evenings, we ate like kings. There were plenty of cooks, and after a sumptuous meal, we all did the washing up under the stars on the terrace, serenaded by the bullfrogs.

I often wondered about Jackie and whether she would ever come here. Would she be able to leave her life of rushing about the world, living in hotels and performing to thousands of people? She had become a butterfly, alighting for a few brief moments before flitting off. Here we were, in this beautiful place where time and the way of life had stood still for centuries. The only things that moved quickly were the lizards, as they darted up and down the walls. Our lives seemed a million miles from hers. At times like these I knew I wouldn't have swopped places with Jackie for anything in the world.

CHAPTER TWENTY-FOUR

Piers

I was so aware my life had no direction. Jackie was world-famous, and Hilary was fulfilling herself with her family, her teaching and the business. But I just didn't know what I wanted to do, let alone what I might be good at. I hated routine, wanted nothing to do with music and needed a goal, something to challenge me. Always, there was the assumption by others that, as a du Pré, I had to achieve something outstanding. I began to dread the question so frequently asked: "And what are you going to do, Piers?" To this there was no answer I could possibly give which would ever meet their expectations. I would be left feeling inadequate and as if I was the runt of the litter.

Then one glorious day soon after coming back from Israel, something happened which was to give me the goal I so needed. Mum was telephoning from the hall, when a jet flew low over the house on its final approach to Heathrow, making such a noise that she had to apologize to the caller. She put her hand over the mouthpiece, looked at me and said:

"Why don't you go and fly airplanes, Ba? You like making a lot of noise."

In that instant, without hesitation, I knew my future. I knew I could do it and it would be something I could be proud of when being compared to Jackie or Hilary. Wondering how to plot this new course, I remembered that Mum taught piano to an ex-BEA Captain. I telephoned him and he told me that the joint BOAC and BEA air training college was at Hamble, in Southampton. When they sent me their prospectus, I found I needed two B passes at A level to qualify. Although I had virtually no chance of such passes, I was not going to allow that to deter me now.

Within a week, Dad announced that he had arranged for me to be taken up for a trial flight in a Cherokee 140 light aircraft at the Airways Flying Club, Booker Airport, High Wycombe. I felt so excited as I walked to the plane with the pilot. Once airborne, he told me to take the control column and fly. My senses reeled. What incredible freedom! Mum and Dad could see from my face when I landed that I had found my future. In my own way I could make music with my flying.

In the middle of August the envelope with my A level results arrived. As I picked it up I knew my career was in my hands. Chemistry—failed. Physics and Mathematics—"concessionary" passes only. Flying began to blur and recede. I hadn't achieved the minimum required.

At the end of August, Dad called me into the sitting room and said in his "serious" voice, "Piers, if you have really set your heart on flying, don't you think you should go and learn? What I mean, Piers, is that we think you should go back to Booker and we'll pay for you to get your Private Pilot's License." A week later, I was airborne in a Beagle Terrier.

During the Hamble interview day my brain was working overtime. This is it, I thought. This is where they find out I don't qualify.

"Now to your exams. I see you have a large number of O levels, and most with good passes. Good," mused the interviewer. "But I see we don't have your A level results. I presume you passed at least two?" I had rehearsed this in my mind many times. "Oh yes," I replied and quickly changed the subject. "But can I just ask something?" Without waiting for an answer I carried on, "On the form I had to state whether I would prefer BOAC or BEA. I left it blank, not really understanding the difference. Can you tell me?"

He did, and forgot the A levels. Two days later, I heard that I had been successful, and that the next stage would be a day of flying aptitude. But before this day was scheduled, I passed my Private Pilot's License. After advising Hamble of this, I received, on February 9, 1968, my prize of gold—a letter stating that the flying aptitude test was unnecessary and that I now had a guaranteed place at Hamble.

★   ★   ★

There was a message from Jackie pinned on the mess board: "Great news. Congratulations. Longing to see you. Lots of love. Jackie."

At last I was being appreciated for being me, not just the baby brother of . . .

I went traveling with my girlfriend, Lin, through Europe to Yugoslavia. While we were there, the Russians invaded Czechoslovakia. Troops and tanks seemed to be everywhere.

We returned to Gerrards Cross to find Jackie and Danny about to give a concert in aid of Czechoslovakia with the London Symphony Orchestra in the Royal Albert Hall on the afternoon of September 2 and the whole family had been invited. The proceeds of the concert were to be shared between the United Nations Association, which was giving financial aid to Czechoslovak refugee students in this country, and the Foundation of Czechoslovak Immigrants. Immediately after August 21, 1968, a trust had been established by Rafael Kubelik to assist Czech refugees in Europe. The concert was to be recorded by London Weekend Television for inclusion in their *Saturday Special* series.

Jackie was playing one of the most celebrated of all cello concertos by, appropriately, a Czech, Antonin Dvořák. Written when the composer was in America in 1894, and inspired by his youthful love, it is a work of ravishing melody, where the cello, an operatic solo voice, sings to the orchestra.

On the morning of the concert Jackie telephoned Mum and told her that she and Danny had received a death threat, but not to worry because there would be special services people everywhere.

"There's even a policeman outside our flat right now, Mum. And he's a cellist as well. I found this out when I called him in for a coffee. I made him try the Davidoff!"

I drove Mum and Dad from Gerrards Cross while Kiffer drove Hil, who insisted upon making the journey even though she might give birth at any moment. Collecting our tickets from the artists' entrance, we found our way to the Green Room.

Danny didn't seem at all concerned. He told us there were marksmen all over the hall.

We were sitting quite high up and to the right of the stage, looking down on the platform. Mum was fidgeting nervously; Dad was trying to reassure her; I was scanning the auditorium, looking for the assassins.

Jackie looked positively defiant as she swept on to the stage with her characteristic bounce, holding the cello high up in front of her. The vision stays with me. There she was in her light-blue lace gown, blond hair flying around her shoulders. Such poise, such confidence. Not a single care about the death threat.

We stood for both the British and Czech National Anthems. As the last chords faded away, Jackie appeared to compose herself more seriously than usual. A look and a nod to Danny, and the concerto began. First the clarinets presented their wonderfully lyrical melody, soon joined by the bassoons, before the solo horn began sounding its haunting theme of romantic longing. Jackie caught these themes and began leading the music passionately forward and deeper. From the moment she started playing, I felt absorbed in a way that I had never experienced before. It may have been because of the death threat or her determination to fight for the cause. For the first time ever, her music struck home. The Dvořák is a beautiful concerto. To me, even more elegant than the Elgar or the Schumann. I felt so proud of her, so set apart from the rest of the audience. There was my sister, being brave and brilliant. But I kept dragging myself back to reality, scanning the boxes for possible snipers. I wasn't going to allow anything to happen to her.

Suddenly, there was a loud crack. I jumped up, expecting Jackie to fall to the floor. At first, she stood, and the audience gasped as Daniel pulled the orchestra to a sudden, awkward halt. Jackie began speaking. It was all right. A string had snapped and she needed to replace it. She left the platform.

The relief was sudden and almost painful. But she seemed to take ages. Danny, concerned, went to find her.

While waiting, Mum and Dad began talking about the pressures of playing. They said Jackie always played better when she wasn't feeling well. In fact, one of the best concerts she ever gave was after she'd had her wisdom teeth out. She had gone to the dentist one morning to have all four out in one go under local anaesthetic, everyone forgetting she was to play in the Royal Festival Hall that evening. She played exquisitely.

Eventually, Jackie and Danny reappeared on the platform. The audience burst into applause.

During the interval, Jackie told us what had happened. She had gone to her dressing room only to discover that she hadn't any spare strings with her, so had had to go to the orchestral Green Room and check every single cello case. Finally, she found the string she needed in the very last case.

The memory of Jackie's playing and how I felt that afternoon has never left me.

Like every other day, February 4, 1969 started with me waiting impatiently at the front door for the postman, only to find that there was still no news from Hamble about when my course would start.

When the telephone rang, I jumped to answer it.

"Bar?"

"Jeets! What's new?"

"Nothing, except I'm going to Berlin. Wanna come?"

"Really? Yeah . . . Sure . . . Love to! When do we go?"

"Today! It's the Dvořák, your favorite, with the Berlin Phil and Zubin. Should be fun."

"Great! You're on!"

I threw a few things in a suitcase, said goodbye to Mum and set off for London.

We traveled together, Jackie, myself and Zubin, laughing and joking for the entire journey, with Zubin calling me "Pee-ars" which amused Jackie hugely.

After the concert, Zubin took everyone out for an enormous meal. The wine flowed and we made merry until the early hours. Afterward, we decided we should all go swimming. When the concierge told us that the pool was closed, Zubin just kept piling banknotes into his hand until he gave us the key.

One or two other musicians joined us in the pool where I realized that bathing costumes were optional. I'd never experienced anything like this before.

Then everyone decided that we should go for a sauna. Again, everyone was naked. This was the first time I had ever been in such a situation and I firmly kept a towel wrapped around my waist. I couldn't wait to get out. It was too hot, in all senses. I escaped and plunged into the cold pool.

Jackie and I didn't talk about what happened. I realized that this was Jackie's world, but I was uncomfortable in it. I think, now, that Jackie allowing me into this situation was her way of telling me what was going on. And perhaps the reason why she so urgently wanted me to go with her was to have me as a shield.

Eventually the final word arrived from Hamble. I shall never forget that day—April 3, 1969. As I ripped open the envelope, I somehow knew it would be good news. And it was. I had to report there on May 16. I felt ten feet tall, and valued for being me.

Hilary

Danny and his friends were the most exciting group of musicians at that time, and he led life at top speed. His days were long and his nights short, and he regularly stayed up until three or four in the morning. Jackie was riding a wave of freedom and fun with him, and her life was overflowing. Late nights, though, were a problem because she had always needed her sleep, preferably nine hours a night, whereas Danny could manage with only four or five. She was becoming exhausted by their hectic schedule.

She often telephoned me, complaining of feeling worn out, so I encouraged her to come to Ashmansworth whenever she could. She turned up unannounced one day in the early summer of 1969. I was in the kitchen with the children, when she suddenly popped her head around the door.

"Boo."

I gasped. "Jackie—Jackie! You gave me such a jump."

"I just thought I'd come and see you. I'm free for the whole day."

"So am I. Hooray!" And we hugged, but it was not her usual exuberant embrace. Instinctively, I knew she wasn't herself. I had always been able to pick up her feelings the moment she walked into a room, and today was no exception. She had put on some weight. I suddenly felt extremely anxious.

She told me she had hailed a taxi in London intending to go

shopping but had changed her mind, so the taxi had brought her all the way to Ashmansworth.

Orlando was now almost a year old and Jackie adored him. In her longing to have her own baby, she became obsessed with him, wishfully imagining he was hers.

"How's my baby?" she asked, looking around for him.

"He's in the garden, sound asleep in the pram. Go and have a peep."

Whatever the weather, at sleepy time during the day, my babies slept outside. In winter the pram was often piled high with snow but the infant was always as warm as toast inside.

Together we crept down the steps into the herb garden. The pram was under the medlar tree, the nearest shaded place within earshot of the kitchen. When awake, the baby loved gazing at the silhouetted leaves moving against the sky.

Jackie stood over the pram and watched the sleeping Orlando. His skin was soft and clear and his fair, white hair gently framed his face. Joy called him a Botticelli angel. No wonder Jackie was entranced by him.

Kiffer was in the garden and it wasn't long before the rest of the household became aware of Jackie's presence and everyone congregated, the children running about excitedly. Theresa, as usual, took charge.

"Jackie, Jackie, come and see our new den . . . come *on* . . ." as she took Jackie's hand and tried to drag her away. But Jackie was pulling a face indicating to me that she didn't want to go. This wasn't like her. Normally the children were an instant tonic for her.

The children led her to their secret place under the stairs, where, with much hilarity, they squeezed and pushed the podgy Jackie into the mouth of the den.

"Hil, I won't be able to get out," she protested.

"Never mind, Jack. Stay there while I make you a cup of tea."

I returned bearing hot tea, and Jackie looked at me imploringly.

"Come on, Theresa, it's time for Jackie to stand up now or she may never be able to move again."

More pushing and shoving and Jackie staggered out.

"How about a quick walk with Kiffer, Jack, while we collect the eggs? I want to get it done before Orlando wakes up."

The children and I went off to the chickens while Kiffer and Jackie walked across the field to cowslip dell.

Jackie was more cheerful after lunch and we sat in the garden, playing with Orlando and watching the three girls splashing about in the paddling pool. She couldn't stay the night as she had a rehearsal the next morning, so in the evening the taxi returned to take her back to London.

Later that night, when Kiffer and I were in bed, we finally had a chance to talk.

"She's exhausted," said Kiffer. "She's fed up with packing bags and traveling all the time. She says she can't cope with it and needs a rest, but her life doesn't allow her to take unplanned time off."

"But she's always found all that difficult."

"Yes, I know, but she says she's not enjoying being with Danny at the moment . . ."

"What do you mean?"

". . . She says they're not getting on and she's too tired to make an effort."

"What on earth can we do?"

"I don't know. Just listen, I suppose. I don't know. Anyway, she said she was feeling better."

She always did feel better when she'd had a walk and a talk with Kiffer. He was positive and strong, and a very good listener. It was a relief for her to talk openly to a man who didn't expect anything from her. She was able to unburden herself on Kiffer, knowing that he made her feel safe.

I didn't see much of Jackie that autumn but when she could visit me her mood of disenchantment seemed still to be with her. She was away for much of the winter, with concerts in Toronto and New York. One morning in early April, the telephone rang and I heard Joy chatting to someone.

". . . Well, just come, dearie. I'll get Kiffy to meet you at the station. What time? I'm sure that's fine." She replaced the receiver.

"That was Jackie. Danny's away and she's fed up, so she's coming for lunch. Someone's named a cow after her! Absurd idea. There's a horse named after Rostropovich, you know."

"I thought Jackie was in New York."

"Just got back. Where's Kiffy? She needs meeting off the 11:56."

* * *

This time, Jackie was in flying form, full of stories of her travels. She had been interviewed for the *New York Times* about women's lib.

This was another world.

"The best part," laughed Jackie, "was the look on the interviewer's face when I said I'd never heard of women's lib—I wasn't supposed to say that."

Over lunch Kiffer produced some photographs of L'île and Jackie was so enthralled we asked her to join us there for a holiday in August.

A few days later she rang to say she would definitely like to come to France but only had a gap of about three or four days between the South Bank Festival and Edinburgh, after which she was due to fly to Australia on a big tour with Danny.

CHAPTER TWENTY-FIVE

Hilary

In high summer of 1970, we set off for France, excited by the thought that Jackie would be joining us a few days later. We made the long journey in our bright-blue Renault 4, the children lying tightly packed together on top of three weeks' luggage, sleeping bags and cooking utensils. The eighteen-hour journey was extremely hot. Oh, what a relief to arrive, and plunge into the river.

Kiffer, who loved working in the heat, enjoyed a siesta after lunch. One day, he stripped off all his clothes and lay flat out on the terrace in the heat of the sun. As usual, he fell into a deep sleep, while I was reading to the children under the fig tree. All of a sudden, I heard footsteps and someone calling our name. I jumped up with the children and ran on to the terrace just in time to see Kiffer stumbling into the dining room. He was obviously still half asleep, and began racing and crashing around the long dining table. The children started to give chase and the postman stood rooted to the spot in utter astonishment. When Kiffer finally came to his senses, I don't know who was more embarrassed: him or the postman.

Two days later, Kiffer drove to Nîmes airport to collect Jackie from an evening plane. It had been a lovely day but shortly after he departed, there was a sudden and dramatic Cévenole thunderstorm. The thunderclaps bounced from mountain to mountain, the lightning forked and flashed, momentarily illuminating the troubled sky, and the rain poured in noisy, banging torrents on to the house. The children slept, oblivious to it all.

I lit the fire downstairs and made supper, weeping stinging tears as I chopped onions. I had our carol-singing lanterns ready to light the way up the mountain.

By 11 p.m. the storm seemed to be abating: the thunder was infrequent and rather half-hearted, and the rain only plinking. I lit a lantern, went on to the terrace and held the little flame up high. There was an immediate hooting from the Renault in the valley below and a long "coooo-eeee" from Jackie.

"Jackie . . . Kiffer," I yelled into the darkness. "Wait there, I'm coming."

I dashed indoors to fetch the other two lanterns and a box of matches and ran, stumbling and slithering down the wet mountain. My heart was pounding with sudden wild excitement. I leapt off the wall, on to the road and into Jackie's arms. What a hug we had!

She was larger and stronger than me and in her excitement lifted me off the ground, squeezing me tightly while burying her head in my neck.

"Hil!"

"Jackie . . . Kiffer! Oh, wonderful, wonderful—you've been ages. Did you come through the storm?"

"We've been sitting in the car waiting for it to stop for about an hour. It was too fierce for us to climb up."

Jackie seemed mesmerized.

"Oh, Hil, where are we? It's all black except for the little glow up there. Let's go up quickly."

We lit the other lanterns and, carrying one each, started the climb. Kiffer led the way, with Jackie's suitcase under his arm.

"Hold your lanterns high, look down there and listen."

We stood huddled together and listened to the river as it splashed and sped its swollen way. The mountain, which had been so dry earlier that day, was now eagerly soaking up the rain. The scrubby holm oaks were dripping, and a calmness and quietness was breathing all around us. Our little candle flames bobbed up and down as we climbed toward the house.

We stood on the terrace in our silent world. The clouds had gone and the sky was spangled with bright stars.

"Jack, we've been waiting for you—you've come home."

Another huge hug and we turned and went into the warm, yellow light, and the smells of wood fire and ratatouille.

We opened the door and crept over the uneven rock floor into the shadowy well room.

"This is where our water comes from, Jackie. Would you like to let down the bucket and fill it up? You have to pull hard when it's full—it'll be heavy."

The bucket whizzed down and the splash echoed in the emptiness. The well had filled up considerably in the storm.

"Come on, I'll show you the house. The downstairs bedroom first. Mind your head. This door was made for the local French!"

We filed into the simple room with its pitted walls.

"You can sleep here if you like, Jackie, but first I'll show you the upstairs room, then you can choose."

Still carrying our lanterns, we climbed the narrow flagstone staircase into the largest room, where Nico and Orlando were sound asleep. Jackie went straight over to look at them.

"Hil, they look so angelic. They won't wake, will they?"

"Not a chance! They all slept through the thunderstorm. Only the morning light will wake them, and they'll be full of energy!"

Jackie held up her lantern and looked around.

"This room is enormous. I love these black and white tiles and the ceiling is so high."

The shadows were dancing with the moving candlelight, and still the children slept. We peeped at Theresa and Clare, in the pink room. Jackie chose the blue bedroom, upstairs.

"Come on, we'll see the rest in daylight. It's supper time."

We sat at the big table in the gaslight glow, our plates heaped with ratatouille and sprinkled with grated gruyère.

"How about some of Portales's red wine, Jackie?" said Kiffer, opening a bottle. "It's perfect with this kind of meal."

"You bet. But who's Portales?"

"He's the chap we bought the house from."

"He lives over there, with his family," I said, pointing.

The glasses were filled.

"You know, Jackie," Kiffer said, "this wine is very important to us, isn't it, Hil?" We smiled at each other. "Yes, it's the reason we have Orlando."

"What on earth do you mean, Kif?"

"Well, you see, when Monsieur Portales discovered that we had

Nico, a third daughter, he was horrified. To the people here, it's vital to have a son to help with the work, and eventually to take over, so he couldn't imagine how we would be able to survive in the long term with three daughters and no son. The remedy was simple. He would give me a barrel of his wine and I was to make sure that I drank a glass every night and within two years, I would have a son. He was right!"

"So, that explains why Orlando is so delicious!" said Jackie.

It was an animated supper. Jackie had been in Israel with Danny and was full of stories.

"You can't imagine what a beautiful place Jerusalem is . . . you'd love it, Hil. And the quantities of garlic they put on their food— absolute Heaven!"

"How's Danny?"

"Oh, he's so busy, as always. He's so lucky he doesn't burn, no matter how long he stays in the sun. Just tans, instead of turning into crackling like me."

It was already midnight and I knew the children would wake early.

It was a short night and, as the bright dawn drew steam from the rain-soaked mountains, the children awoke, full of energy, and were instantly everywhere.

"Mummy, Jackie *is* here. She's in bed. Come and see."

But Jackie had already rolled out of bed and was on her way to our bedroom. Within moments, all four children and Jackie were on our bed in a tumbling heap.

"Let's go for a swim before brekker. I think the river will be bigger today." It was Kiffer's idea, and the children didn't need any encouragement.

"Hil, can I carry Orlando? I'm longing to hold him. Will he mind?"

I gave him to her and Orlando watched her cautiously while she talked to him. She flipped her hair over her face and flipped it back again.

"Boo!" She made him jump and he laughed. The ice was broken, and we all set off down the mountain.

We were a merry band heading for the swollen river. Theresa

and Clare jumped straight in, while Nico ran along the little wall looking for waterboatmen and frogs. Orlando, who was still in Jackie's arms, had entangled himself in her hair and was tugging. "Hil, help, I need rescuing and I want to swim. Help!"

It wasn't long before we were all splashing, diving and jumping in the fresh and chilly water, working up a good appetite for breakfast. We climbed back up the mountain, singing Nico's favorite song "Daisy, Daisy, give me your answer do," over and over again until we reached the terrace. Kiffer had to leave almost immediately to collect our friend, Claire Golding, and her daughter Julia, from Nîmes airport, so he had a quick cup of coffee and left, while we fried eggs and tomatoes, and buttered French bread. The children were already eating yogurt decorated with trails of local lavender honey, so there was a momentary calm.

After breakfast, the children wanted to go to their camps with their recorders. I had taught them to play the recorder so I could hear their whereabouts on the mountain. They disappeared with Jackie, armed with a spare recorder and some folk-songs. A while later, I heard from the far distance "Daisy, Daisy, give me your answer do," obviously performed by Jackie—a very different platform for her.

Many a folk-song floated on to the terrace that morning and it was a contented group of performers who returned for lunch.

"It won't be long before Daddy's back with Claire and Julia, so I've prepared a picnic to have down by the river. They'll be hot after their long journey. Go and find your buckets and fishing nets. Everything else is ready."

Full of expectation, we were on our way to the river again. "Daisy, Daisy," bouncing down the mountain in another colorful and lively performance. The slatey stones rattled as the children ran over them. Jackie carried Orlando and I had the rucksack, the picnic bags, four buckets and the fishing nets. We scrambled over the wall, skirted the little rockface and jumped down to the river's edge. The children immediately slipped into the bubbling, shining water and the valley was filled with shrieks of delight.

Clare was the first to notice three figures on the high wall. "Daddy, Daddy!—Claire and Julia. Look, up there."

The children struggled out of the river and ran to greet them. Julia put on her bathing costume in a flash, and they all dashed back with her into the water. Claire and I sat on the stones and watched the children as they splashed and swam. I decided that food was needed: French bread, cheeses, local farmhouse pâté, juicy tomatoes, salad and dressing, and plenty of water and fruit juices. It was a perfect lunch, ending with extremely ripe peaches.

We spent the afternoon there, just being and belonging in that place. The buckets had been filled but as we left, little fishes and tadpoles were emptied back into the river.

As the golden light was turning pink and the cicadas ceased their creakings, Kiffer, Claire, Jackie and I sat on the terrace with glasses of Muscat and a bowl of black olives. We sipped in silence, chewing the juicy black olives and flicking the stones over the wall and into the valley way below. The flagstones and walls of the house had absorbed the heat from the sun and now, as the light was fading, we were wrapped in the remnants of the day's warmth.

"It's perfect, just perfect. It's been a perfect day," murmured Jackie.

"Oh, absolutely," said Claire. "It's so beautiful. It's heaven on earth."

"I wish I could stay here. I've done enough traveling. I never want to go away again."

"But, Jackie, you've seen such wonderful places, more than I will ever see, and played in fantastic concerts," I said.

"Oh Hil, I know. I love the playing, but I love being with you all much more."

On the day of her departure we all rose at 5:30 to say goodbye.

"Jackie, don't go, please stay, we need you to play with us. Pleeeease . . ." The children were hanging on to her and pleading.

She bent down with tears on her face. "Darlings, I can't. I have to go and play in some concerts. And I'm going to Australia, too, where there are koala bears. I know, I'll send you each a koala teddy! They will arrive by post and when you unpack them they will have been on a journey all around the world, so make them very welcome. I will kiss them before they leave and they will give those kisses to you . . . specially for you."

It was a mournful trail down the mountain as we trudged to the car.

"Hil, these have been shining days that I shall never forget. I love you so much. I'll phone as soon as I can."

Another big hug and we waved goodbye as they bounced along in the little car, over the bridge, around the side of the mountain and out of sight.

A few days after we returned to Ashmansworth Jackie phoned as promised. I knew the parting had been difficult for her; it had for us all. She chatted about the blissful days we'd shared in France, and how the memories were sustaining her while she was so far away on tour. L'île, the children, the bathing, the Mediterranean thunderstorms, Nico's recorder playing—all of it she retained as a private memory, a glowing oasis.

She complained about the inevitable interviews. There were occasions when nerves overwhelmed her, as sweat flowed and her voice dried up. Danny, however, fired on all cylinders and was extremely articulate.

It was to be a while before we saw Jackie again. From Australia, she was traveling to New Zealand. After performing the Dvořák and Haydn concertos with NZBC Symphony Orchestra, she was due to tour America with performances of the Schumann, the Beethoven Triple Concerto, finishing in New York with the Elgar, with Danny.

One day, a large package containing the four promised fluffy koala bears arrived, with instructions from Jackie that they needed hugs and kisses and would, in return, give hugs and kisses from Jackie. The children were delighted with their new teddies and took them on a tour of the house, to meet the other toys, and to see Joy.

Theresa was already playing the violin and as she was showing an interest in playing the piano, too, I asked Mum if she would teach her. I particularly wanted Theresa to have Mum's musical and inspirational influence. Once a week, we would go to Mum and Dad's or they would come to Ashmansworth.

Although he loved living in Gerrards Cross, Dad was finding his city job exhausting. During the autumn of 1970 he began to feel unwell, having recurring bouts of sickness. In mid-November,

Mum and Dad came to Ashmansworth for the day. Dad had taken time off work, which was unlike him.

After lunch, we took a cup of sweet tea into the sitting room for Dad and found him sound asleep in the armchair. He looked wretched. As the piano was in the sitting room, we abandoned Theresa's lesson and crept back into the kitchen.

Mum settled down at the kitchen table.

"Jackie phoned last night. She was in fine form. Guess what? *Harper's Bazaar*, some magazine, is going to take her photo for a series on "great beauties of the day." Jackie said it's made her feel spotty and splotchy."

Mum was full of her stories: Jackie'd gone into a lavatory and found a sign saying "Don't go in here alone. Someone was murdered in here." And a young boy had wanted to shake her hand because he might never see her again. He was going to Vietnam. Someone else asked Jackie if she ever played topless.

As Mum spoke I realized that Jackie was being exposed to a world far removed from the safety of our family.

"Were you aware that you had produced one of the great beauties of today?"

"No, darling. I've produced three actually! I wonder what she'll wear for the photograph? We must ask Dad if he can get a copy of the magazine."

Jackie and Danny had just bought a house in Pilgrim's Lane, in Hampstead, but had hardly been able to spend any time there.

"They're having some work done on it: a sunken music room or something. I'm longing to see it. It's in a very pretty street, apparently, and right next to the Heath."

Mum chuckled as she remembered another incident. Jackie had been presented with a magnificent and exquisitely decorated cake. It was handed to her but she dropped it immediately.

"Jackie said the whole thing crashed on to the carpet like elephant droppings."

Dad slept for most of the afternoon. When he awoke, he looked pale and disoriented, and Mum decided to take him home.

CHAPTER TWENTY-SIX

Hilary

By the end of November, Dad had developed jaundice and was instructed to take three weeks off work. Jackie and Danny were away on a particularly hectic concert tour in America and, from her frequent telephone calls, Jackie knew that Dad was worsening. He sounded miserable and was unable to summon any strength. Jackie's security lay in the knowledge that Mum and Dad were well and happy and that their lives were unworried.

Jackie was extremely anxious about the news of Dad's illness and telephoned immediately to cheer him up:

"What are you up to, fart-face? I hear you've gone bright yellow."

"DZsZeets!"

"Where do you think I am?"

"In the White House?"

"No, old cock. I'm on a telephone in an *automobile*. Unbelievable isn't it?"

She told him to behave himself, to paint himself pink, and to do as he was told.

"I'll be home soon to check up on you. Watch out!"

On Jackie's return from America in early December, she went directly to see Dad and found him in a poor state. His jaundice was severe and Mum was alarmed. Jackie suddenly revealed unexpected qualities.

"Don't worry about anything, Mum. I've telephoned my doctor, Len Selby, and he's coming to see Dad. He's brilliant. He'll know what to do."

Dr. Selby was based in Harley Street and had many musicians

among his patients. Jackie had been introduced to him through Danny.

She tried to lift Dad's spirits by telling stories from her American travels, and Dad was obviously cheered to see her.

". . . We spent our entire time with millionaires! They drip with diamonds like a Tiffany's display case, and their hair is as stiff as dried cowpats. And to cap it all they strive to be civilized."

"What on earth do you talk about at all these dos?" I asked.

"Church Farm, of course!"

"What . . . ?"

"I was telling someone all about the children and you and Kiffer and the countryside, and this awfully friendly lady asked me what you wore on the farm?"

"Diamonds and pearls, of course," I replied, twirling round the room.

". . . and I met some other billionaires who have a huge ranch (as a weekend retreat), and every animal they have is the same color. Like a whole Noah's Ark washed in Omo!"

Dad listened in amazement. "That's extraordinary."

"I know, but I tell you, these rich people don't know how to excite themselves anymore! It's like *Midas*, Dad. Everything has to be gold."

Jackie had always known that Mum's support was readily available to her. Now the roles were reversing and Jackie was controlling and supporting both Mum and Dad. It was possibly the first time she had felt able to do anything for the family and she was firing on all cylinders. She arranged the best possible medical care, paid the bills, and gave a hundred percent of herself with love, energy and joy. Dr. Selby, seeing at once that Dad was seriously ill, arranged for him to go privately into King Edward's Hospital in London. After several days, the doctors advised a biopsy. The results were extremely alarming, and Dad needed an immediate investigatory operation. Mum was petrified. Her worst fears were confirmed when the surgeon told her Dad's liver was covered with cancer, and there was nothing that could be done. He had simply sewn him up again. Dad might have only three weeks to live. Luckily, Jackie was with Mum when she learned this.

Jackie decided it would be best to take Mum to Ashmansworth. She called a taxi.

Mum had become a hollow, gray husk, unable to speak or respond, and just sat by the fire staring blankly. She was profoundly shocked. Jackie was with her constantly. We managed to persuade her to eat a little and, that night, she and Jackie slept in the double bed in the spare room.

While Mum was in the bathroom, Jackie ran down to the kitchen.

"Hil, do you think Mum will be all right? I've never seen her so . . . cracked up."

"She'll be all right, Jack, because of you—you're being wonderful."

"Don't be silly, Hil, anyone would do it. Anyway, she must keep strong for Dad—we all must."

"Do you think we should tell him?"

"No, he wouldn't be able to cope."

We heard Mum coming out of the bathroom.

"Night-night, Hil. Sleep tight."

The next morning, Mum was anxious to return to the hospital, so Jackie called another taxi to take them to London. On arriving, they found a sleepy, half-conscious Dad who was not really aware of their presence.

The shock and the speed of these terrifying events were so great that it caused a strong and immediate redirection of allegiance: Mum's devotion to Dad was complete and irrevocable.

She kept a constant vigil at his bedside, praying for him, both alone and with friends. Dad remained in a stable condition and, after a few days, showed signs of improvement. Another biopsy was advised.

The doctors were literally jumping for joy when they told Mum that his liver was inexplicably clear. Dad was still unaware of the original diagnosis and was perplexed by the doctors' reaction. Mum was jubilant, and when Dad eventually returned home to Gerrards Cross on January 13, he was accompanied by an extremely loving, wholly devoted, wife.

Soon after Dad left hospital, we gathered at Gerrards Cross for a family lunch. As we celebrated Dad's recovery, Jackie seemed withdrawn. There were no jokes, no mimicry, she wasn't looking forward to anything. She was thoroughly flat. I asked her if she was all right.

"It's just everything . . ."

"But you'll have fun with Danny in America?"

"That's the problem. I'm not having fun. I don't have any concerts. I've got to be with him, but I don't want to be."

"Oh come on, it's not as bad as all that, is it?"

"Yes, it is. Not enough sleep, ghastly traveling, ghastly hotels and Danny always seems so irritated with me. I can't do anything right for him."

"Have you told Mum?"

"No, I can't really. She's so wrapped up with Dad now."

A few days later, she departed. The combination of feeling deserted by Mum, of not looking forward to being with Danny, and of being surrounded by musicians but not playing, made her utterly depressed. On one occasion, she joined the cello section of the orchestra just to amuse herself.

Jackie telephoned late one night, very upset. She said she was tired and hinted that things weren't going well with Danny. She sounded confused.

I was so worried I wrote her a long letter, telling her how much we all loved her, and how wonderful she had been with Mum and Dad.

In due course she rang, and we had an emotionally charged conversation from one side of the Atlantic to the other. She was obviously overwhelmed, and comforted to know that the family was concerned. She longed to be enveloped in the cocoon of family understanding and felt lost and out of her depth. She needed us to bolster her again. Many a time she was with us in her imagination. When she was far away, making music, she was as close to me as she could be, pouring out her thoughts and feelings from the other side of the world.

Early in the spring of 1971, the telephone rang. The operator asked if I would take a call from America. I knew it was Jackie, and accepted the charges anxiously.

When she came on the line, she was almost incoherent. "Hil—

Hil . . . is that you? It's me. You've got to come and get me.
You've got to come now."

"Jackie, what's happening? Where are you?"

"I'm in the hotel. I can't remember what it's called. Oh, Hil,
you've got to come."

"Oh course I'll come, Jackie. But try and tell me what the matter is."

"It's Danny," she sobbed. "Hil, I'm frightened, please come."

"Jackie, I've said I'll come. Why are you frightened? What's
happened?"

"They're going to put me in a loony bin and Danny is so angry
with me . . ."

She managed to tell me that she and Danny had been arguing
and she was on drugs to calm her down. Apparently, the doctor
had told her he wanted to put her in a mental hospital for her own
safety. She begged me to go immediately and bring her back
home. I promised I would as soon as I had organized the children,
and booked a flight. She said she would phone me at the same
time the next day.

Within a few minutes Danny was on the phone, in a rage. How
dare I interfere with his marriage? How dare I suppose that I knew
more than him, or the doctor, about Jackie? I was not even to
think of coming over to America—there was no point as Jackie
was perfectly all right and in good hands.

I had to wait for the tirade to stop. Eventually, when there was a
chance for me to speak, I said as calmly as I could: "But Danny,
she's my sister and she sounds unhappy. I don't want to interfere; I
only want to see for myself that she is all right. I am coming to
America and if she is OK, I'll come home again."

He put the receiver down. I was shaking.

The next day I collected a visa from the American Embassy in
London. The queues were long and it took most of the day, but
fortunately Kiffer and Joy were looking after the children. Jackie
and I spoke on the phone again that night and she was still extremely distraught, but relieved that I was going to see her. Everything had been arranged, and I was to depart early the following
morning.

It was with a mixture of excitement and trepidation that I set out. I was terrified of facing Danny. At twenty-nine, the mother of four children, I had never traveled anywhere alone, or been further afield than France, and now I was launching into another world to rescue my sister.

I had only one aim and mission, and nothing could stop me. Jackie needed to come back and we were ready and waiting for her.

When I arrived at Heathrow, trying hard to behave like a seasoned traveler, I received a message over the tannoy instructing me to report to the information desk.

Jackie was to be put on a plane for England, and I should return home.

Kiffer met her at Heathrow and she arrived looking terrible, her face pale and furrowed. Joy and Gran were waiting on the doorstep to greet her.

"Jackie, my dear! Have you had an awful journey? You poor thing."

"Terrible. I just want to lie down . . . Hello, Gran . . . are you all right?"

"Bless your heart. Come inside and we'll make you a nice hot drink."

Within moments of arriving, though, Jackie was surrounded by the children who, despite Gran's efforts at restraining them, soon had Jackie racing all over the garden. There were shrieks of laughter, chases around the outside of the house, and over-excited games of hide-and-seek behind trees and bushes. They all collected flints and soon there were five bottoms in the air around the well, and breathless silence while waiting for the distant thuds far below.

The joyous atmosphere, however, was short-lived. Jackie crumpled in tears and there was nothing anyone could do to console her.

Very quickly I found myself stepping into Mum's shoes. I explained to the children that their beloved Jackie was ill and that we must all be gentle and quiet. It was beyond their comprehension and was hard for them to accept. But, for me, the lifelong pattern of looking after Jackie had re-emerged, and I slotted in easily.

★ ★ ★

That evening, Danny telephoned from America and asked if
Jackie had arrived safely.

"Yes, yes, she's here . . ." I said.

"No, no, I'm not," she mouthed at me from the doorway.

"She seems fine. Yes . . . Kiffer met her . . ."

"Hil—tell him I'm sleeping . . ."

"Actually, Danny, she's sleeping at the moment and I'm not sure
that I should wake her . . . OK . . . I'll tell her you rang."

Over the next few days, Jackie's ups and downs were alarming.

One moment she was rushing about the garden with the children, the next, on her bed, sobbing uncontrollably.

It wasn't long before she told Kiffer that she never wanted to see
Danny again; she loathed him and their marriage was over. In his
absence she flung accusations mercilessly at him and, whenever he
telephoned, she refused to speak to him. I was sympathetic to
Jackie but knew she could be very difficult to live with. I was becoming alarmed that she might use me to hide from Danny which
would be unfair to him.

When Jackie crashed, she would either escape to her room at
the top of the house and shut herself away, or go for a walk with
Kiffer, with whom she felt completely safe. He was at home a
great deal because our chicken business had collapsed. The disease,
Marreks, had swept through the farm.

Jackie was taking the drugs which she had been prescribed and
which were helping her to keep a kind of balance, but still she
fluctuated from great heights to unfathomable depths. Frequently,
she needed to be lifted off her bed and coaxed out of her room.
She seemed to be permanently exhausted.

Kiffer and I had planned a short trip on our own to France. We
had the support of all the grandparents and Olive, but now that
Jackie was completely dependent on us, it seemed obvious that she
should come too. Danny agreed and said he would like to join us
in the hope that, in the peace and quiet of the French mountains,
he would be able to help her.

Jackie, in her despair and unhappiness, was slinging bitter, angry
darts not only at Danny but at Mum and Dad, and she wanted

neither to see nor speak to them. Mum was desperately worried but powerless to help. Her greater concern now was for Dad. She knew that Jackie was staying with us and that we had "taken over." Nevertheless, Mum and Dad wanted to see her before we left for France, so they arranged to come to Ashmansworth.

On their arrival, Mum, as usual, flung her arms round Jackie, who, for the first time ever, pushed her away, glaring with hatred and scorn. Mum stared in disbelief, crumpled and burst into tears. Jackie tossed her head and went to her room.

Dad ignored the situation, absorbing himself with the children, and I tried to comfort Mum.

"Come on, Mum, don't be too upset. She's not well."

Poor Mum, pushed and buffeted by two strong forces, was feeling increasingly bruised and no longer knew how to cope. Kiffer, as usual, did a brilliant job, taking a very upset Mum into the garden and discussing the problems with her, while I retreated to the kitchen with Dad to make him a pot of sweet tea.

It was mid-April and Dad had just returned to work, having been on sick leave since November. He looked well, although slightly pale.

"How's work, Dad? It must seem strange to be back?"

"Oh, so-so, you know. Just as it always was," he mumbled, and took a lingering gulp of tea. "Pass the suzugazoozles, Hibs."

"Do you think you and Mum will be able to come to France with us in August?"

"Mmm . . . Yes . . ." he said, swallowing another mouthful of tea. "Mubs needs a break."

Dad was distracted, staring out of the window, watching Mum and Kiffer in deep conversation in the garden.

"Lots of buds in the garden, now . . ." he muttered. I knew what he was thinking.

Jackie did not reappear that day, so it was with a heavy and bursting heart that Mum waved goodbye.

CHAPTER TWENTY-SEVEN

Hilary

Jackie felt safe, wedged between Kiffer and me. For her, the holiday was a welcome and necessary escape. On the ferry, she was in an elated mood and in this happy state, after a lot of discussion, took her last bottle of anti-depressant pills and hurled them into the sea. We hoped this was the turning point.

Jackie, who had traveled the world in great comfort, often being met by chauffeured limousines and staying in luxurious hotels, was now trundling through France in our bright-blue, push-me-pull-you Renault 4. Kiffer and I knew we had a volcano in the back seat . . . Driving for hour after hour made us soporific, so for the moment there were no dramatic outbursts from Jackie, only occasional quiet weepings.

We were exhausted by the time we arrived in Sumène, but as we wound our way through the valley, our spirits rose in a swift crescendo. As soon as we could see the house, fatigue evaporated. We stumbled out of the car to the sound of goat bells gently clonking on the mountains in the distance and stood motionless, becoming intoxicated by balmy breezes carrying scents of wild thyme, marjoram and mint. The skies were intensely blue and the mountains rose and fell in greens and mauves. There was silence—the kind of silence you can hear.

"Hil?" Jackie whispered. "We're in paradise."

We were stirred from our daydreaming by M. Portales, who, with his mule and cart, was slowly making his way along the little road toward his terraces on the other side of the river. He was surprised and pleased to see us:

"Bonjour, bonjour, ça va?" He beamed and held out a gnarled, hard-worked hand.

"Très bien, merci, et vous? Nous sommes juste arrivés." My brain was struggling to whirl into French action so I could ask him about his family, but it was too sluggish after the long journey. He invited us for an apéritif the next day, waved his hand, slapped the mule and continued his slow way, under the peach trees, down to the river.

The spell broken, we unloaded the car in high spirits and started the tramp up the mountain. We carried the first essential bits and pieces, and staggered our way upward, chattering and laughing as we went. Kiffer was ahead, standing on a rocky outcrop.

"Hil—Jackie—come and look at this!"

We puffed up to him and looked down at the little river winding and bubbling its way, tumbling over the waterfall and splashing into the pool below. There were weeping willows along the edge and the tips of their branches were tickling the frothy bubbles as they sped along.

"Let's have a swim as soon as we've taken all this stuff up."

The idea gave us renewed energy, so on we stumbled, crunching slate underfoot. It was a relief to reach the shaded pathway, the last bit of our climb, and suddenly we were standing on the terrace, surrounded by the gentle mountains breathing their welcome under the cloudless sky. Jackie relaxed and sighed.

"We're the only people in the world. It's so peaceful."

"It's been waiting for us since we last came, Jackie. It will always be here."

Kiffer unlocked the front door. It needed persuasion as it had swollen over the winter months. One more push and we were in, standing in the quiet room with its seven doors, little cubby-holes, ancient shelves, fireplace and gaslights. We dumped our luggage on the big, long table with the straight-backed wooden chairs around it, and raced into the well room.

"Baggy me first. I'll let the bucket down."

Jackie unleashed the rope and the bucket hurtled toward the water and crashed.

"Come on, Hil, help me pull it up."

We heaved and pulled and giggled as it came toward us, and poured the contents into another bucket, splashing water all over the floor.

"No wonder they call you 'Smiley,' Jack, with a laughing mouth like yours."

"That's not why, Hil. It's actually because I'm always crying."

★ ★ ★

There were rummagings in suitcases, searchings for bathing costumes, and off we went, skipping and laughing down the mountain. At times like these we almost reverted to being children and were delirious with joy. Momentarily, we had not a care in the world. There seemed to be no shadows anywhere, just freedom and delight in being alive. I felt sure Jackie was well on the road to recovery.

The pool was still and inviting and Jackie, without hesitation, jumped into the cold water.

"Come on, Kif, I'm waiting. Hurry up or I'll splash you."

"Oh no, you won't."

Jackie slapped the water with her hand, sending freezing spray all over Kiffer. He gasped and sprung from the side, diving into the center of the pool. Jackie tried to escape from him as he surfaced, spluttering and laughing. There were energetic chasings and cavortings, and the merriment bounced and echoed around the valley.

I hoped Jackie would go back to Danny in this frame of mind.

In the house, we unpacked, lit the gas fridge, hauled up more water and made our beds. Jackie was very happy with the blue room, and Kiffer and I chose the downstairs bedroom. While Kiffer surveyed the previous year's building and checked the house, Jackie and I set off to explore the mountain. We raced to the top, stood on the rock and looked down into the valley below.

"Look, there's the Fesquets' house and the onion terraces. And there are their goats and sheep, over there." I paused as Jackie's gaze searched the hillside.

"Here comes!" I warned as I flicked some dried goats' droppings at her. She instantly flicked some back, as we ran off laughing again.

It was time to light the gaslights and make supper. We chopped the vegetables we had bought in Sumène, and grated Cantal cheese on the hand grater. While the saucepans were bubbling away, we drank a glass of Muscat, liquid gold, on the terrace. For the moment, all was peaceful.

In our cozy room at the big table we ate a garlicky meal, accompanied by Portales's wine.

"We'll stink of garlic tomorrow. Dad would hate it," laughed Jackie.

"So would Gran," Kiffer added. ". . . But Joy would love it."

The gaslights were hissing gently and casting their soft yellow glow. But as we finished the meal, Jackie's clouds and shadows began to descend again. Her joy at being in this enchanting place was slipping away and soon she was sobbing again, in increasingly hysterical floods of tears. Nothing could staunch the flow: she couldn't talk, listen, or reason.

We were all exhausted from the journey, and Kiffer and I were longing to go to bed, but Jackie was too frightened to stay upstairs alone in the darkness. So we hauled her bed downstairs into our room; the effort of doing this lifted her mood slightly.

We remade her bed before going on to the terrace with mugs of water to brush our teeth.

It was the most beautiful clear night, completely still, with a star-studded sky. Jackie seemed calmer, so at last we could all go to bed.

I fell asleep quickly, even though I was aware of Jackie's quiet weepings. But it was not long before I awoke with a start. I don't know what alarmed me, a sixth sense perhaps, but I did wake, razor sharp, to find that Jackie was in bed with us. Kiffer was in the middle, lying very still. She was doing her best to rouse him. I, pretending to stir in my sleep, rolled over and put my hand on Kiffer. Jackie immediately withdrew hers. I didn't move. Jackie became restless and tried again, but my hand remained in protective position.

Now it was me who was frantic. Although I knew what Jackie needed and wanted, I was still incredulous with disbelief. How could she? How could she even think of taking my Kif?

My mind was reeling, desperately searching for reasons, comfort, ways out. Still she continued to try, but still I remained immovable. I desperately needed to sleep but was wide awake. I couldn't think straight, didn't know what to do and had no idea how I would face Jackie in the morning. My mind was racing and whirling. I felt that my world was coming to an end. Utterly desperate, I didn't sleep again that night.

★   ★   ★

It was a huge relief when morning came, but it felt like centuries later. The whole valley was aflood with the singing of nightingales. Their miraculous, poignant songs sent darts through my confusion, and I was immediately overwhelmed with sadness for Jackie.

"Come on, let's go on to the terrace and listen to the birds."

We threw on dressing gowns and went outside. Jackie looked gray and awful. No one said anything about the night.

There was an overwhelming feeling of despair, and Kiffer and I tried our hardest to bring her back to a sense of enjoyment again.

"Why don't we have breakfast on the terrace?" suggested Kiffer. "I'll haul some water up from the well, if you two warm the croissants and make the coffee."

Jackie rummaged in the cupboard and found lavender honey while I filtered the coffee. I was bursting to talk to Kiffer, but didn't dare because I knew Jackie would notice the slightest "look" from me to him. We both concentrated on keeping Jackie as happy as possible.

"There's Portales and his son going off to work on their terraces, look, over there."

As we munched our croissants and honey, we watched Ivan Portales trudging along the road, leading the mule and cart with Monsieur sitting in the back. Their days were regulated and dictated by the weather and the seasons, their joys dependent on the quality of their lives. They grew all their own food, vegetables and meats, and, like so many French people, were marvelous cooks. They lived in a tight family bunch, ruled by Monsieur, in a magnificent house with many *caves* and vaults.

They turned off the road on to the slope down to the river and we rushed to the edge of the terrace to greet them.

"Bonjour, Bonjour, Monsieur," we called, waving across the valley.

They looked up.

"Eh!" they called back. Their little dog was yapping. They, with their steady lives, could never have begun to comprehend what was happening emotionally on the mountain above them.

Breakfast and coffee over, Jackie and I left for Sumène to do some shopping and Kiffer stayed at L'île to start his building. We walked down the narrow main street with houses that seemed to lean toward each other. Jackie was again full of chatter and jokes.

"Come on, Jack, let's go in here. You can do the talking."

"Yes, and we'll buy lots of cheese."

"OK, but ask about them first, Jack. You won't understand what they say!"

But she did, and picked up their accent quickly and they loved chatting to her while our baskets filled with provisions.

But as we left the shop, her clouds began amassing and I knew I had to get her home quickly. We barely made it to the car before the tears started again. I drove along the valley with Jackie sobbing uncontrollably next to me.

It was a sad lunch on a gorgeous day. Kiffer and I were completely unable to lift her spirits. Thank goodness it was siesta time afterward. I was so exhausted, I was asleep almost before my head touched the pillow.

When Kiffer and I awoke, Jackie had gone. I tried to seize the opportunity to talk to Kiffer.

"Not now, Hil, we have to find Jackie first. It's too dangerous."

I knew he was right. We decided that Kiffer would hunt for Jackie while I went to the Portales'.

"But, Kif, the dogs!"

"Be brave, Hil, they're harmless and only make a lot of noise. Off you go. Fortitude! We'll wave when you're on the bridge."

We gave each other a kiss, and I departed.

I was very aware of my solitary trampings down the mountain and could hear Kiffer calling for Jackie. I prayed that he would find her quickly. I jumped on to the road and walked over the bridge, straining my eyes everywhere for a sight of Jackie. Kiffer was on the terrace waving to me and signaling that he had not yet found her. My heart was heavy and began to pound as I neared the Portales' house. I knew there would be a rush of barking and I loathed that more than anything.

Fortunately, the wrought-iron gates were shut, and I waited outside while the dogs leapt up and down inside. Hearing the commotion, Madame Portales came to open the gates.

"Madame Finzi. Bonjour. Où est vôtre mari?"

"Il arrivera dans un moment avec ma soeur. Elle a beaucoup de fatigue et a besoin de repos."

I just hoped they *would* come in a moment. Surrounded by yapping dogs we climbed the steps to the terrace where the whole family was waiting under the plane tree. We drank wine and ate little biscuits while I described each of my children at length, to keep the conversation going. I inquired in my faltering French about their winter, and how the planting was coming on. Suddenly the dogs raced down the steps, barking wildly.

"Ils arrivent! Mon mari, ma soeur. Ils sont arrivés!" The relief in my voice must have been apparent but Jackie, Kiffer and the dogs were having all the attention. I had only to glance at Jackie to know that something awful had happened and a look from Kiffer confirmed it. Her face was tortured, her eyes staring and wild.

Jackie managed to pull some manners from behind her distress and shook hands with everyone. I did the introductions.

"Madame, ma soeur, Jacqueline . . . Monsieur, Henriette . . . et Ivan. Jackie est venue pour prendre une petite vacance chez nous."

"C'est la première fois à Sanissac?"

Jackie nodded. I replied for her: "La deuxième fois."

Monsieur turned to shake hands with Kiffer. They were always pleased to see each other and beamed broadly.

We sat in the dappled shade on their terrace, drinking Monsieur's wine.

"Eh . . . Madame, vôtre soeur, qu'est-ce qu'elle fait dans la vie?"

Maybe because she looked so upset, he had not directed the question to Jackie herself. I replied that she was "une violoncelliste." They looked blank.

"Elle est une musicienne. Elle joue du violoncelle."

They still looked blank and diverted their gaze to Jackie who continued to remain silent. Even though she spoke fluent French, Jackie was, at this moment, incapable of saying anything. She watched while I struggled to explain that the cello was a musical instrument, and she played it in big concert halls all over the world.

Monsieur still looked puzzled. After a while he said: "Mais, pourquoi?"

"Jacqueline est très bien connue pour sa musique, et il y a beaucoup de personnes qui demandes qu'elle les visite dans leurs pays avec son violoncelle." That was a big effort for me, and it left them looking blank again.

"Comment voyage-t-elle—en avion?"

"Oui, Monsieur."

Silence.

"Mais . . . c'est fou . . . complètement fou. Et le repos? Et . . . elle a un mari?"

"Oui, Daniel Barenboim."

"Eh . . . qu 'est-ce qu'il fait, lui?"

"Il est chef d'orchestre."

Silence.

I continued. "Il est très bien connu aussi. Il parle beaucoup de langues parce-qu'il est souvent dans un autre pays."

Silence.

I told them Jackie's husband would be joining us the next day and they replied that the weather was going to change.

Later that afternoon, when Jackie was momentarily out of earshot, Kiffer told me he had found her on the hillside, naked and hiding behind some tangled olive branches. She was shaking, her eyes staring, and looking mad. He very gently persuaded her to dress and to walk with him down the mountain, telling her I was waiting at the Portales'. She neither responded nor resisted.

We realized we had brought her to the tranquility of these mountains in the hope that she would be able to think and re-cover, removed from the pressures of her life. But, free to relax, her instability had overwhelmed her and she had broken down. We knew we could no longer let her out of our sight.

That night, although she stayed in her own bed in our room, I was very wary and drifted in and out of sleep. In the morning, she seemed calmer and was able to talk to us again. Kiffer and I agreed it would be better not to refer to the previous day. However, Danny was due to arrive that night and the very mention of his impending visit sent her into paroxysms of tears and despair. It was clear to us that Danny's presence was not a good idea at this mo-ment, but he was already on his way and we had no means of con-tacting him.

I was now dreading his arrival as well as being concerned for his comfort. L'île was a far cry from the well-appointed hotels to which he was accustomed. Here, there were no telephones, no electricity and no loo. Our idea was to improve the house over the years and although we had already done a great deal, it was still extremely basic. Somehow, I didn't think Danny would share Jackie's enthusiasm for being here.

Suddenly, all our plans for her recovery had turned inside out. This just wasn't the right time or environment for a reconciliation.

CHAPTER TWENTY-EIGHT

Hilary

Danny was due to arrive on a late plane, so Kiffer set off to collect him from the airport, leaving Jackie and me to prepare supper. Once again, simple domestic activities seemed to take her mind off her despair: we tried to light the fire but quickly the room filled with smoke, which produced much coughing and hilarity. We chopped onions and wept onion tears, and laughed through it all. We peeled and crushed garlic, and had great fun inventing tastes and dishes for supper. But our merriment was hiding a sense of panic. Jackie knew that Danny wanted a reconciliation: he wanted her to be the Jackie he wanted her to be. He couldn't cope with the Jackie she actually was. She was frightened because she had been carried along on his wave before and now she was in a desperately weak and wobbly state. She knew he could be very persuasive.

Everything was ready when, suddenly, the night was punctured by the rhythmic hooting of the car horn. Quickly we lit the candles in the lanterns, ran out on to the terrace and waved them into the dark distance, calling out over the wall.

"We're coming down with lanterns. Wait for us."

Our voices echoed in the valley as we set off down the mountain, each carrying two lanterns, and tripping and thudding over the slates.

"Hil, don't leave me, don't ever leave me alone."

"Jack," I said softly, stopping and looking straight into her eyes, "you know I won't. I shall stay with you all the time. Come on."

We jumped off the little wall and on to the road, to find Kiffer and Danny waiting for us. Danny and I embraced.

"Danny, how wonderful to see you. How are you? How was the

journey? I'm afraid it's not finished yet. You've got to climb up there!"

"But there aren't any lights! I can't see."

"Yes there are," I replied, handing him a lantern. "This is for you."

Jackie stuck close to Kiffer and said nothing, and we started the steep climb up to the house. Danny and I walked ahead.

"Watch where you put your feet, Danny, it's slippery and uneven."

He was so busy examining the ground in front of him, he didn't notice the evergreen oak branch as it caught in his jacket.

"Ouch! This is dangerous! However did you find this place? No road, and we can't see."

"Wait until the morning, Danny. It's so beautiful. There's a wonderful view from the house and we can swim in the river."

We climbed a rocky promontory.

"Look, there's the house. Doesn't it look pretty with the gas-lights?"

We arrived on the terrace and opened the front door into the warm and glowing room. The fire was no longer smoking and we were welcomed by delicious smells of supper.

"Where's the bathroom?" said Danny, looking round.

"Come with me. There's no loo here, I'm afraid." Kiffer led the incredulous Danny outside again and directed him into the bushes.

The moment he was out of the door, Jackie turned to me. "Hil, I don't want to see him. I'm going to bed."

"Oh no, you're not, Jackie, you're staying here. Just let Kiffer and me do all the talking."

We made supper as cheerful as possible, but Jackie refused even to look at Danny. He was obviously upset. We had decided to give him our room downstairs: Jackie was to sleep in the blue room upstairs and we moved into the big room.

The next day was awful. I was the first to wake and went straight to the window. The weather had indeed changed, it was gray and wet, and the wind was coming from the south—a bad sign. It wasn't long before Jackie came in and sat on the end of our bed. She looked exhausted.

"How did you sleep, Jackie?" I asked.

"I didn't, and I'm going to sleep all day."

"Look, Jack," Kiffer said tenderly. "Danny's terribly upset and he's trying so hard. Please try and be civil. We won't leave you, but you must make an effort. He's as upset as you are. Try and see it from his point of view."

I went downstairs to prepare breakfast: hot coffee and croissants. Danny came into the kitchen. We gave each other a kiss.

"Danny, how did you sleep? Were you comfy enough?"

"Yes, I slept very well, thank you." He looked uneasy. "But what's happened to the weather? I thought you said it would be lovely?"

"I know . . . well, it was meant to be lovely, but I don't think we'll be having breakfast outside today, somehow."

"It'll probably clear up later. Where is everybody?"

"Kiffer is just coming and I think I heard Jackie moving around. I'm sure she'll be down in a moment."

It was cold and we sat round the table trying to warm ourselves with coffee. Danny was obviously chilly but trying, unsuccessfully, to be jolly. Jackie was silent and glum.

Danny sniffed. "I think I'm getting a cold. Have you a heater I can have? I need to go back to bed."

He retreated to his room, and Jackie to hers.

Somehow, Kiffer and I had to keep things afloat, so he went up to talk to Jackie and I went in to talk to Danny. Jackie was sobbing and confused, and refusing to come out of her room, or to have anything to do with Danny. Kiffer tried to persuade her to make an effort, whatever she felt, and to separate her feelings from her actions.

Danny was upset too. He had arrived in good spirits, and had been full of determined hope. "Hilary, I feel terrible. What can I do? What have I done? I can't do anything right, and she won't even look at me."

"Danny, she's extremely exhausted, so obviously she's low. She needs time to recover, and plenty of space. It will be hard, but if you can give her that, it will be the kindest thing you can do for her. She is too depressed to be able to respond to you now."

But neither of them could really see the other's point of view.

The game Kiffer and I had learned to play was keen and fast. Watch, assess, cope and try to steer the moods. Beware of storm-clouds: smell them before you see them.

It must have been hell for Danny to be on holiday with his wife who wouldn't even look at him, and who was making it painfully obvious that she wanted only to be with Kiffer and me.

The rain stopped at lunchtime and, over bowls of hot soup, we managed to persuade them that an expedition would be a good idea. We walked down the mountain, and along the riverbank to find a suitable crossing, where we teetered our way precariously over the water, balancing on the proud stones. On reaching the other side we looked back at Danny, who was refusing to join us.

"Come on, Danny," called Kiffer. "There are plenty of little boulders you can balance on. You won't get wet."

"I'm not coming. I don't want to risk it."

This was red rag to a bull for Kiffer. Quick as a flash, he splashed back, picked up Danny and flung him over his shoulder in a fire-man's lift.

"Put me down," Danny protested, with mock rage.

"All right—here goes," laughed Kiffer in the middle of the river. "One, two, three . . ."

Danny was beating Kiffer's back with his fists, and Kiffer was so convulsed with laughter, he nearly slipped and fell.

"Oops . . . Keep still, Danny, or we'll both get very wet."

I was doubled up with giggles on the other bank.

Once they were safely over, we started the long, uphill climb to the Eagle's Nest, a ruined house, high on the mountain behind L'île. We scrambled over disused terraces, and tramped through ancient olive groves and fig orchards.

"How much further?" puffed Danny.

"Not far," I panted. "Believe me, it's worth it for the view, and we can rest when we're up there."

At last, we were standing on the ramparts of the once magnificent house. Danny was impressed.

"You're right, Hilary. What a view! I wonder who owns this place?"

"It belongs to a local family and has been theirs for generations." Now it was standing derelict, with no roof, and a tree growing in the middle, but it still had its own spring and Roman pipework. Danny became excited and immediately talked of buying it.

"You'd like that, wouldn't you, Jackie? It's full of possibilities. I'd build a proper access road and we'd have a swimming pool and a helicopter pad, electricity and telephones . . ."

Jackie was aghast, but didn't reply. For a while Danny was bubbling again, trying so hard and hoping Jackie would join in his enthusiasm, but she didn't. She continued to ignore him.

That evening, his cold developed into flu-like symptoms, and, feeling thoroughly dejected, he went to bed. There was nothing he could enjoy—he was alone in his room with only me to read or chat to him. He was totally cut off from his world. Occasionally he joined us and we played word games in pairs: Jackie and Kiffer versus Danny and me. The two men approached it logically, whereas Jackie and I, as usual, relied on our instincts. But it was the simple sisters who nearly always jumped to the answers first, leaving the men's careful calculations far behind.

The weather continued to be dismal and, a few days later, it was time for Danny to leave.

Jackie refused even to say goodbye to him.

"Look after her, Hilary."

"I will, Danny . . ."

Danny was warm and friendly, although obviously sad and hurt. We embraced and he left with Kiffer for the airport.

We returned to Ashmansworth to find the children well and exceedingly energetic, having had a wonderful time with their grandparents and great-granny. Even Jackie entered into their infectious spirit, and cheered up when she saw them. A few days later, though, she announced she needed to be alone for a day or two, and wanted to go home to Pilgrim's Lane.

"I'll be back soon. I'll phone."

And she did phone, almost the moment she arrived in London. It was difficult to understand what she was saying, but she sounded demented. Kiffer leapt into the car and sped off.

I knew he was doing the right thing, but it left me a quaking mess. I felt so confused, I don't remember how I coped with the children that day.

When Kiffer returned in the evening, he took me into the garden and I sobbed and sobbed as he told me (but I had already guessed) that Jackie had begged him to go to bed with her—and so he had.

Although we had both expected this to happen, the shock for me was enormous.

I wept in his arms, immensely relieved he had come home, but feeling utterly betrayed.

Jackie was fighting to survive and she knew Kiffer was not overwhelmed by her: therefore, in a crisis, she could turn to him and he would be strong enough for her in a way no one had managed before. When I married Kiffer I had found my life and my love where I felt I could be free and where I knew I was safe. But the only way to make Jackie better was to give her what she wanted. And she wanted Kiffer.

As I struggled with myself, Kiffer said:

". . . And she's coming back tomorrow."

CHAPTER TWENTY-NINE

Hilary

Jackie was arriving on a late train that morning and I went to meet her at the station. I watched as the flat-fronted train came closer and closer. It had stopped at every little station after Reading and had nearly reached Newbury. Another thirty seconds and she would be there. My heart was pounding. I was rooted to my spot on the platform. As the brakes squealed, the little voice inside me nagged, "Come on, Hilary, come on, Hilary. She's more desperate than you." The doors were flung open, and there was Jackie climbing out of the last carriage at the other end of the platform. I flew from my spot and rushed into her arms.

I don't know how long we stood there sobbing and hugging, but at that moment we were as close as we had ever been, sharing silent secrets in our private bomb patch.

The next day I awoke unusually early. It was a beautiful morning and as I lay on my side looking across the yard, I noticed a sleeping bag on the flagstones. My heart leapt.

"Kiffer, look, look, there's a sleeping-bag in the yard."

He rolled over and opened one eye.

"Kif, it's moving. There's someone inside it. Where's Jackie?"

I jumped out of bed, grabbed my dressing gown and ran downstairs. My mind was racing. As I approached the pink bag, I could hear breathing and muffled noises. The bag was being held tightly shut. From inside came a little voice.

"Keep still, it's not time to get up yet."

It was Nico!

I prodded the bag and a surprised Nico popped out clutching one of her beloved chickens.

"Mummy, Mummy, quick, catch Pecker before she runs off."
I dived inside the sleeping-bag and rescued the second chicken.
"They want to see Jackie, Mummy. They're dying to see her."
"Come on, then. We'll creep upstairs and see if she's awake. If
not, they can come and say good morning to Daddy."

We peeped at the sleeping Jackie, and Henrietta escaped from
Nico's arms and clucked noisily as she landed on Jackie's bed.
Jackie awoke with a start.

"Oh . . ."

"Wake up, Jackie," said Nico. "This is Pecker and Henrietta.
Stroke them, they're lovely and soft . . ."

Jackie struggled unwillingly to wake as the two birds flapped
about the bed. Seeing that she was reluctant to stir, I knew we had
to leave her in peace. Sleep was her refuge when she was depressed.

"Nico, darling, I think Pecker and Henrietta are terribly hungry. Let's give them their breakfast now."

Jackie rolled over and went back to sleep.

Thus, Jackie came to live with us at Ashmansworth. She canceled
all her engagements, and it was announced she was suffering from
nervous exhaustion and would be resting until April 1972.

There were four little children in the house as well as my mother-
in-law and my grandmother. Privacy was impossible. Kiffer and I
retreated to the upstairs bathroom where I perched on the edge of
the bath, as he sat on the loo.

"Are you all right, Hil?"

"I'm fine," I replied, with a pounding heart.

"Look, Hil, you must believe that I love you very much and I
will never leave you. There is no question. I will never go."

"I know. And I love you too. I know that Jackie needs to be
here, but I shall still find it awful when you're together."

"Whatever happens, our aim in all of this is to help to make
Jackie better. She needs us both."

Kiffer and I agreed Jackie should stay at Ashmansworth for as
long as she wanted. But each day brought a different requirement,
depending on her psychological state. The bathroom became our
sanctuary whenever we needed to talk about her.

She fluctuated from great heights to bottomless depths. At these times, Kiffer was the only person who could help her, who could support her huge emotional weight. The intuitive, homely world of the du Pré family with its interdependence contrasted dramatically with the sophisticated, international life of the Barenboims— and Kiffer understood this, as he understood Jackie's background.

Jackie slept in the attic, a spacious, light room where she could shut herself away if she needed to. Through the summer months, whenever she needed to be alone with Kiffer during the day, they walked over the fields and downs. Some excursions were longer than others, but invariably she returned in a much better frame of mind.

Kiffer always came to bed with me and, if Jackie needed him, he went up to her later. Sometimes I was able to cope, but, at other times, I felt overwhelmed and wept myself to sleep.

Kiffer and I were both in this together. In my heart of hearts I knew what Jackie wanted and what she was aiming for. Of course, I didn't like even imagining her with Kiffer.

Kiffer and I had talked so much about Jackie and, long before her desperate call from America, I had warned Kiffer of what I instinctively felt and knew. At that time, there was no evidence, no proof of what I was saying, and he quite understandably thought I was exaggerating unreasonably.

It seemed to me that Jackie had unconsciously always been a cuckoo in the nest. First in childhood, when everything revolved around her. Later, in music, as I lost my confidence in the wake of her genius. Eventually, I had escaped and made my new life with my husband and four children. Now, she was in my home, absorbed by my family, trying to take my husband away. And my husband was with her, in her bed.

But, at the same time, I was watching my sister go through hell. She was tormented, frightened and very muddled, and, although I felt extremely sad for her, the duality of the situation was often confusing for me. On the one hand I was glad she had turned to my family for help, but, on the other, I felt robbed and lost. I was under that table again, bewildered and trying to survive. Sometimes I felt I was required to give up everything I loved to Jackie.

There were no half-measures with her and, in Kiffer, she found someone who could meet her fantasies without being completely swept aside. Her impression of his strength had been formed on the day he dragged her out of bed, all those years ago, in Portland Place. Kiffer's ability to look ahead with confidence contrasted sharply with our family's fear of anything over the horizon; just as he had broken the restraining shackles for me, so Jackie looked to him to do the same for her. She had seen me become more and more happy and set free, and she longed for that for herself.

My way of dealing with the situation was to keep life as normal as possible. When Jackie was very depressed, sometimes crying all morning, I didn't want the children to be with her. They found themselves taken out of the house on lots of sprees. Alternatively, Kiffer and Jackie went for one of their walks.

On better days, I seized every opportunity to involve her in the children's activities. When the weather was good, we would pile into the little blue Renault 4 and go bouncing and swaying over the hills to the Gibbet. The moment I stopped the car, the children would tumble out and run like wild colts to the top of the hill, hotly pursued by Jackie and me. They screeched with delight as Jackie pounded along behind them. Theresa always arrived first.

To both sides of the Gibbet were fields sweeping down into the valley, and the children loved roly-polying over the molehills and clumps of tough grass. Jackie, Theresa and Nico landed at the bottom in exhausted heaps, lying spreadeagled on the soft turf. Clare, Orlando and I watched from a distance. Half a field of rolls was enough for three-year-old Orlando. We made long buttercup and daisy chains while waiting for the weary rollers to drag themselves back up the hill.

"I'm starving," said Jackie, followed by a chorus of agreement from the children. "Come on, let's have lunch."

We returned to the car for the picnic and chose the most sheltered spot to eat. Everyone was hungry and thirsty, but as soon as we were all eating our sandwiches, the chatter subsided and there was only the sound of munching. Clare had saved her daisy and buttercup chains for Jackie's hair, and carefully wove them in and out. The skylarks were singing way above us, and we lay back trying to spot them in the bright blue overhead. Sausages, tomatoes, jellies, bananas, all were swiftly and eagerly consumed and, for a short while, there was peace.

But that very food produced another stream of energy which erupted in an enthusiastic game of hide-and-seek. Jackie was "he" and chased the children from their hiding places with excited shrieks, while buttercups and daisies showered from her tossing hair.

Eventually, four very tired children had had enough and collapsed into the Renault, squashed tightly together, with the remains of the picnic thrown into the back. It would not be long before they were in bed and soundly asleep.

When Jackie was in good form, these were halcyon days.

But one day, my feelings overcame me. In the early morning, after a particularly demanding period, when Jackie had been in a slough of despondency, I suddenly found it all too much. Kiffer had been struggling to keep Jackie afloat and was feeling very weary himself, but I was beginning to struggle too and became engulfed with panic and tears. I ran out of the house, across the field to the hedge under the oak tree. I pushed through a gap, buried my head in my knees and sobbed and sobbed.

I should have been giving the children breakfast before they went to school, and I could hear Kiffer calling in the distance, but I just couldn't move. At that moment I was consumed with my own despair, and stayed there until I had cried myself out.

I waited until I heard the school bus go down the road, then slowly dragged my weary way back and went straight to the bathroom to wash my face. It was red and swollen. Jackie was still asleep in bed.

I heard Kiffer coming upstairs. He came in and put his arm round me.

"Hil, where have you been? You look awful. Didn't you hear me calling?"

"Yes, I did," I whispered, "but I couldn't move." I couldn't speak properly, either; my voice was croaky.

"We missed you. The children couldn't understand what had happened to you. Why didn't you come and talk to me first?"

My head was resting on his shoulder.

"Kif, I'm so tired. I need you too. I know Jackie's extremely low, but she wants you for herself. She wants to take you away."

"Don't be so silly, Hil. You know perfectly well I wouldn't let her do that. I wouldn't leave you." He stood me in front of him with his hands on my shoulders.

"Now listen, Hil," he said, fixing me in the eye. "You mustn't lose sight of our aim. I won't let you down. I couldn't, I love you far too much, and we won't let her down either. You know that. Now, come and have some breakfast with me—and you'll feel much better."

"Kif, don't tell Jackie about this morning, please."

"Of course I won't."

"Were the children all right?"

"They were fine. I told them it was my turn to do brekker today while you went up to the chickens. It was chaos!"

I managed a smile.

"That's better. Come on, now. It's going to be all right."

Kiffer was always wonderful in a crisis because he could stand back and see the best way to cope from the practical point of view. He knew I had cried so much that I was ready to move forward again.

That afternoon, Jackie and I went to meet the school bus and there on the grass verge by the roadside was the chicken Henrietta. We could hear the bus coming up the road and slowing down. The door opened and out jumped Theresa, Clare and Nico. Henrietta immediately ran over to Nico.

"Mummy, Mummy, look, she's come to meet me. Jackie, say hello to Henrietta . . . Where's Pecker?"

Everything was back to normal.

Despite Kiffer's reassurance, I was watchful. I couldn't help it. People might say "How could a marriage survive like that?" But Kiffer and I never let go of each other. We were still there together all the time. In the end, marriage, I think, is like a bank balance: the more you put in, the more you can take out. This was an expensive time.

Mum would come over and walk in the garden with Kiffer, worrying about Jackie and her future. Jackie still refused to talk to Mum and kept out of her way. Piers tried again and again to persuade me to tell him what was going on and I knew he suspected something, but at the time I couldn't say anything to anyone.

I'm sure Joy knew what was going on. She was very supportive to Jackie, and regarded her simply as one of the household, but, to my relief, never asked me how I was. If anyone other than Kiffer had shown sympathy, I would have dissolved.

Jackie was dependent on us all. Kiffer as her confidant and emotional support; the children because she adored them; Joy because she treated Jackie as a completely normal person, and me because I understood her and her feelings and allowed her to be whatever she wanted to be. Despite the traumas there were many laughing moments when Jackie and I just giggled.

I loved the hours we spent with the children and, in these moments, I didn't feel pushed out of the way. Cake-making was one of our favorite pastimes. The very mention of it made for an immediate flurry in which flour, eggs, sugar, butter, weighing scales and wooden spoons were found and put on the kitchen table.

Kiffer and I knew it was important that Jackie didn't stop playing the cello entirely during this time, and we did our best to encourage her whenever she felt strong enough. She gave cello lessons to John Saunderson, one of the cellists in the Newbury String Players, and Anna Shuttleworth, a long-standing friend and professional cellist, used to visit and play duets with her. However, Jackie was uninterested, and lent the Davidoff to Anna, who trundled off in her bubble car, the cello crammed into the back.

There was a concert scheduled at the Corn Exchange on May 8, 1971 in which Gerald Finzi's *Intimations of Immortality* was to be performed. Both Kiffer and I were taking part and we persuaded Jackie to join the cello section, where she could sit next to Kiffer on the inside. She didn't want to stay at Ashmansworth without either of us there.

When it was time for the orchestra to go on stage, the players formed a wall around Jackie to hide her from the audience, but she was spotted immediately and everyone rose to their feet in excitement, which was just what she did not want. She was afraid of being recognized anywhere. Normally she loved applause and automatically and willingly responded to it, but now, she couldn't react.

As Kiffer and Jackie sat together in the cello section, I was sure the entire audience "knew" about the situation at home. I sat in the woodwind section feeling utterly miserable, and, consequently, played very badly.

In the heart of the Hampshire Downs, just below the famous Gibbet, lies the straggling village of Inkpen. It is surrounded by softly rolling hills, fields, woodlands and a huge, uninterrupted expanse of sky. It feels as though it is in the middle of nowhere, peaceful, silent and still.

But July 1971 brought excitement to the little rural village. The Inkpen Festival was taking place. The whole village had been spruced up—gardens were immaculate and full of color, the lanes were swept and hedges clipped. There was an air of unusual happenings. The center of all events was the flint church. The village ladies had given their best blooms, and created glorious bouquets and displays with the jostle of July colors. The delicious smell of beeswax mingled with the summer scents, and the wooden pews gleamed in the patches of sunlight.

There had been activities all week with audiences of varying sizes, but the highlight of the festivities was to be a concert, given by the Newbury String Players on Saturday, the 18th. The orchestra was a collection of local amateur musicians, boosted by a few professional players. The great excitement of this concert was Jacqueline du Pré, who was coming to play the Monn concerto.

Fortunately, she was on a wave. For once she was looking forward to performing so the emergency back-up wasn't necessary.

Georg Matthias Monn was an Austrian composer and organist who lived in Vienna in the eighteenth century. This concerto was originally written for harpsichord and transcribed for cello by Arnold Schoenberg in 1932. Jackie hadn't performed it before. Piers decided the concert was an ideal opportunity to try his new recording equipment.

It was a beautiful, high summer evening and the orchestra had been entertained to tea with strawberries and cream in the large house near the church. A quarter of an hour before the concert, we returned to the church to tune and warm up. There was a queue down the church path and along the road. We couldn't reach the church door. But Jackie was with me, and on seeing her the crowds made way, and we went in.

No longer was it peaceful. The church was alive with excited chatter. The pews were creaking and bursting with people jammed together. The players were in their seats, tuning, and Jackie was in her place, inside first desk. Kiffer managed to squeeze to the front with the vicar, and on seeing the dog collar the audience was immediately silent, as though the volume button had been turned off.

We were welcomed warmly by the vicar. Kiffer raised his baton and the orchestra, in their cramped conditions, lifted their bows to begin. It was the first time that a Newbury String Players audience had had to overflow outside into the churchyard. The doors were wide open, and people were sitting on the grass outside.

The strings played a Stanley concerto, followed by a mournful piece for flute and strings by Hunter Johnson—"To An Unknown Soldier." It was based on a poem by Walt Whitman, and Kiffer set the scene by reading the poem to the audience, as I was waiting to play. I wanted to paint the sad and lonely picture with my playing, but was acutely aware of Jackie who was sitting in the cello section about six feet away from me. All eyes were on her.

Reaching the end was a great relief but, as I was about to leave, Kiffer motioned to the audience to quieten and suggested that, as the Hunter Johnson was so rarely played, it would be good to hear it again. It was the last thing I wanted, and I'm not sure the audience wanted it either. I was keenly aware that concentration was not on me. But play it again we did.

The next item was the Monn.

There was a scraping of chairs as the orchestra readjusted to make room for Jackie as the soloist. Piers adjusted the microphones. The atmosphere was electric. Suddenly the church was packed with Jackie and expectations. This was the orchestra's big moment, too, and they were in it *now*. They played their introduction. Jackie took a deep breath, and she was off. The church's flint walls seemed to bulge and the woodwork throbbed. Although the Monn is a relatively light-weight classical work, Jackie played it as though it was a great romantic concerto, with colossal passion and power. The audience was inwardly gasping with the intensity and thrill of her sound, and the lift of her playing. There was total concentration in that little church, and for those twenty-one minutes nothing else existed in the world except Jackie and her miraculous playing.

She transported everyone to an unknown paradise.

We had planned to go to France in August, but Kiffer was still heavily involved closing down our poultry business. Mum and Dad were longing to be there, so we decided I should go ahead with them and the children, and that Kiffer would follow with Jackie two weeks later.

The children gave Jackie strict instructions about looking after the animals and their toys, and she promised faithfully to do everything they asked. On July 25, we departed. I was uneasy about leaving Kiffer and Jackie behind, but as it was the best thing for the children, I was swept along by them.

One morning, not long after our arrival at L'île, I heard the postman calling out from below. Nowadays, he gave warning of his presence for fear of catching us off-guard.

"Madame Finzi, Madame Finzi, c'est la Poste."

It was a telegram from Jackie, asking me to phone. Leaving the children with Mum, I tore down the mountain to the only telephone in Sanissac, with all the change I could find rattling in my pocket. It took a while to connect, but eventually Jackie and I were talking animatedly on the phone.

"Jackie, is everything OK?"

"Of course it is, Hil, I only wanted to chat—to hear your voice."

It was a Jackie special, an honest conversation telling me not only of her love for me but of her love for Kiffer. She had adored the weeks she had spent on her own with Kiffer. She knew it would be hopeless to try to hide the truth from me, and was tender and grateful for the time alone with him.

Despite her need to have Kiffer, she still missed me (as I always missed her) and we sent constant messages of love and reassurance to each other. But I knew, too, that she would find it difficult to be part of the extended family in France, and having to share Kiffer would be a problem.

★ ★ ★

It was only a few days until Jackie's and Kiffer's arrival, and I was relieved. I was missing Kiffer so much.

Mum loved reading to the children and singing with them, and Dad was busy making a huge "Welcome" sign. He cut enormous individual letters out of purl board, which he planned to suspend over the terrace wall. I made certain there were plenty of provisions, and everything was prepared.

We knew they would be driving through the night and I was up at 5 a.m., just in case. I crept downstairs but the children's internal alarm clocks had worked well and they were all awake too.

"Mummy, have they arrived yet?"

"Sshh, darlings, Gow Gow and Wow are still asleep. We mustn't wake them. I'll go down and make a drink for you. Wait in my bed, quietly."

The children tried to be quiet but it was no use—they were far too excited and soon followed me downstairs. Mum and Dad had woken too, and I could hear them chattering in their bedroom.

"Theresa, Clare, Nico, Orlando . . ." called Mum. "Cuckoo . . . we're awake. Where are you?"

Just as I was putting the breakfast on the table, we heard the car horn hooting below. There were immediate screeches of excitement from the children and panic from Dad, as he just managed to hang the last letter in time. The children had already dashed off, pursued by me. They were well ahead and I paused to look at the car which was parked by the cable lift. Kiffer and Jackie were still inside. I knew Jackie was finding the arrival difficult and watched until eventually Kiffer opened his door, went round to Jackie's side, opened her door and persuaded her to get out of the car. Slowly they walked over the bridge, Jackie leaning heavily on Kiffer. I shouted "coo-eee" over the valley and Kiffer waved, although he couldn't see where I was.

Jackie didn't look. Nor did she notice the sign.

Suddenly the children were on the bridge too, racing as fast as they could toward them, Theresa in the lead.

"Daddy, Daddy! Jackie! You've come. Hug me first!"

Their joyful and noisy welcome interrupted Jackie's dolor and she was dragged into reality. I resumed my swift journey down the

mountain and met them just as they were about to start climbing.
My heart was thumping as I flung myself, with huge relief, into
Kiffer's arms, and Jackie flung her arms around us both.

"You must look at the welcome sign," I said. "Dad's spent hours
making it."

We climbed to the first promontory and watched as the letters
of the sign waved about in the breeze.

"It's silly," Jackie grumbled.

"Come on, Jackie," said Kiffer. "Just think how they'll be feeling."

Kiffer called out a hearty "Hello" to Mum and Dad, who were
waiting on the terrace. But Jackie was reluctant to greet them
warmly and stuck close to Kiffer.

"Well, Jackables, how did you like Dad's welcome sign?" Mum
asked.

Jackie didn't reply, but gave Mum a withering glance.

Kiffer interrupted. "How long did it take you, Derek? You've
made it beautifully."

Mum was torn between wanting to be friendly to Jackie and
trying to protect Dad.

"He spent hours perfecting it. He's done it well, don't you
think? And so clever to fix it up like that," she mumbled nervously.

"They've been driving all night, Mum."

"Golly. You must be shattered."

Jackie muttered under her breath, a private joke with Kiffer.

"Come on," said Kiffer. "Let's have brekker."

Between mouthfuls, Kiffer described their journey. They had
driven to Paris to search for Jackie's favorite restaurant but when
they arrived in the city, Jackie couldn't remember where it was.
They had explored for a while and, quite by chance, happened to
find it. They had a sumptuous meal.

"We had piles of wild raspberries and strawberries for pudding,"
he said, smiling with delight. "They were absolutely delicious!"

It was clear that Jackie was finding being *en famille* very difficult.
She had been alone with Kiffer for two uninterrupted weeks, and
having to share him with me was neither what she wanted nor
what she intended. She needed him exclusively, but that was not
possible in this situation. It was possible, though, for Kiffer to slip

into Jackie's bedroom during the night without anyone but me knowing. It was an absolute necessity for Jackie and helped her through the holiday.

The children often saved the day by dragging Jackie off to their secret camps and involving her in their games. When she needed to be alone, she would disappear to her room; or Kiffer, sensing that she needed peace, would take her on a long walk over the mountain. I made sure the children were absorbed with me so they would not follow them.

I knew Mum was extremely worried about Jackie, but some instinct prevented her from the cruelty of cross-examining me. She talked only to Kiffer about Jackie. When Jackie retired to her room Mum always seized the first opportunity for a chat with him. Kiffer constantly reassured Mum that Jackie needed time and space, explaining that she, like us all, was showing her anger to those closest to her.

A few days after their arrival, Kiffer went to collect his niece Lucy, the Golding family, and Olive's grandson, Wayne, from Nîmes airport. The house was full with seven children and seven adults. Clare, Lucy and Julia Golding spent hours brushing and combing Jackie's hair, making arrangements with ribbons and elastic bands. Jackie loved this and was content to sit as the children experimented with ever more wild and extraordinary hair-dos.

Only when she was swept along in a whirl of children's activities did Jackie relax. She continued to be aloof and offhand with Mum and Dad.

CHAPTER THIRTY

Hilary

When we returned from France, the children went back to school and Kiffer continued winding up the business. Jackie and I did everything together: the school run, shopping, cooking and she helped with the few remaining chickens. She was hardly interested in playing the cello.

Danny didn't ring. He was either too wise or too hurt by her.

As time went on, Jackie improved. The troughs of despair became less frequent. She had always wanted to be at Ashmansworth with the family, and now she had Kiffer to support her. The routine of our everyday lives had proved a stabilizer.

In the late autumn, Mum and Dad came to spend the day with us and to give Theresa and Clare their piano lessons. Much to my amazement, when Jackie heard the car pulling into the drive, she rushed to the front door to greet them.

I shall never forget Mum's face as Jackie embraced her.

"Hello, old bean!" Jackie said, beaming. Her eyes were bright and her face glowing. It was the old Jackie again. Mum had tears streaming down her face.

As they stood locked in a long hug, the first for many months, I embraced Dad.

"Kerzuppateseesles, Dad?"

"Mmm. Yes please!"

"Come on, then. The kettle's on."

Dad and I went into the kitchen, leaving Jackie and Mum on the doorstep.

"Jackie looks better, Hil."

"I think she is, Dad. I haven't seen her hug Mum like that for ages."

"Mum would like that."

Jackie stayed with us throughout the day, and was friendly. I expected her to disappear to her room at any moment, but she didn't. I hoped it was the beginning of a big change.

During the months before Christmas, there were times when Jackie was as happy as I have ever seen her. But equally, these times were countered by long bouts of crying. She was totally dependent on Kiffer and her desperate need for him pushed us all aside. He was deeply committed to her and spent many hours of the days and nights with her, and though I sensed this was a strain for him, he always seemed hopeful of finding a way forward.

But as the situation remained static, Kiffer began to feel out of his depth and kept saying that he needed to find an anchor for her to hang on to. A breakthrough came when his friend, Jeremy Dale Roberts, suggested he should read R. D. Laing's *Sanity, Madness and the Family*. This opened a new world of the unconscious for him and he became immersed, not only in Laing's works but in Jung, Freud and others. He was searching for a constructive path out of our tangled confusion of emotional responses.

He knew that it would be useless trying to impose anything from the outside on her, although at that time I know she would have done whatever he told her. Once, when Mum and Dad were at Ashmansworth, I remember Kiffer and Mum having a long and serious talk as they paced up and down the lawn under the fir trees. When I asked him what they had discussed he said, "Jackie, of course. Quite understandably, Iris is desperately anxious about her and needs reassurance that everything will be all right."

He went on, "I told her I too was concerned, and that our only hope was to find a rock of reason that would give Jackie a firm footing."

Within our family, we always knew exactly what the others were feeling without a word being said, just as Jackie and I understood each other instinctively. None of us knew then how to analyze, how to talk logically through a problem. Looking back now, I see our strong, subliminal communication tended to make everyone outside the family a foreigner. Kiffer was the first person to break through our tight circle and he was not perturbed in the least by our family's deep currents of understanding.

I, of course, knew exactly how deeply absorbed he was with Jackie but also understood her desperate plight. This helped me in some way to cope at that time. I also had the children's daily demands to deal with.

One day David Gollins, a friend, and manager of the Watermill Theater near Newbury, telephoned to ask if we would like to host a visit from the Mummers, his troupe of traveling performers. We fixed a date just before Christmas.

For some weeks, the children had been busy making decorations out of shiny, brightly colored paper. The playroom walls were covered with stars and the windows dotted with cottonwool snowflakes. Lanterns of all sizes were suspended from every beam and there were yards and yards of paper chains hanging in loops and zigzagging from side to side. We had excursions along the hedgerows searching for the holly with the most berries and we clipped fronds from the box hedges to dress the kissing bough frame. When the playroom could take no more, the decorations seeped into the house. The Christmas tree was hauled in and bedecked with glass baubles and trinkets, but this year, instead of being in the house, the kissing bough with its hilariously red apples hanging from scarlet ribbons, and the candles around its equator, was aloft in the playroom. It was waiting for the Mummers.

Jackie was tired that day, but she was quickly caught up in the infectious Christmas fizz and made little sandwiches and cheese straws with Joy and the children. We were expecting quite a crowd, having extended an open invitation to many friends. The mince pies were warming in the Esse and the spicy mulled wine was gently heating on the top.

"Jackie, let's light the candles now, before there are too many people about," I suggested. "Theresa and Clare can help you. Here are the matches—catch."

She caught them. "Come on you two, let's light them and then we can sing carols until everyone arrives. Hil, you can play the piano."

There was a rush for the playroom and the candles in the old lanterns were lit, but the kissing bough was left until the last moment.

"Can we sing 'Little Jesus' first?" whispered the awestruck Nico.

We sang it four times: Nico, in my arms, singing a solo twice, and Clare and Theresa once each. There followed many hearty carols as our guests arrived, and they all joined in.

Suddenly, in a lull, there was a jingle of bells from outside.

"They're here, and they're ready. Quick, sit down, everyone."

We all sat down at one end of the playroom and there was silence as the jingling came nearer. The door burst open and in trouped the masquerade led by Saint George on his hobby horse. They were all clad in fantastical costumes and headdresses, covered with brightly colored streamers, and they pranced their lively way through their ancient entertainment. The adults responded with gasps and giggles, but the children were dumbstruck by the extraordinary spectacle and the strange gibberish.

The applause thanked the Mummers and also heralded the entrance of Kiffer and Joy, bearing trays of mulled wine and mince pies.

Jackie whispered in my ear. "Hil, you haven't lit the kissing bough! Do it now while I get my cello."

I climbed on a chair to reach the circle of red candles which were carefully balanced among the box leaves. The little flames brought the suspended orb to life and the polished apples gleamed. I left the chair there for Jackie.

She returned carrying her cello and sat underneath the glowing bough. The children immediately sat at her feet and she started playing carols, as everyone sang lustily. The more we sang, the more powerfully she played, until her sound was so strong the children moved away. There was a pause after "See Amid the Winter's Snow" and in that moment, Jackie launched into Bach. Her sound in that echoey playroom was so overwhelming and the intensity of her playing so direct, many of the children burst into tears and were quickly herded out. But Jackie was carried away on her own wave and we were transported with her as she played underneath her illuminated crown.

The next morning, Clare asked Jackie if she could try her cello. Jackie carefully showed her what to do as the Davidoff towered above her. Clare had always been intrigued by Jackie's playing. I had taken her and Theresa to London to one of Jackie's concerts when Clare was only two and half. The two girls had worn their best dresses and sat in complete silence through the whole performance.

Kiffer and I always had early morning bathroom chats and sometime during early spring he told me he felt Jackie needed more than he was capable of giving her. Although her despairing crying was abating and on the surface she seemed a little happier, we both knew that, deeper down, not much had changed. She was still strongly attached to Kiffer but he felt her dependence on him might be a hindrance to her finding her own sense of direction. He thought he should try and find professional help.

He asked Barbara Gompertz, an old family friend, if there would be any chance of her husband seeing Jackie. Coen had started his career as a professional violinist and was second violin in Max Rostal's quartet. Becoming wheelchair-bound after having a growth removed from his spine, he realized he would never play again. Instead, he studied pyschoanalysis and became a distinguished Freudian analyst.

Kiffer and I took Jackie to London to see him. We had coffee with Barbara while Jackie was with Coen. Afterward, she told us she felt a fraud when he asked her to tell him of her problems, as they seemed so insignificant in comparison with his own obvious suffering. She brilliantly mimicked his Dutch accent and cough, and soon had us laughing with her at herself. A few days later, Coen phoned to say he thought he was not the right person for her but had contacted a colleague, Dr. Walter Joffe, who lived in Hampstead.

Jackie liked Joffe immediately. At first her visits were twice-weekly and she traveled to London for each day. Eventually, a third session was arranged and she started to stay in Pilgrim's Lane overnight because she was too tired to travel back.

In the beginning she related every detail of her sessions to Kiffer, but gradually, as she became more absorbed, the need for this grew less and less. She refused to lie on a couch or sit on a chair out of eye contact, but faced Joffe at all times. He told her that although she was a musical prodigy, there were no short cuts in psychoanalysis and she could not expect miraculous progress.

Jackie once asked him if he recorded their sessions. When he said no, she commented that it was amazing he was able to remember everything without muddling patients' details. He replied that it was just as incomprehensible to him that she never muddled her concertos.

Before she went to Joffe she had told Kiffer she was experiencing patches of numbness on her arms and legs. Later on, the soles of her feet became affected in the same way. When she mentioned this to Joffe he suggested it might be an unconscious resistance to unearthing her painful past and walking over Hampstead Heath to her sessions.

As Jackie spent more of her time in London, life began to resume a normality at home. The more Joffe took the strain, the less important Kiffer was to Jackie. We all felt a huge sense of relief, as though an enormous weight had been lifted. But the impact of our experience with her left us both feeling utterly drained.

Later on Kiffer said he wasn't sure whether he had been much help to Jackie and at best felt he had only temporarily slowed her downward slide. We both knew that if the tremendous weight of her inner despair that he had lovingly shouldered was not supported by someone or something, she must, inevitably, sink further down.

I don't know how Jackie became reconciled with Danny but I can only assume that, after a while, either her confusion subsided or she was better able to cope with it. In December that year, a month before her twenty-seventh birthday, an unscheduled recording session triggered their musical communication again. She picked up her cello and headed for the recording studio with Danny and her sound producer, Suvi Grubb. Much to everyone's delight, they recorded Chopin's Cello Sonata in G minor and Franck's Cello Sonata in A major. They also began the Beethoven Cello Sonatas but Jackie became too tired and had to stop. It was her last visit to a recording studio.

They went to Tel Aviv and performed at the Proms together. In September, they played the Beethoven Piano Trio in D "The Ghost" and the Tchaikovsky Piano Trio with Pinchas Zukerman at the Royal Festival Hall. Some reviewers remarked that "Miss du Pré is back in great form," although others were less enthusiastic.

Once again, we started to see less and less of her, as she swung back into the vortex of Danny's life: concerts, late-night meals, traveling—all the things she had said she couldn't cope with. I wondered how long it would last.

After we had closed down the poultry business, it took the best part of a year to settle the accounts and tidy everything up. Things were extremely tight financially, but we desperately wanted to find a way to stay at Ashmansworth. We had always grown our own vegetables and kept a few animals, and, inspired by the example of the Portales family, whom we had watched with admiration over the years, we decided to become self-sufficient. We acquired three dairy cows, some goats and sheep, and extended the vegetable garden. Having advertized for helpers, we were soon joined by several professional people who, disillusioned with their desk jobs, were dedicated to going back to the land. With this extra help, it wasn't long before we were running our own small farm, providing most of our needs. Fortunately, we also had a small income from my teaching and supplemented this by selling excess produce.

Our new lifestyle meant I was even more tied to home than before, and with Jackie once more consumed by her concert life, we didn't see much of each other. Frequently we wrote, and often she sent presents. On one occasion, she gave me a pair of knickers and said as they didn't flatter her bottom, I might like them. She added salutations from one behind to another.

Piers

In December 1972, Dad organized the Chartered Accountants Students' Society of London Annual Dinner which, this year, would take place at the Park Lane Hilton Hotel. It was to be Dad's last major function before his retirement, and as it was very important to him, we all went.

Jackie was with us and immediately became the center of attention. The others at our table were in awe of her, and she held her audience perfectly. I knew she found it a strain and that the formality of the situation would tempt her to do something outrageous.

Dad made one of his magnificent speeches and then several other eminent members of the Society said a few words. During this time, Jackie reached across the table and took a book of matches from the ashtray. Hiding what she was doing, she fumbled with it under the tablecloth. She asked for a pen. By now, we were distracted by her secret activity and weren't listening to the speeches anymore. I dreaded what was about to happen.

Handing the now bulging book of matches to the most important guest on the table, Jackie watched for a reaction. All eyes were on the matches. There were muffled anticipatory giggles. This was the great Jacqueline du Pré's creation. The guest looked carefully at it before opening it, not knowing what to do.

Inside, all the matches were bent and twisted. He read out what Jackie had written:

"Made by cripples."

There was a shocked silence.

Jackie threw me a victor's knowing glance. But I didn't think her victorious. Somehow, the Jackie humor had soured.

Hilary

Early in January 1973, just before her twenty-eighth birthday, Jackie performed the Lalo Concerto in Toronto. The Canadian press was not ecstatic; this was "good" du Pré but not "exceptional." By the 25th she was back in New York for a chamber concert with Danny. The program included Brahms's Sonata in E minor, and the Debussy and Chopin sonatas. The critics complained of her self-indulgent playing, her rasping tone, and that she often missed notes. Jackie had never before had reviews like these.

She had been noticing for some time that her hands were not responding as they should. It wasn't as though she hadn't practiced or that her muscles were out of trim, but she constantly felt as though her hands hadn't warmed up properly. She consulted various doctors who were anything but helpful. She was told that she was suffering from "adolescent trauma" (at twenty-eight!), which was a cruel diagnosis as she was made to think she was making a fuss about nothing.

Her official come-back concert at the Royal Festival Hall had been arranged for February 8. She was to play the Elgar Concerto, conducted by Zubin Mehta. The press announced that she was returning "after a long illness."

As usual Jackie had reserved good seats for us halfway back in the center aisle of the stalls. I was very aware that we were surrounded by important people from the music world. There was a great deal of chat: "How lovely to see you," "Isn't this exciting?" and "Isn't this wonderful?" and "So pleased she's better."

I sat with Mum and Dad to my right and Kiffer and Gran to my left. Piers had stayed at home to record the concert from the radio. As the orchestra took their places I felt apprehensive. The world was out in force to hear Jackie and I realized, for the first time, I didn't feel secure about her.

Jackie appeared, her cello held high in front of her and, as she ran up the steps on to the platform, the audience burst into frenzied applause. She looked happy and relaxed as she beamed at the crowd. There was absolute silence as she slipped into her deep concentration. Then, with a characteristic backward flip of her head, she raised her right arm and swung the bow across the strings for the opening chords. The sound rose from the cello and swept across the hall, penetrating every soul.

But the first two leaps were much slower than usual: the orchestra was unprepared and immediately sped ahead of her. I froze. Zubin crouched, his arms braced as he tried to pull the orchestra back. There was an uneasy balance between the orchestra and Jackie as they continued out of stride with each other for a few awkward notes. She was exaggerating far more than usual and overemphasizing the glissandi. She was struggling to find herself. That commanding voice, which had once spoken so directly to my heart, and had ruled my emotions with such power and authority, was now floundering desperately and grappling to take control.

Gran had my hand in a vice-like grip, and I didn't dare glance at her or Kiffer in case they acknowledged my fears. My concentration was intense, I stared straight ahead, until the stage faded to a blur. Suddenly I could see Jackie's picture of Elgar, and hear her telling me how his face had always troubled her.

"He had a miserable life, Hil," she said, "and he was ill, yet through it all he had a radiant soul, and that's what I feel in his music."

The audience hardly made a sound at the end of the first movement. I took a deep breath as the voice in my head was saying, "Come on, Jacks, come on." I thought I would snap with the tension within me. Gran let go of my hand, but still I didn't dare turn and look at her.

At first I couldn't identify my unease but gradually I realized Jackie was telling us something that was too much for us to understand or bear. There had always been hope in this music and in her playing but now all the joy had gone. I was witnessing a crucifixion. In a solemn and final reckoning, all I could hear was my sister's farewell.

That night's performance was a heavy burden. To me, the message was unmistakable. But no one wanted to hear it.

After the final sforzando chord, Zubin's arms flopped to his side and the audience rose to its feet, like a huge tidal wave. I found myself swept on to my feet too, and pushed forward by the sheer volume of cheers and applause. Jackie's face broke into her huge smile and she stood with her adoring, but utterly uncomprehending, audience at her feet.

CHAPTER THIRTY-ONE

Piers

My training long since completed, I was now a First Officer with two-gold-band epaulettes. I had married Lindsay (née Dickson) on July 15, 1972, and we were now living in our one-bedroomed, semi-detached bungalow in Bourne End, Buckinghamshire. Lin was teaching at the local primary school in Flackwell Heath.

On April 10, 1973, I woke early, excited by the prospect of a sumptuous lunch with Jackie. Where would it be? Looking out of the window, I saw it was a great day: sun shining, the sky completely blue, no clouds in sight. Brilliant! The perfect day for a drive in my TR6—hood down!

I told Lin, "I'm going to pop by and see Mum and Dad on the way, and I have to take Jackie to the airport later, so I don't know what time I'll be back. Won't be late."

"Give her my love."

I flew along the main roads to Mum's and Dad's house. The wind was cool and invigorating as it whipped around my face. The air was sweet with the expectation of a glorious day and the car, strong and powerful, took each bend in her stride. A beautiful day, a great car and a lunch with Jackie to look forward to. What a life! And I was actually paid to practice my hobby—to fly airplanes.

Mum was in the laundry-room doing battle with the washing machine. It always took her ages to make it work. She would press every button and twist every dial until she happened on the right combination to make it start. I made her jump.

"Oh, hello, Bar. I still don't understand this beastly thing."

"Here, I'll do it," I said. "What setting do you want?"

"I don't mind, just make it go, will you?"

Mum put the kettle on, made us both a cup of coffee, and sat down at the kitchen table with me.

"Blow," she announced, as the kitchen clock caught her eye. "Is that the time? I'm teaching in a few minutes and must change. I've got some things for Jackie. Some ironing, a blouse which Gran has mended and, oh yes, she needed some new pads for her dress. It's going to be very hot in Tokyo, you know. Here you are."

Mum was still taking care of Jackie's clothes and washing.

"I hope she's going to be all right. It's strange, though," she said, reflectively. "She's very tired, you know."

"Don't worry, Mum. We're going for a nice lunch and I promise I'll make sure she gets on the plane, complete with luggage."

Jackie was practicing as I reversed the TR into her driveway. The moment she heard the car, she rushed to the front door.

"Bar, you're here at last! Great." She flung her arms around me. "I've booked Villa Bianca. Come on," she said, reaching for her door keys.

Haverstock Hill was teeming with people enjoying the sunshine. Jackie strode along the pavement.

"How's Mum?"

"Fine."

"And how's Lin?"

"She sends her love."

"Send mine back! I'm starving, aren't you?"

As we entered the restaurant, the waiters seemed to stand to attention. It always happened when we went to restaurants together, whether they knew her or not. She had such a commanding presence. We sat at the table by the window.

Jackie ordered for me and chose the richest and juiciest of foods. This time it was avocados with lashings of dressing, and veal. I chose the wine. We ate well, right through to desserts from the trolley, coffee and truffles.

"Why can't you fly me to Tokyo, Bar? We could charter a plane."

"Not possible, Jacks. Far too expensive! Nice thought though . . ."

"Last time I was there," she went on, "I got a huge standing ovulation and was called back on to the platform four times.

Finally, I gave up because I was so exhausted. Then a little man rushed into my room in a panic. 'Miss du Ple, Miss du Ple,' he said. 'You must come back on stage—the whore house is crapping!' "

Mum had told me that things hadn't gone well in America for Jackie. When the coffee arrived, I asked her what had happened.

"Oh, Bar, it was ghastly. First of all, I couldn't get the cello out of the case. I just couldn't hold it. My hands didn't seem to want to work. And when I finally managed it, I realized that my left hand was completely numb. I told Lenny that I couldn't possibly play, but he just brushed it aside."

Jackie contorted her face to impersonate Leonard Bernstein's American accent. " 'Don't be such a goose,' " she drawled, pretending to take a drag from a cigarette. " 'You're just nervous.' "

We laughed. But then she was serious again.

"The rehearsal was terrible. It was obvious everyone was talking about it."

"How awful."

"Yeah, it was. And the concert was even worse. I couldn't feel the strings at all, so I had to judge where to put my fingers by sight. It was a nightmare."

"Did you see a doctor?"

"Yes, I did all that. They say that it's just stress and I need to rest . . . so I've been resting."

"Are you OK now?"

"Yeah . . . I'm fine."

"Sure?"

"Uh ha!" came the wistful response, after a short pause. But she wasn't able to look me in the eye and I knew it wasn't true. She changed the subject by asking for another coffee.

Jackie paid the bill in cash and we walked back to her house laughing like kids playing truant from school. But, within a block of her street she suddenly stumbled in such a way that she just couldn't stop herself. She crumpled and fell. I put out my hand to break her fall and thought, Oh no, we've overdone it. Too much wine. In our struggles, we both started giggling. But after a while my giggling turned to concern. She couldn't move and I couldn't lift her.

"Come on, Jackie, brace your legs!"

"I can't!"

People started gathering around to see what was happening, and eventually someone helped me lift her up. Once on her feet she was extremely unsteady. I hooked my arm underneath hers to support her.

"We're OK now. We live right here. Thanks. We're OK now." The crowd dispersed. When we were back in her home, I made her a cup of tea and she seemed to recover her mobility. The rest of the afternoon was spent packing, but a sense of uncertainty and seriousness had replaced the fun. We both knew something was wrong, yet there was no time to do anything. Jackie had a plane to catch and the incident was put on one side.

Hilary

Not long after Jackie's return from Tokyo, Kiffer and I were invited to lunch with her in Hampstead. The atmosphere was without strain and she seemed in good form, giggly and chatty. She had prepared a meal and we tucked into bowls of steaming soup.

"Jackie, this is delicious," I said. "One of your best."

"Hmmm, I love it," Kiffer enthused. "But it would be even more lovable with some salt."

Jackie picked up the salt cellar with her right hand and tried to pass it across the table, but her arm would not go toward Kiffer. It just bounced in mid-air.

"He's over there, Jacks," I joked, but very quickly realized, from her frightened face, that she was not playing around. Her arm continued its directionless bouncing.

"I can't, Hil. It won't go."

We were stunned into an awful silence. I immediately put my arm round her.

"Jack, *please*, will you *please* go and see the doctor? It's silly to be frightened and without help."

Piers

In May, Jackie canceled her appearance at the Brighton Festival because of an "inflamed wrist tendon." When I arrived at Pilgrim's Lane, she was resting in bed and, since it was lunchtime, I had to cook.

In the kitchen I found some veal and a bottle of Marsala.
I shouted upstairs to Jackie: "How about veal Marsala à la Barzi
con sel?"

She blew a loud raspberry, which I took as acceptance.

I hadn't a clue what to do. I put far too much butter in the pan,
poured in excessive quantities of Marsala, waited until it was
frothing and added the veal. Rather than being fried, it ended up
being boiled in the depths of the steaming wine.

"Mmmm . . ." said Jackie, "the gravy's lovely and . . . well, it's
very rich."

It tasted revolting. Stoically, we finished it all.

I had my flying schedule with me and we realized that I was going to be in Los Angeles in June when she was in San Francisco.
We arranged that I would fly up and see her.

As it turned out, this was impossible. When I checked into the
hotel in LA there was a message from Jackie to call collect. I had to
ask the receptionist what this meant. I telephoned, reversing the
charges. When I explained I couldn't make the journey to see her,
she burst into tears, and kept on and on asking me to come. I
found it hard to know how to respond. The tears and the pleading
left me feeling wretched—cold and weak. She needed me but I
just couldn't help. As I replaced the receiver, I was shivering. She
had sounded really desperate and frightened and I, her only
brother, had been useless to her. Something was badly wrong and I
had let her down.

When we were both back in England, I telephoned her and,
wanting to make it up to her, made a date to meet. The film *The
Day of the Jackal* had just opened to rave reviews and, thinking a
distraction would help, I suggested we should go and see it. We
settled on a date, July 17, and I booked the tickets.

Lin and I met Jackie at the Westbury for an early dinner where,
thankfully, Jackie seemed on great form. After a hearty meal and
an extremely expensive bottle of wine, Jackie settled the bill with
cash and we set off for the cinema.

Jackie was enthralled and became engrossed in the story to the
extent that when the Jackal was about to strangle his lover, she
stood up and shouted, "No, no, no. Don't!" much to everyone's
amusement.

She didn't mention her upset in America and I assumed that, because she didn't mention it, she didn't wish to discuss it.

A month later, Jackie attended the Edinburgh Festival but again was unable to perform because of a "mystery illness." Eventually she went to see her doctor, Len Selby, at the beginning of October, and the true story of what had been happening slowly began to emerge.

She reported to him that a year earlier she had noticed difficulty in using her hands. There had been times when her left hand was unable to press down the cello strings, and her right hand had difficulty holding the bow. She was also aware of numbness and tenderness in her legs and her back was weak. For the last three months she had experienced occasional blurred vision in her left eye.

Dr. Selby suspected a neurological disorder and made an appointment for her to see Leo Lange, a neurologist, who advised that she should go into the London Clinic for tests as soon as possible. Meanwhile, the Yom Kippur War had started and Danny had gone to Israel with Zubin to play to the troops. When I went to London for dinner with Jackie on October 10, she didn't say anything about seeing Lange. She just told me she had seen a doctor and had to go into hospital for some tests. From the way she spoke, I knew she was full of fear; she knew something was wrong but didn't want to talk about it. A few days later, she was transferred to the Lindo Wing of St. Mary's Hospital in Paddington to be under the supervision of their senior neurologist, Harold Edward.

On October 16, multiple sclerosis was finally diagnosed.

Jackie's immediate reaction was to telephone Danny in Israel but not to tell him the truth. He was due back soon and she didn't want to make his last five days in Israel more difficult for him. She said her results had not yet come back, and changed the subject to ask how his concerts were going. Danny, however, sensed something was wrong, and made some telephone calls which confirmed his suspicions. He was soon at her bedside. He made Jackie promise she would always tell him the complete truth. She was delighted he had come home, especially knowing that he had put her first.

I was with Mum and Dad at Gerrards Cross when Jackie telephoned.

"I have a fatal illness, but don't worry, I haven't got it very badly. It'll be OK, and so will I."

None of us knew what multiple sclerosis was.

Devastation

CHAPTER THIRTY-TWO

Hilary

I first heard the diagnosis on the news. I had returned from France late the previous night and the wireless burst into automatic action at 6 a.m. with the alarming statement: "It has been announced that the cellist Jacqueline du Pré has multiple sclerosis . . ." I was too shocked to remember what else was said. I waited until a reasonable hour before telephoning Mum.

We went up to see Jackie *en famille*. The children were excited and Jackie was full of bubble. She had bought pretty, ankle-length dresses for each of the girls and they had fun racing up and down the hospital corridors pretending to be princesses.

Jackie was relieved to have a diagnosis after all the strange things that had been happening to her and, as a result, was buoyant. It was also a huge relief to her that, at last, there was a sustainable reason for avoiding everything that she wanted to avoid. We had a jolly time together. None of us, not even Jackie, knew of the awful possibilities, and we all took it for granted that she would recover.

It was another ghastly shock, therefore, when the newspapers announced that Jackie would never play again:

A heart-rending tragedy has ended plans of Jacqueline du Pré, Britain's foremost cellist, to return to the international concert platform. Miss du Pré, 28-year-old wife of conductor Daniel Barenboim, has been told that she is suffering from multiple sclerosis and will never play in public again.

Daily Mail,
Tuesday, November 6, 1973

Jackie and Danny immediately countered the reports by insisting that Jackie was fine, and they were photographed together, going to one of Danny's concerts. We were told that MS was not necessarily fatal and that there could be long periods of remission. Because Jackie didn't look ill, we hoped that she had only a mild form of the disease.

At first, life continued as normal except that Jackie needed a great deal of rest. Danny was still very busy but made sure Jackie had everything she needed. She coped on the few occasions they were at home together, but was having increasing difficulties in the kitchen. Danny had never learned to cook, but was soon making hot Indian curries, which she adored.

Mum visited her as often as possible. Whatever the emotional weather (and there had been some turbulent storms), Mum had always made herself available for Jackie, and still did. Mum would shop, clean, do the washing, or just be with Jackie. She was especially vigilant when Danny was away.

I made several visits to Pilgrim's Lane. Preparing four children between the ages of five and ten for a day in London was quite a palaver. Jackie always had delicious treats for them—crisps, biscuits and fruit juice—things they didn't normally have at home, and special surprises, too. On one occasion she gave each of them a soft pink bag containing a machine with a small button which, when pressed, emitted lecherous laughter. They thought these presents were absolutely wonderful. I remember Nico wending her way up and down the crowded station platform activating the machine which was concealed in her pocket, and being completely oblivious to the effect she was having on all the commuters. Another time, Jackie produced a gadget to fix underneath the loo seat. When an unsuspecting person sat on the seat an awful voice said, "I'm watching you," and then burst into frightful laughter. Gran nearly died when the children tried it out on her.

The children loved Jackie's house with the sunken music room and the colorful Italian tiles in the bathroom. But best of all was the little summer house at the end of the garden. After energetic games on the lawn, Jackie always produced a scrumptious tea with special tiny plates and cups and small cakes and biscuits.

Piers

Now that Jackie was ill, Mum's and Dad's plans to retire to more distant places were abandoned because the need to be close to Jackie was once again paramount. Moving nearer to London was not an option, financially. Instead they decided that the maximum distance from Jackie should be no more than one hour by car. The preferred direction was west, near Hilary. After much searching, they found Birch House in Curridge, near Newbury. Given the support Mum and Dad now needed, I told them that Lin and I would move to the Newbury area as well, as soon as we could.

Mum continued to teach the occasional pupil at home, and no sooner had she started attending their local church at Hermitage than she was asked to join the Parochial Church Council and commandeered to run the choir.

Once they had finished organizing their new home, I went to install their hi-fi system which included a new pair of BBC monitor loudspeakers. Dad was out in the stonery and Mum was busy in the kitchen. As soon as it was ready to test, I chose the record of Jackie's Barbirolli Elgar Concerto and turned the volume up high. The sound was superb.

I closed my eyes and could see Jackie performing it at the Royal Festival Hall: how she moved and how her hair flew. After a while, I went into the kitchen, and there was Mum, bent over the breakfast table, her head in her hands, crying. I rushed to turn off the music.

In the kitchen, I put my arm round her. "I'm so sorry, Mum, that was so foolish of me. I should have thought."

She wiped her eyes and blew her nose.

"Did I really bring Jackie up the wrong way, Bar? Should I have insisted on a normal life for her? Should I have stopped her playing so much? . . ."

Mum had often been criticized for her single-minded encouragement of Jackie and her playing. Now, Jackie's illness had made many people very angry. Why had Jackie been cut down in this way? Clearly someone had to take the blame. The scapegoat was Mum. People love to speculate. Was Jackie's illness stress-related? Was the stress caused by Mum pushing her from such a young age?

I had never heard Mum talking in this way before. She had never questioned the way she brought any of us up. Now that Jackie was ill, the pressure on Mum was compounded and she was beginning to blame herself, as any mother might, for what had happened. She had just turned sixty, and I think the combination of Jackie's tragedy, moving house and her advancing years, had become too much for her. Mum had put everything into ensuring that Jackie's gift could flourish and prosper. But now it had all been blown apart by the unknown force of this terrible degenerative disease. The realization was too much for Mum to bear and she was finally giving in to all the criticism.

I tried to reassure her and, gradually, she calmed down. Suddenly we heard Dad walking along the patio. Mum quickly pulled herself together and we both tried to act as if nothing had happened.

"I must make him a cup of tea," she said, picking up the kettle and heading for the sink. Then she turned to look at me.

"Thank you, you old monkey."

Over elevenses, I showed them how to use the stereo, but I had hidden Jackie's record away.

Mum was never again able to listen to Jackie's playing.

Hilary

The year of 1974 brought many changes. Joy had decided to leave Ashmansworth, eventually finding an exquisite cottage the other side of Newbury. We had lived together for thirteen years and she felt it was time for her to "move on."

It was a struggle to make ends meet, but with friends, we took the opportunity of having a stall at the Friday and Saturday markets in Winchester and Southampton. We already had cows, goats, sheep and pigs, as well as chickens, and Church Farm was functioning as a busy small farm. Although the stalls flourished, we decided a shop would be more practical. Eventually we found suitable premises to lease in Newbury and opened Sunstore. It was an early version of a health food warehouse, specializing in wholefoods of all kinds. The shop was immediately successful but, even with the help of several people, this way of life—the shop, the farm, the children—was a tremendous tie.

It wasn't long before Jackie needed help at Pilgrim's Lane. One evening, Danny was particularly exhausted and decided to go out for a meal. He arrived at a restaurant just as it was closing. As he turned away, someone tapped him on the shoulder. He turned to face a kindly middle-aged woman.

She was Olga Rejman, who worked at the restaurant. A music-lover, she had recognized Danny. She invited him in and produced a meal. They talked, and subsequently she left the restaurant and was soon employed as housekeeper in Pilgrim's Lane. Not only was she a wonderful cook, but also sympathetic to Jackie. With the added support of agency nurses when required, Jackie was now surrounded by helpers.

But as Jackie's life was settling down to an organized routine, disaster struck again. On May 8, 1974, Walter Joffe died suddenly of a heart attack. To Jackie, it seemed like the end of the world and she was both heart-broken and angry about his death. His place as Jackie's psychoanalyst was taken immediately by Adam Limentani, an Italian Jew. Jackie told me that Limentani knew all about her. Joffe had never given him her name, but had kept him well briefed. Limentani had guessed the identity of his famous client. It was a while before Jackie felt as comfortable with "the Lemon" as she had with Joffe. Eventually, though, she grew very fond of him.

There was a great deal of media interest in Jackie's illness and she made it a rule never to discuss her symptoms, for fear of frightening others. Being such a well-known celebrity, she was inundated with advice about cures which ranged from diets to meditation, from drugs to bathing in special waters. She received fan mail from all over the world. There were many sensible ideas, but others were crazy. One claimed: "I know the answer to MS, you must be suspended in a parachute for 30 minutes and you will be cured." Other letters would start off reasonably, "I'm a great admirer of yours, I love your music," and gradually degenerate into a sexual assault. Many of the letters, though, were from fellow sufferers for whom Jackie was a role model. She was a huge inspiration not only because she was famous but because she was coping with a devastating illness. As long as Jackie could cope, other victims of MS could cope also. Sometimes, she found this a terrible pressure, because she had to keep a brave face.

Jackie's devoted friend and secretary, Sylvia Southcombe, painstakingly replied to many of the more genuine letters on

Jackie's behalf. There were many, of course, who were truly interested in Jackie's welfare and many, too, who wanted something
from her: to use her name, money, or the prestige of being able to
say "I know Jacqueline du Pré."

When Christmas came, it was clear that Jackie would not be
with us.

Jackie was heart-breakingly brave. As someone who adored
shopping, she now had to ask a friend to do it for her. She expressed herself as vividly as ever but could no longer write clearly,
so had to type instead.

By April 1975, eighteen months after the disease had been diagnosed, she could still walk but could manage stairs only by going
up and down on her bottom. She had been to St. Mary's Hospital,
Paddington for steroid treatment and felt much better for it. But
when the treatment stopped, she worsened quickly. For some, the
improvement was longer-lasting. Jackie was back in hospital within a month.

Danny wanted to keep his concert engagements as close to
England as possible, to avoid being too far away from Jackie.
When Sir Georg Solti resigned from the prestigious Orchestre de
Paris, Danny was offered the music directorship. It was a wonderful opportunity to have his own orchestra again, after several years
of appearing as a guest conductor. Although it would mean
spending over half the year in Paris, it was within commuting distance from London, enabling him to go home every two weeks.
As Jackie was adjusting to her new circumstances, Danny was taking the first steps to a very different life.

CHAPTER THIRTY-THREE

Piers

Jackie knew that most of the "cures" suggested were useless, but she still felt that some were worth trying. The Rockefeller Institute in New York was pioneering a new treatment using oxygen and Jackie's doctor, Len Selby, advised her that this might be helpful. Even though she hated traveling and being away from home, Jackie left London in a hopeful frame of mind. Despite problems with coordinating her legs, she managed to walk on to the plane unaided.

A few days later, while I was laying floorboards in the two attic rooms in our bungalow in Bourne End, the telephone rang.

"Bar? It's Jacks! What are you up to? No good, I suppose?"

"No. Actually," I replied indignantly, "I'm building a house, thank you very much!" And for once, I blew the first raspberry.

Before I could ask her how she was, she launched into the whole miserable story: the treatment was horrible and painful; she had no one to visit her; she felt isolated and lonely. "How soon can you come over? Bar, I'm dying to see you. *Please* say yes. No one else has come to see me."

Hearing the very real cry of her heart, I called British Airways Crew Scheduling. Explaining that my sister was having experimental treatment for MS in New York, I asked if they would reorganize my flying roster so I could fly out to see her. Later that day they called back to say I could swap my next day's planned Antigua trip for one to New York. This was wonderful news. It meant I would have three days with Jackie, and could return as a passenger so there was no pressure to be rested for flying. I rang Jackie immediately. She sounded relieved.

"Don't bring any money," she said. "I've got plenty. We'll have a ball, cha-cha-cha. But do please wear your uniform because I want to show my brother off to everyone."

Once in New York, the British Airways Station Manager confirmed I could stay for four nights. The Manager of the Berkshire Hotel turned out to be a big fan of Jackie's, and offered me a room free of charge. I phoned the moment I arrived.

"Hi Jacks. Guess where I am."

"Bar, are you really in New York?"

"Yes. And I can be with you within the hour."

In my excitement, I chatted on for a few moments until I realized that she was completely silent.

"Jacks, are you still there?"

She was crying. She wept and wept.

"Don't worry, Jacks, I'm on my way."

I had hardly put the phone down, when it rang again. It was the hall porter to tell me that my car had arrived.

"But I haven't ordered a car."

He asked me to hold on.

"I understand that Miss du Pré has sent a car to collect you, sir."

Remembering what Jackie had said about my uniform, I quickly washed, changed and presented myself at the front of the hotel where the car was waiting.

"Mr. du Pré," said the chauffeur. "I'm to take you to your sister." Even the doorman looked impressed. It was a huge black stretch limousine, with blackened windows and enough room inside for a billiard table. I climbed in and lost myself in the plush leather seats.

The Institute was awesome. As I walked through the front door, I was immediately aware of that ghastly hospital smell of antiseptic which seems to say: "This is a place where people are in pain and where people come to die." There was a hushed atmosphere which made me self-conscious as I crept along the corridor, searching for Jackie's room, trying to stop my highly polished leather shoes from squeaking on the spotless, gray-tiled flooring.

I tried to feel positive and look bright, but, as I neared Jackie's door, became anxious about how I would find her and feared that I would not be able to keep a brave face. I stood outside for a few moments, practicing my happy smile, before knocking decisively.

"Come in, Bar."

But as I opened the door, I felt my throat tighten. She was in bed on the left side of the room. I had wanted to make a big entrance, do something funny, make her laugh. But instead, I just went straight over to her and hugged her, not least to hide my face, which was now crumpled with tears. Neither of us could say anything. We just held each other and sobbed. After what seemed ages, Jackie began to speak.

"I'm going to die," she said. "The doctors have told me I'm going to die. And I can't walk anymore. And they say I'm going to go mad. I'm not mad, am I? Am I mad already?"

She looked at me, searching my eyes for an answer. What could I say? The last thing I wanted to do was give false hope. I just didn't know. She held on to me tightly and talked and talked. I listened.

This was so incredibly different from the tough exterior of "Jackie coping" that she usually presented to the world. She used to brush the disease to one side, joking about it, saying how much more fortunate she was than others. But now her true feelings of helplessness, frustration, loneliness, and fear of dying, were overwhelming her. Jackie was in jail, on death row.

The doctors in England had been over-protective. They hadn't told her about the progression of the disease. Obviously, they didn't want to frighten her unnecessarily, especially since MS is so unpredictable that it is impossible to say with certainty what may happen next. All we had been told was that it is possible to recover totally after an attack and not have a relapse for years. But it was becoming clear that, in Jackie's case, the disease was advancing at a much faster pace than usual. It seemed to me that the American doctors, in assessing her condition, had inadvertently painted a full picture of what the future might have in store for her, holding nothing back, and she had been left to face up to all this on her own, isolated in a hospital miles away from home. She was terrified. Now, instead of having hope, she was completely engulfed by fear, spending hours alone thinking about every symptom.

To pass the time between treatments, Jackie had to attend the Occupational Therapy Department. This meant sitting in a day room surrounded by other patients, most of whom were grossly obese, and in a far worse condition. They had been making leather belts. She produced one that she had made for me, inscribed with the words: "If flying be the food of love, eat up, and ffly on to N.Y. on B.A."

"Sorry I couldn't spell 'ffly' but at least B.A. and Bar sound the same."

I admired her fine workmanship, and she muttered gruffly, "It's supposed to be good for me, but I don't want to make belts for the rest of my life, so why do they make me do it?"

That evening, the hoods' car returned and took us to the Russian Tea Room. The doctors had forbidden Jackie to drink alcohol and had put her on a strict diet. But I knew she would disregard this without a moment's thought and I was right.

Jackie ordered a large vodka. Not wanting to be seen drinking in uniform, I took my jacket off, quite forgetting about the epaulettes on my shirt. We spent the whole evening giggling and laughing, drinking "Navy Grog" while Jackie mimicked the doctors and we exchanged the latest set of risque jokes.

The next day, I wheeled her downstairs for her occupational therapy class. It was in a long, narrow room, with brightly painted walls, and, just as Jackie had told me, was completely packed with the fattest and most helpless, sad-looking people I had ever seen. They sat in rows, monotonously and silently punching holes into leather belts. A strident voice called out to us across the room:

"Please take the place at the corner on the second table on the left, and continue with yesterday's work. You'll find the leather straps and hole punches in the wooden box in the center of the table. I'll be over in a minute to see how you're getting on."

Everyone stared at us as we took our places.

"Let's see how clever we can be today," said the nurse, in a well-meaning, yet condescending tone.

Jackie obediently picked up her tools and set to work. But I couldn't. Instead, anger and frustration welled up within me. Jackie looked utterly beaten and helpless, her vibrant personality and great talent, so used to being free and full of life, had been beaten into submission and locked into a minute cage. I could take no more. Without a word, I wheeled her straight back to her room. No one could have stopped me. I was never going to allow anyone to subject my sister to such degradation ever again.

Lunch consisted of some anaemic food and a very indifferent

cup of coffee. Not long afterward, there was a knock on the door and a nurse and two men in hospital uniforms came in, pushing a trolley. On it was a light blue rubber contraption, with some electrical equipment with wires, gauges and a hose-pipe.

Before I could react, Jackie reached for my hand and whispered. "Now see what they're going to do to me!"

I challenged them immediately.

"What on earth is this for?"

"This is going to help Miss du Pré to walk. It's a suit that she wears rather like a wet suit. These things are like small hose-pipes which run vertically up and down on the outside. We pump compressed air into the tubes. Since she can't use her legs, they stiffen the suit, which then holds her up. It helps her to stand and therefore helps her to walk again."

As he spoke I thought, what do you mean "walk again"? She could walk when she came to New York two weeks ago and now you say she *can't* walk! What have you done to her?

The suit had been made especially for her and had to fit exactly to be effective. It functioned like a pilot's "G" suit. Standing up allows gravity to drain blood from the body to the legs. Normally, the leg muscles prevent this. But Jackie's muscles could no longer prevent the draining, and consequently it was a tremendous strain for her heart to keep pumping sufficient blood to her brain. By making the leggings fit tightly and increasing the "squeeze" with air pressure, they hoped to keep blood flowing naturally through her entire body.

Jackie lay flat on her back on the bed as they dressed her in the suit. It seemed to take forever. Then, connecting the hose to the unit, they plugged the compressor into the electricity supply in the wall, and switched on. The motor buzzed noisily, and the pressure gauge began to climb.

As the tubes filled with air, Jackie became more and more rigid. I couldn't believe what I was witnessing. It was like something out of a horror film. They helped her into a sitting position, with her legs over the edge of the bed. All three of them had to hold her up, one standing on the bed behind her, and one on each side. It took a great deal of effort. As the suit became fully inflated, they gently inched her off the bed until her feet were touching the floor. But she still couldn't straighten her legs—they kept buckling at the knees. The compressor was now laboring to push the last little bit of air into the tubes. Finally, the nurses hoisted Jackie to a full standing position, although her knees were still slightly bent.

"Try using your legs," they urged, again and again, encouraging her to walk.

"I can't," said Jackie impatiently.

I stared in amazement. My sister, looking like the Michelin Man, was being pushed and shoved around the room.

Eventually they gave up and put Jackie back on the bed. As they left the room, they were reassuring themselves by commenting on how successful the whole exercise had been.

That evening we went back to the Russian Tea Room and had more vodka, more rich food and more laughter.

The standard-issue, white hospital clock on the wall opposite the bed was showing the moment was drawing close when we would have to say goodbye. Our last day together was over. In spite of the surroundings, or possibly because of them, the time we had spent together had been outstanding. Now I had to leave to go back to my hotel before catching the British Airways "red-eye" home that evening.

I was fighting the feeling that I should rescue her from the hands of these people. I wanted to take her back home with me. Jackie was frightened by what the doctors were saying to her and hated their injections.

She was desperate to leave. But it was not to be. After one of those special, long, family hugs, I turned and left her gray room. No words. In the corridor I began to retrace the steps I had made when I had arrived three days before. Still the smell of antiseptic was hanging in the air; still my shoes squeaked on the floor; still the tightness was in my throat. No one was around. I hesitated when I got to the lift. The pull of going back to fetch her was huge.

As the lift slowly took me to the ground floor, I could hold it no longer. I had to allow the intense grief and pent-up emotion of the last few days to show itself. My mouth opened and I sobbed loudly. I held my handkerchief hard over my mouth to quieten the noise. I forced myself to stop and was wiping my eyes as the lift doors opened. I almost ran out of the hospital. A cab took me to the Berkshire Hotel, where I picked up my suitcase and left for the airport.

I felt like a traitor.

A few weeks later, Jackie telephoned to say that she was returning to London Heathrow on a Pan Am flight and we agreed that I would meet her personally on the aircraft and escort her through the airport. In my uniform, and with my British Airways ID card, this would be easy to organize. I contacted Pan Am who told me Jackie would be in a wheelchair and the only way to escort her from the aircraft to the waiting ambulance would be for her to exit from the forward galley door, be wheeled on to the galley support services lift and lowered to the ground. This would happen after the last passenger had disembarked. Hence, I could wait on the tarmac to greet her.

I was at the airport in plenty of time, and was directed to where the aircraft was to park. I introduced myself to the Red Cap and explained why I was there. Yes, he had been briefed about me, and confirmed that Jackie would be taken off last, on the galley lift, just as I had been told. I sat on a pallet. How unreal it all was.

Pan Am arrived on time as did the ambulance which was to take Jackie to the British Airways Medical Center where she would be examined before being allowed to continue her journey to London. I went and sat with the ambulance driver. After a while, the small galley door opened and the lift moved into position. Trolley after trolley of used catering supplies and rubbish were unloaded. I waited. The lift went silent. Jackie will be next, I thought. I left the ambulance and went over to the lift. All the passengers would surely have disembarked by now. What was the delay? Where was she? I went and found the Red Cap.

"She's probably been kept on board until everyone else has been taken off. But I'll check."

He called someone on his radio.

"Apparently she's already been taken off the usual way. She was the first to disembark."

"What?" I yelled. I rushed across the tarmac to the terminal building dodging between ground support vehicles. I held up my ID badge, and ran. Up the stairs and into the arrivals corridor, I pushed past weary travelers. Passport Control didn't stop me—

they couldn't have. Eventually I made it to the ground floor and into the Medical Center.

"I'm here to greet Jacqueline du Pré. Where is she?" I asked the receptionist.

"You've just missed her," she said, smiling as though it was my fault. "She left a few moments ago."

I looked out of the window and saw her being pushed on a stretcher into the back of a private ambulance. I yelled at the top of my voice, but the triple glazing was against me. Nothing could be heard through it. Again I ran. As I arrived on the pavement the ambulance was driving off past Terminal Three.

Out of breath and fuming, I stood there in utter disbelief. What would Jackie be thinking? She expected me to be there. "Jackie, Jackie, Jackie," I said, half under my breath. I walked to my car and drove home feeling utterly useless and dejected.

When we managed to speak on the phone, she said she knew I must have been there.

"I kept trying to tell all these soppy airline people," she said. "But they wouldn't listen."

I went to see her and noticed the space suit bundled in a heap in the corner of her bedroom.

"Did it ever work properly?" I asked.

"No," was her immediate reply. "And I don't ever want to try it again."

"Well, it certainly won't work here," I said, examining the instruction leaflet.

"Why not?"

"It's the wrong voltage. The motor is labeled 110 volts. We use 240 volts in England."

Jackie blew a loud and very long raspberry.

CHAPTER THIRTY-FOUR

Hilary

Jackie needed to convalesce after her experiences at the Rocke-feller, so it was decided that she should go into the Lindo Wing of St. Mary's Hospital, Paddington for a few weeks, to rest and recuperate.

There was chattering and laughter as she settled into her room, which was already full of bouquets from friends and well-wishers. Her voice could be heard all the way down the corridor.

"This goes to Rutland Gardens, this goes to Pilgrim's Lane, this goes to Rutland Gardens."

She was sorting out her clothes.

The mews house in Rutland Gardens belonged to the ballerina, Margot Fonteyn, and was to be Jackie's new home when she left hospital. It had been clear for some time that the house in Pilgrim's Lane was no longer suitable for her. Margot Fonteyn had met Jackie socially, and had offered her Knightsbridge house, which had already been appropriately converted for her husband, who also used a wheelchair.

Jackie continued to laugh and joke boisterously with Mum and Dad, who were visiting. A nurse came round the door of Room 9. It was Ruth Ann Cannings. With a jovial laugh and a warm, broad smile, she commented that it was two in the morning and other patients were sleeping. Jackie was apologetic and Mum and Dad left immediately, promising to return later that morning. Ruth Ann settled Jackie for the night.

Ruth Ann had heard about Jacqueline du Pré, and had been to one of her concerts, but had never met her before. Her first im-pression of Jackie was that she was extremely strong because she seemed so full of life. Ruth Ann felt instantly that Jackie was not the sort of character to respond to the wrong kind of sympathy or pity. She observed Jackie very carefully that night as she was preparing her for bed and noticed that she was still able to help herself in many ways. For example, she could flip her feet over the side of the bed to sit up. Ruth Ann made a conscious decision never to invade Jackie's independence. It was important for Jackie to do what she could for herself, for the sake of her dignity.

Jackie was, by this time, incontinent. She would ring the bell frequently. One day she remarked to Ruth Ann, "Every time you put your head around the door you're smiling, no matter what you come in for."

Ruth Ann looked at her. "Are you doing this on purpose?"

"Of course not!"

"Well, then, why should I be angry with you? Come on, let's just get you sorted out."

Jackie was in the Lindo Wing for three weeks and, by the end of her stay, Ruth Ann had become her favorite nurse. They made a promise to keep in touch, and wrote to each other from time to time.

The Fonteyn house was in Rutland Gardens Mews, a quiet cul-de-sac off Kensington Gore in Knightsbridge. Jackie moved there from the Lindo Wing in July while Danny was away. She was joined by Olga, the housekeeper from Pilgrim's Lane, and the usual succession of agency nurses.

Danny's commitments in Paris absorbed most of his time, but he came home regularly to see Jackie. He would take her out to Hyde Park, usually pushing her along the road rather than the pavement. When passing a bus queue, Jackie would call out, "Full up, no room!"

In October she made her first official public appearance in a wheelchair, when Margot Fonteyn took her to the Royal Opera House and pushed her into the Crush Bar. Once she had overcome the hurdle of being seen in a wheelchair, her courage strengthened, making it easier to accept her new situation.

At Christmas, Jackie heard she had been awarded the OBE (Order of the British Empire) in the New Year Honors List and she began 1976 with renewed enthusiasm. Having been reluctant to give interviews, she suddenly started accepting invitations for radio broadcasts, TV appearances, even a concert engagement, and busied herself with teaching and seeing her friends.

She broke her unwritten rule not to speak about her illness and appeared on BBC Television's *Tonight* program, where she expressed only positive thoughts. She had realized it was up to her to make something of her life—there was still a great deal to do and enjoy.

In February she appeared at the Royal Festival Hall to launch "Crack," the young people's movement within the Multiple Sclerosis Society. Sitting in her wheelchair on the stage which had been the scene of so many of her musical triumphs, Jackie gave a performance of a different kind. She delivered a speech to an audience of MS sufferers and journalists, insisting that life can start from a wheelchair and telling the audience about her teaching and her intention to rethink her life.

In June, Jackie took part in a BBC radio documentary about her life entitled *I Really Am a Very Lucky Person*, talking about her career and the end of her playing life.

I'd played whatever I wanted to play, I'd played with the people I'd admired and in that sense there were no stones left unturned. I don't have to look back and say, "Dammit, why did it all happen before I got properly started." I'd already had several years of a very full artistic life. Although I am sad not to be able to play, I do feel that I am ready to start a new career as a teacher.

Danny arranged for Jackie to play the drum in a performance of the *Toy Symphony* by Haydn (now attributed to Leopold Mozart) conducted by Rafael Kubelik, in the Royal Albert Hall, on July 1. The occasion was to celebrate the centenary of her agents, Harold Holt Ltd. She was excited by the prospect, but I thought it was immensely brave of her. To see her sitting in the orchestra banging a drum was shattering, even though she performed with commitment and dignity. It was a very different Jackie from the little girl who broke the drum with her enthusiastic blows all those years ago at the BBC. But she seemed to enjoy it, and certainly loved being on the platform again. It was a terrific boost to be applauded by her adoring audience once more.

Later that summer, Danny was conducting Beethoven's Ninth

Symphony on the steps of St. Paul's Cathedral and Ruth Ann, noticing the advertisement for the concert in the newspaper, decided to go along, hoping she might see Jackie again. The whole area was packed and all the places near the front taken. Way ahead, by the front row, she saw Jackie in her wheelchair. The moment the concert ended, she tried to move toward her, but there was a sudden surge of people, all trying to reach the front. Ruth Ann pushed her way through the scrum, to find Jackie surrounded by friends and fans. The crowd cleared as Danny stepped down to greet Jackie, placing his hands tenderly on her cheeks. At last Ruth Ann was close enough to say hello, but, feeling awkward in the crowd, turned to struggle away. Danny spied her and asked his mother, Aida, to pursue her.

Aida told Ruth Ann they had been experiencing difficulties with agency nurses and that Jackie herself had asked if Ruth Ann would come to look after her.

Ruth Ann didn't know what to say. She had never thought of herself as a home nurse. She had just been offered a good job at the Wellington Hospital and owned her own flat. At thirty-one (the same age as Jackie), she had plans to live in America. Hoping not to insult Aida, she asked for a few days to think about it. Aida telephoned her every other day.

Eventually, Ruth Ann said she was interested but would like to talk about the job in more detail. She had two reservations: the first that she and Jackie had become friends, so it might be awkward to live in her house as a nurse; the second, her faith. Ruth Ann is a devoted Christian and Jackie was a convert to Judaism.

Apart from these anxieties, Ruth Ann was clear about her relationship with Jackie. Jackie should feel free. In a clinical environment, the nurse was in control, but not in the home. Jackie was the mistress of her own house, and had total say in everything to do with her life, except medication. These were Ruth Ann's conditions, and Jackie said, "Fine."

By the time Ruth Ann met Danny a few days later, she was almost sure she wanted the job. She reiterated her worries to Danny and together they organized a practical schedule of hours. Ruth Ann felt she would need two days off a week, not only to refresh herself, but also to give Jackie a break. She saw the job as a huge challenge, feeling sure she could offer Jackie more than nursing skills. But she recognized the possibility that she might not fit into the household, and requested Danny always to be absolutely honest with her. She asked the Wellington Hospital to keep her job open for six months, and moved into Rutland Gardens.

Olga, the housekeeper, continued to cook and look after the day-to-day running of the house. There was a cleaner and, if a car was required, a chauffeured vehicle was hired from Avis.

Ruth Ann knew that being confined to one space encourages introspection in MS sufferers. She wanted Jackie's life to extend outside the home environment as much as possible. The agency nurses had been arranging her daily schedule, and she was underoccupied. Ruth Ann felt it was important for Jackie to take charge. So, on her first day, she sat down and asked Jackie how she wanted to manage her day.

Jackie hesitated for a moment.

"Well, I would like to go to concerts and the theater, but I can't get in because of the chair."

Ruth Ann was delighted and replied positively:

"We'll find a way."

She visited the local theaters to check the best access for the wheelchair. Many didn't have facilities for disabled people, so she found a suitable seat on an aisle, and lifted Jackie from the chair into the seat. She made a careful note of the seat numbers in each theater, so as to know which ones to ask for. Usually the boxes were more convenient, although the chair was sometimes too wide to get through the door. But Ruth Ann quickly discovered that if she unscrewed the outer wheels of the chair, it would usually just squeeze through. This meant she had to remember to carry a screwdriver everywhere. There were other important considerations as well, such as being able to take Jackie out quickly if there was a fire, or if she felt unwell. Ruth Ann was determined Jackie should enjoy life, and live each day to the full.

Ruth Ann moved ahead of Jackie to facilitate her decisions. She hoped that by trying to eliminate problems before Jackie encountered them, Jackie would not be aware that changes had been made to make access easier.

She wanted Jackie to choose what she wore, and where and when she went out. Jackie still loved to go on wild shopping sprees, and Ruth Ann made sure she always had the check book and credit cards with her. She loved seeing her friends, so Ruth Ann arranged for visitors to come frequently.

On her first day off, Ruth Ann stayed in her room, catching up with her correspondence. Suddenly there was a knock on the door. It was the agency nurse, delivering a little note from Jackie. Ruth Ann sent a note back. And so they continued to exchange notes throughout the day. After a while, Ruth Ann went out on her days off enabling them to have a break from each other.

With such a positive new energy of organization in her home life, Jackie seemed to go from strength to strength. During the next five years, she appeared in public, at concerts and the theater. She gave masterclasses, continued to take private pupils, and entertained almost every evening. Honors from various universities were bestowed upon her. She was creating a new niche for herself in the world.

CHAPTER THIRTY-FIVE

Hilary

I was longing to spend sometime alone with Jackie and managed to arrange a visit. The day was miserably cold, so I decided to wear my warmest winter clothes: a pair of thick corduroy trousers, a guernsey sweater, and some sturdy, navy-blue walking shoes, which were particularly broad across the toe, and extremely comfortable.

When I arrived, she was still in bed, waiting for her physiotherapist.

"Jackie, you look wonderful." And she did. Ruth Ann had washed and brushed her hair and told me that Jackie had eaten a good breakfast.

"Not as hearty as you, you old country bumpkin," she replied, looking me up and down. "How do you keep your face so red? Must be all that wholemeal bread?"

We were off, flinging jokes and laughing at their stupidity, when the physiotherapist arrived and quickly set to work. Jackie loved her visits, and found the treatment very comforting, so I left them in peace and went downstairs. Ruth Ann was in good form, bustling about in the kitchen and chatting away. She had made coffee which I consumed gratefully, as she explained the plans for the day. Once the physiotherapy was over, it would be time to go to Jackie's psychiatrist, the Lemon. We would come back to the house for lunch and, in the afternoon, there was to be a special visitor: Margot Fonteyn.

As the physiotherapist left, Ruth Ann went upstairs to wash and dress Jackie. The driver arrived and I could hear the wheelchair being pushed into the lift. At least I would be able to talk to Jackie in the car.

I watched as Jackie was levered into the front seat by Ruth Ann, and the wheelchair folded and put into the boot. I sat in the back with Ruth Ann and couldn't speak to Jackie because she spent the whole car journey talking to the driver about his holiday. On arrival at the consulting rooms, Jackie turned to me.

"Look, Hil, the Lemon won't want to see you because you are family, so Ruth Ann will take me in. I'll see you afterward."

Finally, at lunchtime, we were alone together.

"Guess who came to see me the other day, Hil—Prince Charles, and no one was allowed to know."

"Really! Why?"

"Well, he had never seen my film and asked if I would arrange a viewing for him. So I did. Here!"

The detectives had been to check the house earlier in the day and Prince Charles arrived in the evening.

"He watched the film with tears streaming down his face. I was very touched. I asked him if he remembered me telling him off, when he was a little boy. He laughed and said, 'Yes, I was riding your cello like a horse and you didn't like it!' "

Jackie's face was glowing with excitement.

"You know, Hil, he told me that he used to play the trumpet, but one day he was taken to a concert of mine and when he went home, told his mother that he wanted to play the cello instead. He said he was allowed to make the change, but it didn't take him long to realize that he wouldn't be as good as me! . . .

". . . And I just couldn't call him 'sir,' so I called him Charles," she giggled. "And he said he didn't mind."

There was a bowl of fruit for dessert but as soon as Ruth Ann was out of the room, Jackie whispered: "Hil, see that box of chocolates over there? Quick, let's have some."

"But, Jack, you're not allowed . . ."

"Oh, don't be stuffy. I'm starving and I love them. Quick."

We tucked into the box eagerly. I'm sure Ruth Ann knew what we were doing, but she pretended not to notice. It was time for Jackie's afternoon rest, so Ruth Ann took her upstairs and I waited downstairs. I began to wonder what Margot Fonteyn would be like, how she would be dressed, and what she would talk about. Perhaps she would want to see Jackie alone and I shouldn't be there? But as I didn't want to leave without saying goodbye, I decided to wait until Jackie woke.

About an hour later, just as Jackie re-emerged, there was a knock at the door. I answered it, and greeted Dame Margot whose whole being was effortless, but disciplined. She smiled exquisitely as she floated past me into the hall. She glided straight up to Jackie and embraced her. I suddenly felt immense and hugely out of place in my bulky, country clothing. I tried to emulate Dame Margot's delicacy, but my heavy walking shoes clumped at each step, and her precision made me feel hopelessly uncoordinated. As I followed I inadvertently kicked a chair over and, when I sat down, knocked the low table with my knee. I consoled myself by thinking that at least I couldn't do any more damage while sitting.

"Margot, this is my sister, Hilary." Jackie made a large gesture which meant, Up you get, Hil, and go and shake hands.

I struggled to my feet and tried to step elegantly between the wheelchair, the low table and Dame Margot, who was sitting with her legs in a twirl, her dainty feet neatly pointing, in ballet position.

"Dame Margot, how lovely to meet you." I was trying to be my gracious best, but was glowing with nervous perspiration and over-heating inside my guernsey sweater, while my face was reacting like a belisha beacon. She didn't reply but offered me a cool, limp hand and gave another perfect smile.

Ruth Ann appeared with tea, the tray set with the finest bone china, and a plate of fancy biscuits. It was put on the table next to me and for an awful moment, I thought I would have to be "mother." Fortunately, Ruth Ann must have sensed my apprehension and immediately set about the task of pouring and passing.

The conversation flowed between Jackie and Dame Margot, which was just as well since I felt far too hot and flustered to contribute anything. I watched and listened as she and Jackie chatted. Eventually, Dame Margot left, and it was time for me to leave too.

"Hil, don't go yet," Jackie pleaded.

"Jackie, I must. The children will be waiting for me."

"One evening won't matter. They'll be all right."

"But Jackie, you're going out tonight anyway." I stood up, embraced her and turned toward the door. "Look, Jacks, I'll do some ballet for you before I go, so you can remember me."

With unpointed shoes I skipped and pirouetted around the room, straining to fling my heavy legs into the air above my head. Very quickly I lost my balance and fell over, on to the sofa. We were both hysterical with laughter.

"OK, you fat daughter of a porpoise. You can go. But you'd better come back soon."

On the way home I realized that I hadn't talked to her about anything.

Clare had made such excellent progress with her cello that Anna Shuttleworth, who was teaching her, suggested she should enter for the Suggia Gift. The audition was to take place at the Wigmore Hall and I was to accompany her.

It was a strange feeling walking on to the platform where, sixteen years before, my sister had made her astonishing début. To find myself there with my eleven-year-old daughter playing the cello, was a parallel too close for comfort.

Clare was awarded a prize, and suddenly I found myself facing the same decisions that Mum had faced with Jackie all those years ago. Clare had announced that she wanted to leave school because she needed more time to practice, and I had no hesitation in agreeing. She was extremely disciplined, rising at 5:45 every morning to start practicing. She achieved all her academic work, too, and I had no doubt she should follow her dreams.

One day, the door burst open and in came Aunt Muriel.

"Clare!" she shrieked, in her customary excitement. "You've done so well, Mummy must be so proud of you . . ."

I certainly was.

". . . First you are the second child, like Jackie. Then you had measles, just like Jackie. Then you won the Suggia like Jackie, and now you're not going to school, like Jackie—whatever next!"

There was a horrified silence.

Although she started teaching and giving masterclasses, Jackie loathed them. In public she said she loved teaching, but privately said she was unimpressed by the standard. She complained, saying, "God, they're so hopeless, these people." She could be very scathing. She knew that teaching was a way of performing, but her heart wasn't in it. Sometimes, when other cellists were mentioned, she dismissed them by blowing a loud raspberry.

She loved listening to her own recordings but wasn't interested in anyone else's. It was almost impossible to persuade her to listen to new music. She needed to have a personal connection and, if she didn't, she simply couldn't concentrate on it. Listening to her recordings was her way of reliving the most important aspect of her life and was a powerful reminder of her own value.

Gran was becoming increasingly concerned about her future and didn't want to be a burden to Kiffer and me. For someone who had devoted her whole life to the family, in the broadest sense of the word, it was an extraordinary concern. One day she announced her surprise decision to enter an old people's home and, through her doctor, found Ticehurst, near Aldershot. When a vacancy materialized in June 1977, she moved immediately. I visited her at least once a fortnight and she came back to Church Farm for high days and holidays.

In the summer, Piers and Lin moved to Upper Bucklebury, a few miles away from Mum and Dad. Orchard Gate was a more spacious house than Bourne End and was surrounded by two and a half acres of land.

Jackie had a busy summer, giving masterclasses, teaching and occasionally trying to play the cello, for which she had to be lifted out of her wheelchair into a high-backed armchair. Bill Pleeth visited her and they played together. Even though she could make only a weak sound, she still needed to play: regular physiotherapy had helped to strengthen her wasted muscles. Her legs, however, were almost completely paralyzed. On good days, she could totter around the bedroom with the help of a walking frame.

In December, Jackie and Ruth Ann went to stay in Curridge with Mum and Dad for four days. It was an upheaval making the house comfortable and practical for Jackie. Mum and Dad created a bedroom downstairs in the dining room. We gathered several times during her visit. Jackie was in fine form, and Mum loved having us all together again.

Dad, though, was withdrawn. As we were washing up, I

mentioned this to Mum who was also concerned, and had noticed that his handwriting was smaller and uneven. I laughed.

"But, Mum, his handwriting has often been impossible to read!"

"Yes, I know. But it's more than that. His hand freezes when he writes and I know it troubles him. And he keeps stumbling."

"Have you spoken to the doctor about it?"

"No. I wasn't sure if I should . . . it's probably just old age. He is nearly seventy, you know."

Danny would sometimes fly to London specifically to take Jackie out for dinner at one of her favorite restaurants—Mr. Chow's, Ceccioni's, or the Westbury, often arriving bearing flowers. Jackie recognized that he gave her the security she so desperately needed, while, inevitably, her home was becoming a prison.

Early one morning I arrived at Rutland Gardens Mews. Ruth Ann had prepared breakfast and Jackie and I ate it in her comfortable bedroom. I did not realize Danny was at home. After breakfast, I carried the tray downstairs and was bounding back up to Jackie's room when, to my utter surprise, I met Danny on the stairs.

"Danny!" I gasped, with genuine astonishment. "What are you doing here?"

He looked disbelievingly at me and walked past without saying anything. Whether it was a surprise shock to see me, or the unfortunate words I uttered, I don't know, but I didn't see him again that day.

In July 1978 I discovered a lump on my thyroid and was told it needed to be removed. I wanted to tell Mum and Dad at once but on my arrival found them sitting at their kitchen table in a state of shock. Before I could say anything, Dad announced he had Parkinson's Disease. They had just returned from their doctor. Dad was frightened and his reaction was to cling to Mum even more.

Jackie had been brave and staunch over Dad's jaundice, but now, in stark contrast, showed no interest in his plight. She was terrified that something might happen to Mum or Dad so, for her own security, dismissed his illness.

★ ★ ★

Jackie's need to find a new means of communicating and expressing her inner world led to a fascination for words and she started to read the dictionary. This desire was fueled by her teaching which, as she could no longer demonstrate on the cello, demanded that she should express herself in words.

As Jackie had always adored performing, and loved having an audience, Danny arranged for her to narrate Prokofiev's *Peter and the Wolf*, which seemed an ideal opportunity for reappearing on the stage. The concert was to launch the new Jacqueline du Pré Research Fund, which she had set up with Danny's support after the press reported that most of the funds raised for the Multiple Sclerosis Society were spent on administration. Danny, Itzhak Perlman, Pinchas Zukerman and Clifford Curzon agreed to donate to the fund their fees for four concerts a year. The date for *Peter and the Wolf* was fixed for August 15, 1978, at the Piccadilly Hotel, and Jackie eagerly set about learning the script.

I was at the performance. Jackie was excited about it: she needed a platform and here was a chance for her to perform again. But I found it all desperately sad. It was awful seeing this giant of an artist being manhandled on to the platform in her wheelchair. I wondered if there was any point in putting her through this indignity. But she spoke beautifully, making the story more vivid than I had ever heard it before. In the past, that kind of intensity from Jackie would have been accompanied by her familiar movements—swaying body, flying hair—but now all she could do was to wobble her head. She couldn't bow and sweep off the platform in her own inimitable, energetic way. Instead, she sat and waited until her handlers lifted her awkwardly down.

Twice, I looked after Jackie while Ruth Ann had a short break. I had been given careful instructions and Ruth Ann had taught me how to lift her, which was quite a skill. Jackie needed to have everything done for her.

As a novice nurse, I felt anxious for Jackie's comfort, but Ruth Ann had trained me well and Jackie was in giggly form. My efforts to emulate Ruth Ann's efficiency, and my general fumblings, created great mirth. At last, I was able to do something useful for Jackie.

CHAPTER THIRTY-SIX

Piers

On April 2, 1979, our second son, Diccon, was born. Amidst all the excitement of the new baby, two events occurred to cause us both sadness. The first was when we took Diccon to London to show him to Jackie. Although she made the usual comments, it was clear she wasn't at all interested, and if there was so much as a squeak from him it seemed to be an unbearable irritation to her. The visit was short and seemed oddly formal.

The second was when Mum and Dad came to Orchard Gate in June. Both Lin and I were surprised to see how much Dad's Parkinson's had progressed. In the house he quickly became disoriented and clung closely to Mum. It was a shock to see him so enfeebled and to realize that, outside the familiar environment of his own home, he was no longer able to adjust to his surroundings. Mum looked tired. We had been watching Jackie deteriorate, and now we were witnessing the same with Dad.

Jackie was giving a series of four televised masterclasses at the Guildhall School of Music in London. Although she had given several before, this was the first time on television. Not only were they reported as a remarkable demonstration of her musical genius, but her determination in the face of MS was much admired. Confined to her wheelchair, unable to play, and with MS occasionally affecting her speech, she was beginning to struggle to form words. When asked how she managed to cope without demonstrating on the cello, she replied that if she had been able to play, the students would simply have copied her without forming their own interpretation. Instead she had to unravel the music with words and watch the students unfold their own musical revelation.

. . . the poor pupil comes along and his morale can be shattered as his playing is matched against the master. I hate it when they do that. I think it can actually do harm to the person. I didn't find masterclasses a great help when I was a student.

Jackie never showed her impatience to the students, but instead was always gentle and sympathetic, often waiting for them to stop playing rather than interrupting. The audience loved the classes, feeling as though they were eavesdropping on hidden secrets of great performance. Jackie's ability to open doors in the musical imagination gave her pupils a feeling of true performance, a sense that they were colluding in how best to make the music speak to the audience.

Jackie was horrified when she saw the BBC TV programs replayed. She thought she looked fat. "Those damn steroids," she said, and told me to stop the video.

Our visits to Jackie as a family were to cease. The children obviously caused her distress, which in turn caused Lin distress. Now I went on my own. By the end of the year her speech was becoming slurred and the effort of speaking was very tiring for her, making sustained conversation difficult, so I tended to do most of the talking. Yet she hadn't lost her sense of humor and always wanted to hear rude jokes, the more risqué the better, and as many flying anecdotes as I could remember. But among these stories and our laughter, she was beginning to interject vicious remarks about other people, typically cutting comments about Ruth Ann, "Miss Chastity," as she now called her. She also began to target Dad. I hated this, didn't understand it, and couldn't stop her.

I began to feel deeply sad, realizing that her personality was changing. As the disease progressed, she was becoming belligerent, especially about the family and those closest to her. I found that visitors to the house were often fed stories of how her family had deserted her, and how Ruth Ann was cruel to her. So totally unfounded and untrue—but many seemed to choose to believe her. So far her vituperative remarks had not been directed at me. I also began to notice that her short-term memory was failing. She would often forget that various members of the family had visited her, complaining that no one came to see her anymore.

The Jackie I knew was gradually slipping away, being replaced by someone of opposite qualities.

My visits to Jackie usually included one of our favorite pastimes, going out for a "push." On one particular day after we had been for a long "push" through Hyde Park, Jackie suddenly decided she had nothing to wear. We set off for "Harabs of Saudi Kensington," as she called her local corner shop. Before crossing the Brompton Road, we passed a shop which had bright dresses in the window.

"Let's go in here," said Jackie.

I changed direction. Once inside I realized that it was a designer clothes shop, with rows and rows of extremely expensive outfits.

"How may I help you, Sir? Madam?" asked the petite and pretty assistant.

"Can we just look around, please?"

"Certainly."

I wheeled Jackie over to the first rail and she started examining the colorful dresses. The assistant was hovering.

"Look and see what size this is, Bar," she said. I looked, and then took the dress from the rail and handed it to her.

"See who the designer is, Jacks!"

She looked and after a few moments was able to read the name. When she did, she burst out laughing.

"Is anything wrong, Madam?" asked the assistant, looking worried.

We quickly excused ourselves and made a speedy exit. As soon as we were out in the street, Jackie could contain herself no longer. She let out a hearty guffaw and we both collapsed with giggles.

The designer was EMESSE.

In the summer, Lin and I invited two close friends, John and Gill Sandeman, to stay for the weekend. When they arrived, something was seriously different—they were carrying Bibles. During lunch, they went on and on about their new-found faith as Christians.

Over breakfast on Sunday, John suddenly asked:

"Piers, why don't you and Lin come to our fellowship meeting this morning?"

"No, John, I must get on with the house." I was not going to be drawn into this.

After breakfast John asked me again and I refused once more. Then, as they were packing the car he asked me a third time. To my astonishment, I found myself saying "OK."

Lin looked at me in disbelief as I went to change.

An hour later, we arrived at a modern single-story council building in Marlow and I immediately began to feel out of place. I had dressed in my Sunday best as if for church—everyone else was casually dressed. Church was always a beautiful building. This certainly wasn't. Inside No. 1 Meeting Room, everything felt wrong. There were no hymn books or prayer books, only printed sheets with songs. The Pastor stood up and began the service. The Worship Leader picked up his guitar, played a few chords and everyone started singing. I tried to follow the tune, but didn't manage very well. When it finished I sat down just as everyone else began singing it again. The reading was about the sower and the seed which fell on stony ground. I felt as if it was directed at me. After the sermon and more singing, the service ended. This was my cue. I was off.

But you can never escape unnoticed. Bob Woollard, the pastor of the fellowship was by the door and introduced himself. When I told him who I was he said, "Oh yes, we've been praying for you for months."

My pride rose within me. How dare anyone even think I needed prayer?

"How nice of you. Thank you," I replied through gritted teeth. After a few more moments of conversation he just looked at me and said, "Why don't we pray together, right now?"

And then it happened. I burst into tears. A chair was found for me but I couldn't stop crying. A number of people were saying "Hallelujah" and "Praise the Lord." Bob asked if I would like to give my life to Jesus. I said, "Yes."

That night, on the way home in the car, I suddenly realized I was praying out loud, something I had never done before. The moment I returned to Birch House, I found Mum's Bible. I began reading the New Testament. I couldn't put it down. For the first time I could clearly understand what I was reading. What I

previously knew as a religion was fast becoming a vibrant relationship with God through His Son, Jesus. I hardly slept that night.

A few days later Mum and Dad returned from France and I
couldn't wait to share my excitement with them. I knew the best
time would be once they had a cup of tea in their hands. The moment they were in the kitchen I said:

"I've got something to tell you."

"I know you have," said Mum. "It's been obvious ever since I
first saw you. Your face is all lit up. Tell me, monkey doodles."

I told the full, unexpurgated version.

". . . And I can tell you exactly when it happened! August 17 at
1:10 p.m!"

Mum had caught the excitement. "I've prayed so much for you,
you old scallywag," she said.

Dad was not quite so certain, but after a look from Mum,
agreed it was good.

Mum and I spent many wonderful hours reading and exploring
the Scriptures together. I had never been able to take part in
Mum's music, but now at last we had something which we could
share and feel passionate about together.

Hilary

It was through Jackie's friendship with the cellist Moray Welsh that
she was invited to take part in a series entitled *With Great Pleasure*
for BBC radio. The idea was to invite a well-known personality to
choose their favorite poetry and prose. Penelope Lee, an actress
friend of Moray's, ran the Upottery Festival in Devon, and it was
decided Jackie should present her selection of poetry at the festival, and the BBC would record it.

It was sometimes difficult for Jackie's friends to find anything to
talk about. They would eat dinner and listen to her recordings.
Sometimes she played a recording over and over again, making it
unbearable. So, when Jackie expressed an interest in poetry, Moray
was delighted that she had found something new to occupy her
imagination. However, she knew only the poems she remembered
from our childhood.

Moray arranged for Penelope and other acting friends to visit
her in the evenings to read poetry to her. She put her favorite po-

ems on one side, and read them over and over again until she knew them by heart. The idea of being in front of an audience and making people laugh was so much a part of her psyche that she responded excitedly to Moray's plan. Sometimes she giggled so much when reading the poems, she collapsed and had to stop. She practiced her reading on everyone who visited her.

She telephoned me regularly to recite the poems over the phone: "Hil—what do you think of this one . . . ?"

> "Thank you for the flowers you sent," she said
> And sweetly smiled and coyly turned her head.
> "I'm sorry for the things I said last night.
> I was wrong and you were right.
> Please forgive me?"
> So I forgave her
> And as we wandered through the moonlit hours
> I thought
> "What bloody flowers?"

We both roared with laughter.
"Isn't it brilliant?"
"Where did you find that one, Jacks?"
"I don't know. It's by someone called Anon!"

The trip to Devon in August was planned down to the last detail: how she would travel, where she would stay, access for the wheelchair, her food. It took the best part of a year to make all the arrangements for this one recording. There was no doubt it was a risk for her to make the journey: the disease was now attacking her brain stem and affecting her speech, which was beginning to slur. The journey would obviously tire her, and the recording might be stressful and embarrassing if her speech failed or if she became unwell during the performance. But she had been looking forward to it eagerly. The disappointment of canceling it after so long would have been equally destructive.

The event was a huge success. She read the poems beautifully, as though she were playing her cello. The English language had now become her music, although, as she said, a very poor substitute. She told little anecdotes about her life, and made fun of her disability, dissolving into giggles when she couldn't pronounce some of the words. Her audience was enchanted.

Piers

On September 1, I went to London again to have supper with Jackie on my own. I had been bursting to tell her everything but thought I would wait until we were face to face.

"Guess what!" I said.

"What?"

"No, guess what's happened."

"You're having another baby?"

"Nope!"

". . . You've bought your own plane?"

"If only, if only . . ."

"I can't guess. Come on, Bar, tell me. It's obviously something wonderful."

"It *is* wonderful. I'm a Christian! . . ."

Jackie smiled, but didn't say anything.

". . . I'm a Christian, Jacks. I've given my life to the Lord and it's the best thing that's ever happened to me. It's the best thing that could ever happen to anyone."

"Bar. What can I say? That's wonderful . . ."

"Thanks, Jack."

We hugged each other.

". . . Tell me what happened . . ."

I explained how life had now totally changed for Lin and me. Jackie became excited for me, and asked questions about the Bible. Amazingly, I was able to answer almost everything.

Much later we talked about Mum and the Hermitage Organ Fund that I had become involved in too, and I asked Jackie if she would be the Patron. I needed someone important as a figurehead.

"Of course I will—but why don't you ask the Duchess of Kent as well?"

"Do you think she would do it?"

"Yes, I'm sure she would. You should write to her."

By October, Orchard Gate was finished and we moved into our splendid new home. Following the loss of British Telecom's monopoly, I had decided to establish my own telecommunications business, and I set up my office in the dining room. Once we had settled in, I quickly arranged the letterhead, visiting cards and invoice forms for the new company. I placed an advertisement in the *Newbury Weekly News*, and employed a secretary. I was ready to make my fortune.

By 4:30 p.m. two days later I had made my first sale, and had the check in my hand. As I drove home it dawned on me that business was a game plan, so different from flying, where one's skills are focused on conquering the elements.

Being in the training section of BA (by now BOAC and BEA had merged and was called British Airways), I could regulate how much or how little I flew. Every day seemed to be consumed by commitments. It was impossible to go to London more than once a month to see Jackie, which made me feel horribly guilty. Mum and Dad continued to visit her every Friday.

On November 23, the Hermitage Organ Fund was announced publicly, with the Duchess of Kent and Jackie as joint Patrons.

Two weeks later, though, we were all plunged into utter sadness. Gran died. The person who had been the prop for the whole family in countless situations had gone.

CHAPTER THIRTY-SEVEN

Hilary

As Jackie became more incapacitated she took an even greater delight in shocking people. Many a male visitor would be alarmed by the greeting, "Fuck me." Some were able to deal with it and turn it into a joke, while others were frightened away. Maybe it was Jackie's way of saying she was still a woman and had not lost her sexuality. We were watching the toll MS was taking on Jackie's personality. The fun-loving girl who had so enjoyed risqué jokes was now becoming coarse. Her anger was vicious and terrifying. She seemed to want to wound others. This was not the Jackie we had always known. She felt frustrated and trapped. The worst thing about being in a wheelchair, she told me, was that she could never escape any situation.

The phone rang one day and I answered. It was Jackie. She wanted to speak to Kiffer.

"He's outside, gardening, Jack. Shall I call him?"

"Well, please tell him to come to London now because I need him to make love to me."

I was stupefied.

"Jackie, I can't tell him to do that. You must speak to him."

"Go and get him, then, so that I can ask him myself."

With a pounding heart, I ran outside and called Kiffer to the phone.

"It's Jackie. She needs to speak to you."

Kiffer listened to Jackie for a while without responding. After a long silence, he replied:

"Jackie, we can't go back in time. It wouldn't work. I'm sorry, but no."

She slammed the phone down.

I was shaking.

"Kiffer," I whispered. "I think that's the first time anyone in the family has ever said 'no' to her."

Jackie never spoke to Kiffer again.

By 1982 Jackie's health was deteriorating quickly. Swallowing was becoming difficult, and as her speech was increasingly hard to understand, only her most faithful and resilient friends visited her regularly, but Ruth Ann made sure her diary was always full. Jackie continued to teach a few long-standing pupils, but was naturally increasingly frustrated by her limitations.

Theresa, now living in London, visited Jackie occasionally on her own, but disliked it because of the constant criticism. Mum and Dad continued their weekly visits, but Dad's concern for his symptoms infuriated Jackie. She still had no sympathy for him. Jackie was in a far worse condition, and Dad appeared to have no sympathy for her either.

Dad's dependence on Mum intensely annoyed Jackie and she seized every opportunity to crush him. Her poisoned darts caused not only Dad to crumple, but Mum too. Neither of them could cope with Jackie's bitter anger, nor did they have it in them to protect themselves from her verbal onslaughts. Yet again, Mum was the worm between two blackbirds, both seeking her exclusive attention. Mum's sense of guilt was exacerbated by her powerlessness to help and comfort, so the visits to Jackie became weekly torments. She couldn't bear seeing Dad being smashed and felt helpless in the face of the emotional battering. It was slowly destroying her.

Fortunately, Dad's interest in geology came to his rescue. Lalla arranged for him to spend one day a week in the Geological Museum in London, working alongside the staff. For him, it was an escape from Jackie. For Mum, it was a relief she didn't have to deflect the blows aimed at Dad. Her times alone with Jackie were a sad and lonely strain. After a day in London, she returned an exhausted wreck. Jackie's tragedy and her cruel rage were too much for Mum to bear. I tried to persuade her to reduce the frequency of her visits, but she would not.

I could not confront Jackie either, and became increasingly

frightened when she turned on me. I always returned home feeling completely drained. She attacked my musicality and made my
lack of success a target, but what really hurt me was the abuse she
hurled at our family. Having to listen to her damning and incessant
criticisms was driving me away.

I could understand so well what Mum was going through.
Jackie attacked me from the side, but Mum received the vicious
blows head-on. Anyone who had been close to Jackie became the
victim of her verbal barrages. Just as once she had been violently
bitter about Danny, now she was vile about her family.

Piers

In the autumn of 1981 I had been declared unfit for flying duties
due to a sinus infection. Two months later, I was told the Boe-
ing 707 fleet was being reduced and I was to be stood down from
active flying on full pay until such time as the aviation industry
picked up. On the one hand I was upset since I loved flying, but
on the other, it meant I would have more time for my business.
This was the state of affairs until the winter of 1982 when I was
asked to attend a meeting with British Airways personnel, after
which we began negotiating the details of my severance.

Hilary

By 1983, Jackie was able to do very little for herself, and the house
in Rutland Gardens had become awkward for her. Ruth Ann
was concerned that being marooned in her bedroom upstairs
would make her feel even more isolated. Ruth Ann suggested
to Danny that a flat on one level would be more practical. Olga
had left and was replaced by a vivacious French girl, Anne-Marie
Morin. Jackie was fond of Anne-Marie and enjoyed speaking
French with her.

Danny heard that the flats at 36-38 Chepstow Villas, Notting
Hill, were in the process of being rebuilt and final specifications
could still be made allowing the architect to incorporate any special requirements. He wanted to surprise Jackie with the keys to
the flat, but Ruth Ann, forever practical, felt that Jackie should be
involved from the beginning, making her own choices about the

décor and furnishings. One flat would have been too small, so Danny bought two adjoining ones, linked by an archway.

He continued to meet all Jackie's needs: a special telephone line had been installed in his Paris home which was reserved solely for Jackie. But his visits became less frequent. Jackie kept up her sessions with the Lemon but, as she became bed-bound, he visited her in the flat. More and more, her physical disabilities were controlling her life.

Piers

In September, Lin and I went to visit Jackie in her new home. We dropped off our children with Hilary just after lunch, arriving at Jackie's in the late afternoon.

Lin, who was in the early days of pregnancy with our third child, was feeling tired and retired for a rest. I had made myself a cup of coffee and returned to be with Jackie, but when I sat down she asked quietly:

"What's a bigot?"

"Sounds like a big version of a spigot," I said.

"What's a bigot?" she repeated, as though she hadn't heard my reply, and the tone of her voice hardened. "You're a bigot, so what's a bigot?"

I felt the words lance into me deeply. I had seen this type of venom before, but it had always been pointed at others, often those who considered themselves Jackie's closest friends. Everything within me began to retreat. I couldn't believe it. It just couldn't be Jackie speaking.

My mind was racing. This was the first time she had leveled anger toward me. It was also the first time I had heard her use this word. As I tried to think of something diversionary, the silence became ghastly.

"What's a *bigot*?" she persisted, her words slurring horribly. "Of course, if you don't know, why not ask Miss Purity—Miss Chastity? She's a *bigot* as well."

Lin came into the room. Jackie changed the conversation immediately and, with a broad smile and lifted voice, asked Lin if she had managed to rest.

I was stunned. For the first time ever, Jackie had thrown an Exocet missile at me. For the first time, she was trying to hurt me. Always, always, we had been close, and able to share anything and everything.

The next time I went for lunch, she did it again. She made her voice sound mean, as though she knew what she was doing and really wanted to hit home. I tried changing the subject. She wouldn't let me. I tried telling her about the business but she didn't listen. I tried asking her about her music, but she didn't want to know. All she wanted was to drive the point home. *Bigot.*

I felt as though all the special things I had ever told her were being thrown back at me. Whenever others came in the room, her countenance would change. As soon as they left, she would turn on me again. I tried so hard to regain that special family connection, but it was not to be.

I didn't see Jackie during the winter.

In October I had moved the company into proper business premises at the Eight Bells in Newbury, an old disused pub. I was suddenly busier than ever and, still smarting from Jackie's vicious attacks, I was glad of an excuse not to have to see her.

After a long period of no contact between us, she telephoned me. She was finding it very hard to speak.

"Why don't you come and see me anymore?" she asked, in a terribly labored and stammering way.

She sounded genuine and upset.

Lin and I went up to London the following week. It was now March 1984 and Lin was a month away from giving birth. Once again, she retired to another room to rest. The moment she had gone, Jackie began the same attack again. I couldn't stop her. I tried appealing to her, but all she would say was "bigot," over and over again.

She seemed to be making sure that the barrier between us was securely in place.

On April 10, our third son, Adam, was born. I was utterly miserable about Jackie and couldn't bring myself to take him to see her. I knew she wouldn't be interested and I didn't want to see her. I felt betrayed.

CHAPTER THIRTY-EIGHT

Hilary

In the summer of 1984, Clare, who had been studying the cello at the Royal College of Music for two terms, announced that she couldn't play the cello anymore because of a problem with her back. As the months went by, even though the back problem improved, she had no inclination to play. Kiffer's cello, which she had used for some years, was left in the corner of the music room and she decided, instead, to go to university.

Mum had been suffering from indigestion and general malaise for some time and when she was unwell, both she and Dad had stayed with us at Ashmansworth for a while. Then, in February 1985, I received a phone call from Dad, who asked me to go to Curridge immediately. Mum was in bed again and Dad was in a panic. When he was out of earshot, Mum told me that she had what appeared to be menstrual bleeding. I called the doctor, who advised them to go to Ashmansworth with me. A few days later, I took Mum to a gynecologist who advised a D and C: a routine operation to clean the womb.

On our arrival at the hospital, we found she had been allocated a private room, but Dad became increasingly disturbed, and she asked me to take him away. His body had become rigid.

"Come on, Dad. Why don't we have a cup of tea while the nurses are making Mum comfy?"

Reluctantly he took my hand and I guided him out of the room. Since he could now only shuffle, and stumbled frequently, it took us a while to negotiate the long corridor to the canteen. I found a chair and settled him down. He was broken, the embodiment of sadness, sitting awkwardly in his seat. A mug of warm, sweet tea revived him slightly.

"Hil . . . this is it, isn't it? It's the end. I know it's the end."

When we returned to say goodbye to Mum, she was in a hospital gown, sitting up in bed, supported by several large white pillows.

Piers

The April date set for Mum's operation happened to coincide with our monthly company review. In the middle of one particularly sensitive discussion, the telephone rang. Annoyed, I stood up, walked over to the, wall phone and picked up the receiver.

"Yes?" I asked impatiently.

It was Hil.

"Piers . . ."

There was silence.

"Yes?" I said, with a sudden feeling of dread settling deep in my stomach.

"Mum's got cancer."

"Go on."

"The surgeon has just telephoned. He can't find anything in her womb. He's found secondaries and wants to find the primary."

"What did you say to him?"

"I said he could, provided he phones to tell me exactly what he finds."

Hil was choked with tears, and could hardly speak.

I put the phone down and left for Church Farm immediately.

When I arrived, Hilary was in the doorway. I tried to be brave as I climbed out of the car, but when I looked at her we both burst into tears and fell into each other's arms. Dad was distraught. He kept saying he had known all along, and seemed to swing between desperation, bewilderment and anger.

The three of us set off for the Royal Berkshire Hospital in Reading, where we found Mum asleep, looking pale and sunken. Dad talked to her, desperate for a response, but she didn't stir. He stroked her head and murmured to her. I was glad she didn't open her eyes. She would have guessed immediately what was going on.

When the surgeon was ready to see us, I found myself interrogating him with question after question. By the time he had finished explaining, it was clear that there was no hope. It really was terminal. Mum would die.

Hilary

When I telephoned Jackie to tell her the awful news, she did not respond at all. I called back later and spoke to Ruth Ann. She promised to tell Jackie, again, as gently as possible.

I decided that Mum and Dad should continue to live with us at Church Farm. They both needed a great deal of nursing and I wanted to do it for them. We arranged for all the animals to go, and as the last three cows were loaded into the lorry, I calculated that their absence alone would give me at least four extra hours a day. I never found those spare hours.

A few weeks later, Mum was admitted to Newbury Hospital for a blood transfusion and Ruth Ann arranged to bring Jackie to see her. The news of Jackie's intended visit cheered Mum and she could talk of nothing else. It was early September 1985 and Jackie was having difficulty holding her head up and forming words. The disease was now affecting the control of her neck muscles.

Piers and I were already with Mum and Dad when we heard Ruth Ann talking to Jackie as they came along the corridor. We rushed out to greet her, and although it was the first time she had seen Piers since the "bigot" episodes, she was very warm to him, as though nothing had happened. The three of us, Jackie, Piers and myself, made our entrance to the ward. Mum's bed was by the big doors and there were our gray but smiling parents, delighted to see the three of us together again. Mum held out her arms.

"Jackables, Hullaballoo, Barzidoozers!" she called.

We pushed Jackie in her wheelchair as close to Mum as we possibly could on one side, and Dad, who was in his wheelchair too, stayed as close as he could on the other. Jackie could hardly speak and Dad could only whisper. There was little conversation. Piers and I, choked with emotion, sat helplessly watching these three fatally ill people, Jackie, Mum and Dad. They all needed one another so desperately, yet were completely unable to give any help or comfort.

Ruth Ann tried to induce a feeling of merriment and produced a camera. Piers and I squashed between the wheelchairs and the drip paraphernalia.

"OK! Are you all ready? Smile!"

We all smiled and the shutter clicked.

It was the final family photograph and the last time we were all together.

Piers

A few days later, Hilary called me during the night. Without hesitation, I dressed and drove over. Beryl Radcliffe, a dear Christian friend of ours from Marlow, was there. She was a nurse and loved Mum. She gave me a big hug, and told me the time was near.

Dad's bed was next to Mum's. He was holding her hand and looking into her eyes. I held her other hand. It was cold and felt awful but I didn't want to let go. Eventually her breathing began to catch in the back of her throat. I prayed quietly, "Oh, please, dear Father God, let her die in peace." Every breath seemed to be her last, but then there would be a pause before she suddenly took another. The only other sound within the room was the occasional buzz of the wretched morphine machine.

Dad started to talk to her, begging her not to leave. He wanted her to go back to La Coupe with him to hear the seagulls.

Mum died shortly after dawn on September 27, 1985.

Hilary ran into the garden and picked some sweet-peas and laid them on Mum's chest. After a long time, I let go of her hand, said goodbye and went out to the kitchen. Beryl was there and gave me another hug.

"There goes the only person who really knew me," I said.

Hilary

When I rang Jackie to tell her Mum had died, she shrieked. She couldn't believe me and wailed repeatedly. Eventually, Ruth Ann took the receiver from her.

It was several days before Jackie was able to accept Mum's death as a reality. Dad was profoundly distressed and dazed, needing a great deal of support. I had to summon huge resources of strength to survive the next few days.

The funeral was a week later, on Friday, October 4. Mum had wanted the service to take place at Gold Hill Baptist Church, and to be buried in the cemetery above Chalfont St. Peter. I didn't want it to be just an ordinary funeral service, but a glowing testimonial celebrating her life, her achievements and the unconditional love she gave to so many. We arranged for her beloved piano to be taken to the church. Rory Kindlon, a pupil of Mum's, to whom she had bequeathed her Blüthner grand piano, had agreed to give a short recital. Piers and I decided to speak about Mum, Piers about her Christianity, and me about her as a mother, and her music.

On the day itself, the weather was glorious and I was completely absorbed in the spin of the event. I ran into the church. No one was there except for Mum in her simple coffin. I stayed with her, offering silent love, heartfelt thanks and cherished memories, my eyes swollen with tears. I had wanted Mum to have a wonderful day and hoped that everyone would be able to enjoy her again. For months I had been with her, almost one hundred percent of the time, but now she was completely alone.

Eventually I went outside where there was a bustle of activity. Jackie was there with Ruth Ann, and others were arriving in droves. They all seemed to come up to me, even complete strangers, to say how much they loved Mum.

During the service, the family sat together: Dad, Jackie, myself and Piers. None of us could sing the hymns. I couldn't even make a sound; I opened my mouth, but nothing came out. Then it was time for Piers and me to give our appreciations. Piers spoke first, clearly and eloquently, and I marveled at how well he held himself together. I was trying to control myself but could think only of the lonely image of Mum in her coffin. Eventually this thought completely overwhelmed me.

I could see Dad and Jackie sitting close together, yet so far apart.

I was unable to speak, and broke down sobbing in front of everyone. Piers put his arm round me and whispered, "You can do it." Gradually, and feebly, I said my words, speaking of Mum's warmth and strength, her dedication to her children, the love she had for her pupils and her teaching, and her capacity to bring out the best in everyone. I ended by saying there could be no greater tribute than for Rory to play on the piano Mum had left to him.

How he managed to do it in those emotional circumstances, I don't know. But he did.

The pallbearers lifted Mum into the hearse and slowly we drove through Chalfont St. Peter, up the hill to the cemetery. The grave was at the far end, overlooking autumnal woods, along a path lined with hundreds of bouquets. Mum was lowered gently into her tomb.

She never saw her eighth grandchild, Piers and Lin's son Toby, who was born five weeks later.

Neither Jackie nor Dad could believe or accept Mum's death. They both needed her exclusively for their own survival. The tower and force which had built and supported them was no more, and the person they had spent their lives fighting and tussling over had gone.

Before Mum died, she had arranged for Dad to live at Rock House, a Christian home attached to Gold Hill Baptist church. Although he needed full-time nursing, even at night, he stayed with us until Christmas before moving into his new home. It was an agonizing time. He didn't want to go, yet I knew I simply couldn't look after him on a long-term basis. I had to have more time for Kiffer and the children and my teaching.

We all visited Dad regularly, took him on outings and to visit Jackie. He came to Ashmansworth whenever he wanted, and stayed with us at Christmas. But he never recovered from Mum's death and lost all will to live. It was not long before he was calling me "Mubs," his pet name for Mum.

After Mum died, Jackie slid downhill very quickly: she could no longer feed herself or drink from a cup unaided. It was impossible to have a conversation with her as she couldn't organize her tongue. But she could still hear perfectly, even though she couldn't reply. Her head was permanently bouncing up and down and her arms flailing.

In early 1987, Piers and I went to visit Jackie together. She was in her wheelchair and ready for us. Talking was almost impossible for her now and her eyes were wide open with the strain of trying to see. Her faithful driver, Doug, was there, and together we thought it would be good fun to go on a jaunt. What was even more fun was the suggestion that we three should go alone.

It was quite a palaver getting out of the flat, but by the time we were on the pavement, Doug had the car ready. He helped us hoist the chair into the car and handed the keys to Piers.

It was an extraordinary feeling. We were on our own, no one else around and no one to interfere, and we could go anywhere we wanted. We felt like schoolchildren playing truant. We giggled and flung jokes back and forth. Jackie tried so hard to talk, but could only join in the laughter. It was the first time in years that we had felt so free together. We had escaped.

As the months went by, visits became more and more difficult. I used to dread the first moment of seeing her, because each time she was so much worse. Ruth Ann always greeted me with a warm smile and her distinctive "Hello," emphasizing the end of the word, making it so welcoming. On one occasion I found Jackie slumped in her wheelchair looking utterly miserable, her head dipping and bouncing. She tried to say "Hello, Hil," but her tongue wouldn't function properly, and only a croaky gurgle came out. I put my arm round her head and held it close to me.

"Hello, Jack."

She tried to put her right arm round me, but it just waved in mid-air. I caught it and held it across my shoulder. A huge lump had formed in my throat and I couldn't speak either. So we both remained there, silently clinging.

Ruth Ann came in with a cup of coffee for me and some juice for Jackie. She held Jackie's head and guided a long, angled straw into her mouth, while Jackie tried to suck and gulp. Ruth Ann chatted away merrily, giving me all Jackie's news. I wondered how on earth she managed to keep her spirits so buoyant when she was surrounded day and night by such hopelessness.

Jackie blew an unmistakable raspberry and my heart leapt a beat. The old Jackie was still there somewhere. As Ruth Ann went out to the kitchen to prepare lunch, her exit was followed by another loud snort from Jackie.

"Jacks, how is Danny?" I said, trying to deflect her scornful attack on Ruth Ann by changing the subject.

Another raspberry.

"The children send you their love. Clare is loving Bristol." I chatted about the family.

More snorts.

"Have you seen the Lemon recently?"

I could just make out the word "No."

"And who has been to see you?"

She gurgled, "No one."

Lunch was ready and it was time to wheel Jackie to the table, which had been beautifully laid for two. It was a relief to have something to do. Ruth Ann cut Jackie's lunch into tiny pieces and left us.

She had prepared a special liver dish which we both loved, but every time I tried to put food into Jackie's mouth, her head movements became more violent, making it impossible to position the spoon in her mouth. So, I stood beside her, held her head firmly against my body with my left hand, and slipped a spoonful of food into her mouth with my right. Because she couldn't control her tongue, chewing was difficult, so each mouthful was a huge effort, followed by a gulp of water through the straw. She looked frightened, but was hungry, so we had to go through the process over and over again. She was becoming exhausted and, because it took so long, the remains of her meal had become cold. Eventually she had no more energy for eating.

Ruth Ann returned, cleared the table and put on Jackie's recording of the Schumann Concerto. We sat in silence and listened. I could not believe that the person I had just been attempting to feed, who was now shaking uncontrollably beside me, was the same person who had created these heavenly sounds.

It was not too long before it was time for Jackie to have her afternoon rest. We embraced each other again, and she was wheeled away. I left the flat, walked down the stairs and wandered into the street. The last few bars of the Schumann Concerto were still running through my mind. Everything seemed hopeless.

CHAPTER THIRTY-NINE

Piers

Ruth Ann telephoned on Thursday, October 15, 1987 to tell us that Jackie was suddenly much worse. Hilary and I immediately drove to London to see her. She was suffering from pneumonia and was unable to talk, swallow, speak or see. When we arrived, Ruth Ann had flipped Jackie over to the side of her bed and was massaging her back to release the liquid that was collecting in her lungs.

I knew it was important for Hilary to be alone with Jackie, so when Ruth Ann said she needed to go to the shops, I offered to drive her and we left Hilary and Jackie together in the silence of the flat.

Hilary

Piers and Ruth Ann departed. Suddenly I began to wonder, What if she needs to cough? What if she chokes? What should I do? Jackie was flailing about, her arms banging on the bed, her eyes rolling, and her ears twitching. Her heels and elbows were protected by shaped muffs to prevent soreness from the incessant rubbing. Every part of her was on the move. She was a gyrating mass.

I had just returned from Jersey where I had been with Aunt Myrtle who was scattering Uncle Norman's ashes. I had hired a little car, and stayed overnight in Lalla's beautiful house.

I started to remind Jackie of Lalla's farmhouse which we knew so well. The cows with their mackintoshes on and the race to see who could spot them first. The smell of Jersey, the idyllic weather, the warm, pink granite. I told her about my visit to Archirondel with its red and white Martello tower, and about clambering up

the great granite pier to the top from where I could see St.
Catherine's Breakwater. I described St. Agatha where Gannie and
Pondles used to live, and my drive along the Pine Walk, around
the coast to the breakwater. I ambled down the slipway and dipped
my fingers in the sea, where we had spent many hours diving and
swimming. Then on to our favorite bay of all, La Coupe. I parked
the car at the top of the hill, ran down the little winding path past
the occasional fig tree, and jumped on to the granite pebbles,
scrunching over them to the sand. I chattered about the warm
wind and the smell of the sea, and reminded her of the feeling of
the sand between our toes. I went into our little cove—it was always "ours"—down to the rocks where the shells hid, put my hand
under the slippery seaweed, felt the purple anemones, found cowrie shells, top shells and winkles. I gazed into the rock pools. The
colorful lichens, barnacles, limpets and darting shrimps were just
as I remembered them, and I listened to the voices from the past.

After I'd been talking for a short while, Jackie became completely calm and still; her eyes were open, her whole body relaxed,
and her arms and fingers motionless. Suddenly my sister was with
me again and I was with her. It was one of the most intense times
I had ever had with her. I had to go on talking. I didn't dare stop.

I reminded her of Dad's little boats carved out of cork, of our
sand barrages, our races over the rocks, our picnics, the fuschia
hedges, the *cotees*. I reminded her of tea with Gannie and Pondles,
of ice-creams from Mrs. Lecouteur, of "frogs in bed, frogs in bed,
all the way to raspberry jam, frogs in bed." Of our times playing
on Lalla's farm and riding on the carthorse, of watching the Bre-
tons harvesting the potatoes. And back to the sea, the shells and
the bathing. I found myself talking of lowtide fishing and
Guernsey sweets . . . I don't know how long we were there.

Suddenly the door latch clicked and Jackie's thrashing instantly
started again.

I squeezed her hand and said, "Thank you, Jack."

She could not reply. But for that time, we had been as close as
any two people could be, just as we always had been in our bomb
patch.

The following morning, at home in Ashmansworth, I awoke to find
enormous destruction caused by the hurricane which had swept the

country in the early hours of the morning. Trees were down and blocking the roads. I couldn't believe I had slept through it.

That evening, we were told Jackie had stopped eating and was unable to keep fluids down. Dr. Selby saw her and explained to Ruth Ann that if Jackie didn't die that night, she could possibly last another week. She hoped Jackie would die quickly, knowing that if she lingered she would be fed artificially.

Ruth Ann telephoned early on Monday morning to say the end was very close. Piers and I left for London.

The roads had been cleared of fallen trees and there were no delays. It was a dismal day, Black Monday in more ways than one.

There was no one with Jackie apart from Ruth Ann. Jackie was hardly breathing and seemed to be only just conscious. We gently held her hands, whispered to her, wept and were silent.

Even in death, this once vital and powerful personality was still tying me up in emotional knots. All over again I felt lost, bereft, bewildered, confused and overwhelmingly sad. For forty-two years we had been through such an extraordinary gamut of situations and feelings. I loved her so much, yet had been profoundly hurt by her. I was extremely proud of her, and we had had enormous joy and fun together. I had longed to be the performer she was, and she had longed for the children and life I had.

At midday Danny arrived from Paris. A silent kiss from both of us for Jackie, and Piers and I left her in peace with Danny.

Piers and I sat in the car not knowing what to do, but eventually drove to the coffee shop of the Lancaster Gate Hotel. Piers ordered food. Neither of us could speak. We just stared. Sometime afterward, the waitress came back, put her hand on my shoulder.

"Are you OK?" she asked.

Our food was cold and congealed. So were we.

We returned to the flat later in the afternoon, and were stunned to find it bursting with people. I felt shocked and upset. This should have been a private time, a quiet time, but it wasn't. Since she had become well-known, Jackie's life had been taken over. But I was not ready for this.

The Duchess of Kent had been one of the first to arrive. Bill Pleeth and Tony, his son, were there, as were Jackie's rabbi, Len Selby, friends and musicians. Someone had put on one of her recordings and yet everyone was talking. Selfishly, I was unable to think of the emotional needs of others who were in the house. I could think only of my own overwhelming feelings, and my own immediate need for peace and stillness, which I knew Piers would share. When Mum had died at home, although it was harrowing, it was wonderful, too. With only the four of us there, it was private, peaceful and gentle: we were able to be ourselves in our own way. I felt so sorry for Danny. He looked awful, as though he had aged a hundred years, and, understandably, did not want to speak to anyone. He had retired to be on his own, but people kept going to see him.

Ruth Ann organized the gathering. As we filed one by one into Jackie's room, Ruth Ann instructed us to say our names. She believed that Jackie could still hear.

Piers and I stood at Jackie's bedside. She looked tranquil, at last.

After a while, Ruth Ann came in. I thought Jackie had gone. In fact, she was still alive, but unconscious. Wearily, Piers and I left the room, as Danny went in.

He was the last to be with her.

Jackie died at 8:30. Feeling out of place in the crowd, Piers and I were almost the first to leave. Neither of us spoke in the car on the way home.

Piers turned on the radio. The opening headlines of the news were being read: ". . . and the cellist Jacqueline du Pré has died, aged forty-two." It was only half an hour since we had left the flat, yet someone had already telephoned the BBC.

One of the nurses at Rock House had heard the announcement and had broken the news to Dad. I thought he would be distraught, but he seemed strangely unperturbed. Since Mum's death the situation between Jackie and Dad had been even more difficult. Ruth Ann explained later that Jackie couldn't cope with her parents' illnesses: she needed them to be strong.

In keeping with Jewish traditions, the funeral had to take place as quickly as possible. Kiffer didn't come. For him, mourning is a very private thing. He had said his farewell years before and felt his presence could be an embarrassment to Danny. The Jackie he had known and struggled so hard to keep had passed away long ago.

As I stood by Jackie's coffin, alone with the rabbi, listening to his profound words, a great sense of peace and relief came over me. But suddenly the doors burst open, and in poured the great and illustrious, led by Rostropovich, followed by many famous faces, and finally Piers, Lin and Dad.

Since there was no designated place for the family, we gathered round a spot suitable for Dad's wheelchair and sat in tight, squashed rows. I remember thinking I was almost the only person without a hat.

The funeral service was simple and moving and the rabbi spoke with great warmth, sketching a picture of the Jackie we knew before her illness. He spoke of the golden years with Danny and their great achievements as they created a partnership of life and music. Then had come the darkness.

Few people knew of the greatness she achieved then, of the nobility and inner development as she discovered new strength and vision within herself even as her body became her prison. It is a comforting half-true legend about multiple sclerosis, that the sufferer is enveloped by a quiet serenity and happiness which copes with the illness. But we cannot deny the frustration, the bitterness, the enormous anger which could and did erupt during her long night of suffering. It was balanced by her humor, by her compassionate work for fellow sufferers and by her continuing joy for life. Jackie had a unique place in our lives because she belonged to that rare group of individuals who blessed the world. Arthur O'Shaughnessy wrote:

> We are the music makers,
> And we are the dreamers of dreams
> Wandering by lone sea-breakers,
> And sitting by desolate streams!
> World-losers and world-forsakers,
> On whom the pale moon gleams:
> We are the movers and shakers
> Of the world forever, it seems.

Piers

After the service, the pallbearers, led by Danny and Pinchas Zukerman, carried Jackie's coffin out of the synagogue and there was a rush to follow them. Everyone was jostling and pushing to be at the front. I couldn't keep up, having to look after Dad and push him in his wheelchair. The grave was completely surrounded. The rabbi saw Dad approaching and asked people to make room for the wheelchair at the head of the grave, but as I pushed Dad closer, the chair sank into the uneven ground and could not be moved. Everyone began to crush around us again.

I never managed to be close to Jackie that day.

Hilary

Jackie was lowered into her lonely, dark cavern. Danny's flower was thrown on to the coffin. I had been told my rose would be there, but I couldn't see it anywhere. We stood while the rabbi intoned. Afterward, everyone was asked to throw earth into the grave. Dad tried but was too far away and his handful fell to the ground.

Soon, it was all over and slowly the crowd began to disperse. The custom is for the bereaved family to stand while everyone files past, offering their condolences.

I believed Danny would not want to see me, so decided to slip away. As I made my move, I felt a hand on my shoulder. It was Charles Beare.

"Hilary, where are you going?"

"Home."

"Oh no you're not," he said and pulled me with him to stand in the queue.

We gradually moved closer and closer to Danny, and eventually it was our turn. Danny shook my hand without looking at me, and I moved on to Enrique, his father, who did the same.

It was a relief when it was over. I talked to Charles for a while: he spoke with gentleness.

Suddenly, I needed to say goodbye to Jackie again. It was drizzling and gray and I was half running toward the grave when I saw Danny there alone, bent and motionless. I instantly rooted to the spot and just could not move. I suppose we were about ten yards apart. He had not seen me. I waited, still unable to move. After some while he turned and slowly, slowly dragged himself up the path. I still remained rooted, but assumed he would pass me without looking. Gradually he came nearer, and still did not look. As we were side by side, he suddenly collapsed on to my shoulder and we both sobbed and sobbed. As we held each other in our arms, it was as if all the years of awfulness had never existed. The years that started with Jackie's frantic phone call from America pleading for help. The awfulness of Danny's despair, of my efforts to restore my broken sister. The guilt and confusion over losing my enjoyment of her, and of my inability to do enough for her. Danny's understandable anger.

Suddenly the great force had gone, leaving a void where, for many years, those emotions had been overwhelmingly important. After a while, we parted, Daniel walked away and I went down to the grave.

It was festooned with expensive bouquets. I thought Dad would like to see the flowers, so I found him and pushed his wheelchair down the path. As we approached, he said: "Mum had more flowers than she did." After a few moments, we turned and retraced our steps. I never discovered what happened to my rose.

It was a long, slow journey back home that evening, in complete silence: there was nothing any of us could say. We were heavy with emotional exhaustion and saturated with tears. Dad was welcomed gently and warmly at Rock House, and was immediately absorbed by the carers and their attentions. I had left my car at Piers's house, and drove back to Ashmansworth on my own, my mind in a fog, my face swollen, my nose blocked but dripping. I arrived home at about 9:15, dragged myself out of the car and into the sitting room, where I collapsed into an armchair.

Theresa, who had returned from the funeral before me, came in, and seeing me slumped in the darkness and beyond speech, pushed the television in front of me and turned it on. The news was coming to an end and I was dimly aware of the weather forecast, followed by an announcement about a special tribute. Suddenly, there were Pinchas Zukerman, José Luis Garcia and Zubin

Mehta, eulogizing Jackie. I struggled to focus and then I saw her, my Jackie, to whom I had just said goodbye forever, but now very much alive on the screen in front of me. There she was, larking about, as vibrant as ever, laughing and joking with fellow musicians. I felt as if I'd been hit by a sledgehammer.

I don't remember going to bed that night, but I do remember waking up the next morning and feeling as if the world had come to an end.

Revelation

CHAPTER FORTY

Hilary

After Jackie died, there were the inevitable newspaper articles and Nico, who was working in London, collected them and posted them to me. When I read that Danny had been living with the Russian pianist, Helena Bachkirev, in Paris for the past five years and that they had two children, I was, at first, astonished. I had no idea of his "other life," but on reflection understood completely how vital it was for him to have the support of a family. In fact, it made no difference to the tenderness with which he had looked after Jackie: he had made certain Jackie had everything she needed.

Danny's other family had been the best-kept open secret in the music world. I don't know if Jackie knew, although someone told me that she telephoned Danny one day on their private line and heard a baby crying.

Danny introduced me to Helena at the Royal Festival Hall in London after one of his concerts. She was delightful and so were their two little boys, who were running around the Green Room. The older, David, was a miniature Danny. I was happy he had a flourishing family after all those years of sadness.

Piers

The thanksgiving ceremony for Jackie's life was held on what would have been her forty-third birthday, January 26, 1988, three months after her death. I drove Dad, Hilary and Lin to Westminster Central Hall. There was little conversation. At least it wasn't raining.

Dame Janet Baker sang, the English Chamber Orchestra played,

and the actresses Joanna David and Janet Suzman read. Zubin was
to make the address. Walking slowly to the front of the stage, he
looked at his notes, paused and began reading from them. But after a few moments, he hesitated and, as if with second thoughts,
folded the paper, looked up and said unsteadily:

"I can't continue to read what I've written. Everything I want
to say can be told in this story. Recently, I was conducting the Elgar concerto in New York. Toward the end of the third movement, I just couldn't conduct anymore. The cellist looked up and
said, 'You're thinking of her aren't you?' 'Yes,' I replied. The
thought of Jackie playing with me in London for the last time in
1973 completely overwhelmed me. At that point I knew I could
never conduct the Elgar again. There was no one like Jackie and
no one could replace her. There is nothing else I can say. There is
nothing else to be said."

He has not conducted the Elgar again.

Danny and the orchestra re-assembled for the final tribute to
Jackie: Mozart's Piano Concerto No. 27 in B flat major. It was the
performance of a lifetime.

Hilary

After the memorial, I received a message from Danny that he
wanted to see me in the Green Room. I found my way behind the
platform and could hear voices coming through the door. Someone came out and I asked if Daniel was there.

"Yes, but he's having a meeting."

"He said he wanted to see me. Shall I wait?"

"What's your name? I'll tell him you're here."

"Hilary."

The person went back into the room and Danny immediately
called me in. He tried to introduce me to the other people in the
room, but we were both very quickly overcome by tears, just as
we had been at the funeral. Neither of us could utter a word. We
could only weep, and everyone else discreetly crept away.

When eventually I spoke, Danny was overcome again. I suspect
that he found me so similar to Jackie in voice and mannerisms that
seeing me was too much for him.

★ ★ ★

The months immediately after this have faded into a blur. Our great force had gone from our lives. Later that year I attended the stone-laying ceremony but, otherwise, plunged myself into my family and my teaching, and buried my sadness.

Jackie's estate went to Danny. The cellos are now in the hands of other artists: Yo Yo Ma plays the Davidoff and Lynn Harrell the Brown Strad. I don't know what happened to the Gofriller and the Peresson.

Dad continued to live at Rock House. He became disorientated even when visiting Ashmansworth. Although he desperately wanted to go to Jersey and come with us on our holidays in France, we were advised that it would be unwise: he couldn't walk and needed constant skilled nursing.

In March 1991, Joy tripped and fell down in her house, breaking her leg. It was the start of her decline, and she determined to die. She was in hospital for a while, but eventually came back to Ashmansworth where she lived until her death in June.

Dad died nearly four months later in Rock House. His hearing had remained as acute as Jackie's, but his voice was reduced to an inaudible whisper, and his eyes looked terrified.

Dad was possibly the most sensitive person I have ever known. He seemed to have no capacity for coping with any hurt, however tiny. The smallest thing would pierce him like a dart and torture him mercilessly. He was acutely aware of others' feelings and thoughts, and this awareness was often a burden to him. Because he was so vulnerable himself, he was often unable to react. As he grew older he built a protective wall around himself, but that very wall became a prison. He was exceptionally talented, but gradually the man who had braved wild seas and climbed impossible mountains had been engulfed by fear.

Piers

As Christmas was approaching, I was having a business lunch with a friend, and we began talking about our hobbies. I mentioned reel-to-reel tape recording and his immediate response was to ask where I kept the tapes. When I told him, he was horrified.

"In the attic? And some of these are of Jackie?"

"Yes," I said. "And they form a solid base for the squirrels to play on."

Colin proceeded to tell me that tapes deteriorated with time, becoming sticky, deformed and fragile, especially if not stored correctly. I really ought to check them as soon as possible and certainly move them to a more stable environment.

That evening I rescued the boxes which in themselves looked intact, although appallingly dirty. I cleaned them and took out the tapes. They looked fine to me. I had just purchased a DAT recorder, and decided to copy all the recordings on to DAT, for safety.

I loaded the first reel on to the big Revox. It was Hilary playing Hunter Johnson's *To An Unknown Soldier* at the 1971 Inkpen Festival. It was so bright and clear. The tape was perfect. I was there, reliving the performance.

Over the coming days I copied tape after tape, until only one remained. This I had left on purpose until last. It was the February 1973 Elgar with Zubin Mehta conducting the New Philharmonia Orchestra, when Jackie made her comeback which turned out to be her last performance in the U.K.

I had to hear this tape by myself. I didn't want interruptions and I didn't want to share it with anyone at all. It was far too special, and I knew the memories it would evoke would be so strong and personal that I wanted the freedom to show my feelings openly. I decided to creep downstairs early when no one else was about.

I woke at 5 a.m. It was pitch black outside. Downstairs, I made myself a cup of fresh coffee and disappeared into the dining room where I had the recording equipment. Carefully, I took the tape out of its box, placed it on the Revox, loaded a DAT tape and put on the headphones.

As the BBC announcer began setting the scene I realized, with gratitude, that this tape was in as good a condition as the others. The audience began clapping as the leader appeared, followed by a crescendo of expectant applause. I could imagine Jackie striding on to the stage carrying her whopping creature.

A few moments of tuning, a short pause, and she began. I suddenly jumped. She was slowing the tempo down. A few more bars and it became vividly clear. I knew exactly what was happening.

Jackie, as always, was speaking through her cello. I could hear what she was saying. No longer was she on the polished wooden platform of the Royal Festival Hall performing to an audience. Instead she was playing in the open air, as if in a huge grass field, and in front of her was a grave. No one else was there, not even an orchestra. She was alone. Everything was still and silent except for her music. All I could see was Jackie with her cello, playing intensely to an empty grave. The grave was hers, and she knew it. I could almost see tears on her face. She was saying goodbye to herself, playing her own requiem.

I stared out of the window, the dawn light now breaking over the gravel driveway, my eyes blurred. Whatever had happened was over. She had said "farewell" in the same magnificent way as she had once said "hello" at the Wigmore Hall in 1961.

Rediscovery

CHAPTER FORTY-ONE

Hilary

Multiple sclerosis attacks the central nervous system by breaking down the myelin layer, an insulating sheath which covers each nerve fiber. The sheath is replaced by scar tissue (sclerosis) which prevents nerve signals from traveling normally. The damage happens in widely scattered areas of the nervous system, although the scar tissue tends to be concentrated in the brain and spinal cord.

There are now strict criteria for the diagnosis of MS: there should be two episodes affecting different body systems and they should be temporarily separated. For example: a problem with the eyes, followed by a problem with the hands, each occurring at different times.

Because any part of the nervous system can be affected, any part of the body can therefore be affected. Every person has a unique experience of the disease.

There have always been many interpretations of Jackie's MS. One was that she had exaggerated the effects of the disease to find attention when her career was supposedly failing. Another, that she didn't want to play the cello anymore, and the only way she could escape with honor was to be known to have a high-profile disease.

Jackie herself was always reticent in talking about her illness, knowing that whatever she said would be reported in the press. She feared, for example, that if she complained about tingling in her hands, everyone with that symptom would fear they have MS.

Piers

Professor Ian McDonald, the senior neurologist at the National Hospital for Neurology and Neurosurgery in London, told Hilary and me that about 80,000 people in the U.K. have multiple sclerosis (there are approximately 350,000 sufferers in the United States) and it is generally diagnosed between the ages of twenty and forty. More women than men have it, no one knows why. The cause of MS is still a complex puzzle, and a huge amount of work is being done in an attempt to solve it. Current investigations are examining environmental influences, viruses and the nature of the genetic factors involved. There has been real progress but there is still a long way to go. When I heard this, I smiled to myself because this was exactly what we were told when Jackie first became ill, a quarter of a century ago.

Significant steps have certainly been made since 1983, when MRI scanning revolutionized the diagnosis. After this, not only could pictures be taken of the brain showing the lesions, but the course of the disease could also be tracked through regular scanning.

Attempts to isolate a virus have failed. Measles and glandular fever might be possible culprits but expert opinions differ. Although the disease is not inherited as such, you sometimes see families with more than one case. What may be inherited, though, is the susceptibility. Exposure to whatever the agent is—it could, for example, be one of any number of common viruses—might produce an abnormal antibody response in those people who have the genetic susceptibility. As it happened, we had just found one of our distant relatives, of Jackie's generation, who had MS.

The majority of patients begin with what is known as the relapsing and remitting form of the disease. In other words, they have attacks from which they often seem to recover completely. Each separate attack is known as an "episode" and, having recovered, it is possible to have a relapse with similar or different symptoms. After a varying period of time—say, eight to ten years—the deterioration can start to be continuous and when this happens it is referred to as "secondary progressive."

It was gradually becoming clear to Hilary and me that Jackie must have been experiencing symptoms much earlier than we had thought because after MS was diagnosed in 1973 she deteriorated very quickly, and was in a wheelchair within eighteen months.

I asked Professor McDonald if stress could be a contributory factor and he told us that there was no evidence to suggest that it was. Jackie could also tolerate extreme cold, especially when swimming, and I wondered if this had anything to do with it, but apparently not. On the other hand, hot climates and being overheated can indeed aggravate the symptoms.

Because the loss of movement and independence are often the most devastating problems with which MS patients have to deal, the physical side has tended to be at the forefront of medical consultations. But Dr. Dawn Langdon, a neuropsychologist, specializes in the effect of the disease on the brain and therefore the psychological reaction to it. This aspect of the disease is now receiving increasing clinical and research attention.

We were interested to hear that there are cases of people who at first experience problems with memory and concentration. Understandably, there is a reluctance among the spokespeople for MS to acknowledge that psychological difficulties can create problems since this attitude might undermine MS sufferers who may feel that they would not be treated as sensible and dignified human beings. But now there is a great deal of work being carried out in the area of psychology to ascertain the effect of MS upon intellectual skills. It is not yet known if rage and emotional distress are directly related to the disease in terms of brain dysfunction or are a reaction to having to tolerate and endure a degenerative illness. It is possible that anger and exaggerated emotion are a sign that malfunction is developing in the brain before any symptoms show themselves physically. Being able to remember music, and coordinate the very fine movements required to play the cello, suggest that Jackie was not experiencing significant intellectual difficulties before the physical signs of her MS were in evidence. But when did the first symptoms really occur in Jackie's case?

The textbook pattern of MS is that the language skills—of conversation, reading, speaking and naming—tend to remain intact most of the time. Instead, it is the recall memory, concentration, reasoning skills, judgment, problem solving, understanding and the ability to think ahead—which can be affected. Langdon refers to this as the submarine factor. Because language skills tend to remain intact, it is possible to talk to people with MS and be persuaded that everything is fine. But behind the mask of competence, the reasoning and recall memory are not as good as they should be. Research has shown, though, that lesions in the brain can cause a cognitive deficit which is temporary, and that this can then disappear. It doesn't have to be all downhill. Langdon gave as an example the story of a young woman who worked in a bank and experienced a serious relapse. A scan revealed a new lesion in the left side of the brain, which affected her ability to count and do arithmetic. However, within three months she had recovered her numeracy and a further scan revealed that the lesion had disappeared.

Hilary and I also went to see our friend, Len Selby, who had been Jackie's GP for so many years and cared for her throughout her illness. He told us he had first attended Jackie in 1970 when she decided to have twelve skin moles removed.

"Daniel telephoned me from the Edinburgh Festival and asked if I could do him a favor and come and examine Jackie at Heathrow airport because they were on their way to Australia and didn't have time to come into town. At the airport, as Daniel rushed around confirming the flight bookings, I looked for a suitable place to examine Jackie. In the end, I examined her in the ladies' toilet. I didn't find anything actually wrong with the moles, but because of the danger of them turning malignant Jackie said that she would be happier without them. I said I would sort it out for her, and off they went to catch their plane."

Dr. Selby referred Jackie to a consultant plastic surgeon at University College Hospital and the operation was arranged for February 1971 under general anaesthetic. This was just after Jackie's twenty-sixth birthday and shortly after Dad had been diagnosed with cancer.

When Jackie came round from the operation, she complained of numbness on the left side of her body. It lasted a few days and then went away.

Hilary

Dr. Selby now believes that the numbness Jackie felt after the anaesthetic could have signaled the onset of her MS. I couldn't help wondering whether the disease could also have been fueling the psychological difficulties which precipitated her violent emotional crisis and breakdown. She had not told us anything about the operation to remove the moles, or its after-effects; but it wasn't long before I received that terrible panic phone call from America, after which she came home to stay at Ashmansworth in the spring of 1971.

Piers

The next time Jackie saw Len Selby officially was on October 8, 1973, eight months after the fateful Carnegie Hall concert when she couldn't lift the cello out of the case. He read to us from his notes of that meeting:

> She told me that a year earlier she had noticed difficulty in using her hands and that she was unable to compress the strings of the cello. She also had trouble in her right hand and had difficulty holding the bow. Four months prior to that, she had experienced tenderness and numbness in her legs and her back was weak. Three months prior to that, she complained that her left vision was blurred on and off—it wasn't consistent. With this story, I then suspected MS and referred her to Leo Lange, a consultant neurologist, and he confirmed my suspicions.

I asked if Jackie could have already been developing the disease when she was much younger. Also, had they identified it sooner, could anything have been done to prevent it from developing?

"We do have some cases of MS in the late teens, but it is very unusual. But even if she had been diagnosed earlier, the course wouldn't have been any different because even in this day and age, we still don't have a specific treatment for it. It's a 'wait and see' policy, although a lot of patients do respond well to steroids. The standard treatment Jackie had is still given now. At the time, though, I just hoped and prayed there would be a remission, but it never came."

"How did you explain the disease to her?"

"We tried to explain to her what MS was and what it does, that some people have one attack and never have another. One doesn't paint a dark picture, because there seems to be no point in frightening the patient when many do get over it. MS is the most variable disease in medicine."

I asked if Jackie had been a good patient.

"She very seldom complained, and always seemed to look lightly on it. I think underneath she was perhaps afraid and concerned, but she always greeted me with a smile. We were very close friends, you know, almost like sister and brother in the way that we spoke to each other. She never lost her sense of humor and always had a funny story to tell me. She had such a lovely nature and couldn't hurt a fly."

The conversation lapsed into reminiscences about Jackie and we mused over her anarchic humor and crazy sense of fun. He then gazed into the distance:

"You know, I'm sure the answer is going to come, but the problem is, one feels so useless. I mean, she would come and see me and we would just talk, and every time she walked out I said to myself, 'What good am I doing?' It was like having my hands tied behind my back. But she always said that it helped to talk."

Dr. Hatchick had been our family doctor when we lived in Portland Place, and was also medical adviser to Dad's Institute. When we saw him again recently, he reminded us that the first time he met us Hilary and I were sliding down the banisters, and had nearly knocked him over.

Mum had taken Jackie to see Dr. Hatchick in 1969, when she was twenty-four, two years after her marriage to Danny. Jackie and Danny had been on tour in Australia and Jackie had come home complaining to Mum that she had been bothered by a constant urge to urinate, which was particularly inconvenient during a concert. There was a history of cystitis in the family, and Mum had always suffered from it. Jackie had been taking tablets for cystitis, but the symptoms persisted.

When Dr. Hatchick questioned her, he suspected that she might have been suffering from a neurological bladder complaint, meaning that the discomfort was caused by a malfunction in the nervous system, rather than in the bladder itself, and, because of this, he referred her to a neurologist, Anthony Wolf, who later confirmed the diagnosis. Dr. Hatchick had suspected that this could be an episode of MS, but as Jackie hadn't reported anything to him except the bladder complaint, he was hesitant about his findings and kept quiet.

"She presented her MS in an odd way. If a young woman comes to you and complains of mist in one eye, this is usually the first sign of MS. But Jackie didn't have any symptoms other than discomfort with her bladder."

Hilary

With every doctor we consulted, the date of the onset of MS seemed to be getting earlier and earlier.

Piers

The next step was to find the eye specialist, John Anderson, who had met the nineteen-year-old Jackie at the Wigmore Hall in the spring of 1964. Kate Beare was performing and John Anderson was a guest of Kate's husband, Charles.

John had a bag of sweets with him, and in the interval, when a young golden-haired girl came swinging down the aisle toward him, he caught her eye and held out the bag. "Have a sweet?" She took one, and said, "Thanks."

"Do you realize who that was?" said Charles, watching her as she strode away. "Jacqueline du Pré."

John was a keen string player himself and held regular chamber music evenings in his house, inviting many eminent performers to play. Guests wrote their names in a diary and listed what they had played. The diary now reads like a *Who's Who* of the great and famous, including names such as Heifetz. Jackie's first entry was on May 27, 1964, and she played Haydn, Mozart, Beethoven and the Purcell Chaconne. Her name appears about twenty times and on one occasion, typical of her, she has written it upside-down.

John and Jackie quickly became close friends during those years when she was finding her independence in London and before she met Danny. She was also friendly with John's brother, Robert. Together, she and Robert would play duos and, at Christmas, tour the ward of Bart's Hospital, entertaining the patients. The chamber music sessions continued throughout 1965 until Jackie left for Russia to study with Rostropovich.

When she returned from Russia, in June 1966, she asked to see John at Moorfield's Hospital in High Holborn because she had been experiencing a problem with her eyes. She told him she had had trouble with her eyes not tracking together, but she told others she was suffering from blurred vision. By the time she had her appointment with John, the problem had gone away. It was then that she contracted glandular fever.

We met John recently and he confirmed that when he had examined her, she definitely did not have a condition called retrobulbar neuritis (inflammation of the optic nerve) which would have led him to suspect MS. In fact, he couldn't find anything wrong with her eyes at all.

John lost touch with Jackie after she met Danny. Jackie was swept away into a different social arena, and John went to live and work in Africa. They wrote to each other occasionally, and met again briefly in 1971, at the beginning of Jackie's "marriage difficulties" as John put it. On that occasion, Jackie told John two extremely significant things: the first, that her marriage was over, the second, that she knew she would be paralyzed and not able to play the cello.

MS was not diagnosed until two years later.

Piers

Counseling for both patients and families has become an essential aspect of modern treatment of MS but, when Jackie was ill, there was no such thing readily available. We didn't seek it, and it wasn't offered. I now realize that, had we had the opportunity to express our anxieties in an environment where we could share our experiences with others, we would not have felt so isolated and alone.

Psychoanalysis afforded a very important lifeline for Jackie, although there is no scientific proof that this is in any way helpful to MS sufferers. I suspect she used her sessions with Dr. Limentani for conversation rather than counseling, and relied on them more than any of us knew.

The methods of rehabilitating a patient between relapses have also changed. The therapy which Jackie endured at the Rockefeller Institute is no longer considered helpful. Instead patients are shown how best to recover and achieve the functions and skills which apply to their own daily lives. Tragically, in Jackie's case, it would never have been possible to retrieve the fine movements and hand control required to play the cello.

Hilary

Meeting Julia Segal, author and leading counselor, was a revelation and I realized how much I wished that she had been available to us when Jackie was ill. Julia became involved with MS patients when she worked for a charity called ARMS, which began as a self-help group of patients, their families and doctors. Their focus was how to live with MS rather than to cure it, and they soon clarified their priorities. Physiotherapy and dietary advice were at the top of the list. Julia was brought in to add the idea of counseling, a new concept at that time. Apart from writing books about how children cope when their parents have MS, Julia has also produced a booklet about emotional reactions to MS.

I told her our story, leaving out the Kiffer part of it, and she listened and commented. It was comforting to find many of our experiences with Jackie were so understood and so familiar to her in her own work. And then I told her about Jackie's emotional explosion when she came home from America after her "marriage difficulties." Julia's response stunned me.

She said that people who have bladder problems might also experience sexual discomfort, and can have difficulty in achieving a satisfying sexual experience. Jackie was bound to be suffering from lack of self-esteem at this time, and might have reacted by throwing herself at the first man who came into her life. I just quietly gulped and said, "Yes, that sounds about right." Jackie had told me privately that the main reason for her break-up with Danny was her lack of sexual responsiveness to him.

I couldn't bring myself to tell Julia about Jackie's obsession with my husband.

I recounted the story about the time in the bomb patch when Jackie had told me she wouldn't be able to walk or move when she grew up. Could Jackie have had MS from the age of nine? Julia replied that she has had experience of children with MS, although it's rare.

As I traveled back to Newbury on the train that evening my heart was heavy. I couldn't stop thinking about that time in the bomb patch. Jackie's words were haunting me. Surely there must have been some motivation for such a powerful and terrible statement from a nine-year-old?

Perhaps if she had consistently seen one doctor, who had the full picture, she might have been diagnosed earlier.

We will never be able to prove exactly when MS first struck Jackie, and now I don't think it's important to know. But it is likely she was ill much earlier than we previously thought, and that she was battling with unknown difficulties for many years before the crippling symptoms finally took over.

CHAPTER FORTY-TWO

Hilary

Rabbi Friedlander had met Jackie and Danny in the street one day, when Danny was pushing Jackie in her wheelchair. The rabbi lived with his wife in a flat above the synagogue at the entrance to Rutland Gardens. A lift, just the right size for the wheelchair, made it possible for Jackie to visit him there. More usually, though, the rabbi would go to Jackie's house, meeting with her at least once a week.

Piers and I decided we would like to make contact with him. I hadn't seen him since the funeral and wanted to thank him properly for his profound words, which had stayed with me and been a constant comfort to me.

Piers

The rabbi talked about the time he spent with Jackie.

He had read Scriptures to her. "She liked to talk about the people in the Bible, and the poetry. She would say things like, 'What a spoilt brat Joseph was, with his coat of many colors.' It would be a mistake to think of her as a devout Jewish person. Her relationship was more to do with being a part of the Jewish community, because so many of her friends were Jewish. Jackie could see herself as *belonging*, but hated any kind of fanaticism—fanatical Jews as much as fanatical Christians. Music was her religion. Other things were ancillary to it."

Jackie had told Rabbi Friedlander that she had not had a chance to learn as much about literature as she would have liked. He therefore organized people to come and read Shakespeare and poetry to her, listen to music and talk about it.

I asked him what had been fueling Jackie's anger toward our family. I knew the question had touched a nerve, since he thought for some time before answering. He told us that two things had greatly disturbed Jackie's peace of mind. The first was when Mum had apparently told her that her illness was a consequence of renouncing the Christian faith, and the second was when I had apparently given her a Bible.

Hilary and I were aghast. I had never given Jackie a Bible.

After our meeting with the rabbi, we learned from Ruth Ann that Jackie had indeed received a Jerusalem Bible in the mail with a letter telling her that if she renounced the Jewish religion and turned back to Christianity she would be cured. Jackie had opened the letter herself and been woundingly shocked by it.

Hilary

This book began with a letter, "to my dearest, darling Mum." It was nearly eight years since she had died. I wrote it by hand and could hardly write fast enough. I found I was able to say anything to her. Once the flood gates had been opened, the story of our lives with Jackie just poured out. It took me four months and I didn't show it to anyone, not even Kiffer, until I had finished.

I invited Piers to Ashmansworth to read my long letter and made him comfortable in the music room. Three hours later I returned to ask if he would like a cup of coffee. I had never before seen a man so consumed with tears.

"Yes," he said. "That's how it was."

Now I needed to talk to Daniel. He had been such an important part of Jackie's life. I wrote to him asking if we could meet to talk about Jackie, but wasn't sure he would want to. I didn't expect a reply, but in the late autumn of 1995, the telephone rang:

"Hilary, how are you?"

I recognized his distinctive voice immediately and replied with an excited shriek. "Danny! How lovely to hear from you . . . I'm fine. How are you?"

There was a silence before he spoke. He told me he'd received my letter, and he would like to meet.

He was coming to London the following week for a few days,

and suggested we should meet at the Hyde Park Hotel at 6 p.m. on Monday.

I arrived far too early, and had an hour to wait. I paced up and down the reception area, and went nervously in and out of the ladies', trying to make the time pass. I stood by the dressing-table in the cloakroom which was covered in a chintzy fabric, decorated with creamy-pink roses reminding me of the rose I'd chosen for Jackie on the day of her funeral. I stared at myself in the mirror, and could almost see the many panicked thoughts racing through my mind. Since those days in France with an unhappy Danny, I had never felt at ease with him.

As I continued to gaze into the mirror, I silently rehearsed what I was going to say to him. Suddenly it seemed as though Jackie's face was staring at me from my own mirror image. The cloakroom attendant came in, her presence jolting me from my daydream. I glanced at the clock: it was time.

The receptionist contacted Danny.

"Hilary!"

I turned and there he was, smiling at me; that powerful figure from my sister's past. We fell into a spontaneous embrace. I felt an instant warmth toward him.

We settled in comfortable chairs in the bar and he lit a huge Havana cigar, which enveloped me in a cloud of smoke. He waved his arms furiously, trying to bat it away from my face. "I'm so sorry. Excuse me."

There was silence, as we both waited for the other to speak.

"Danny, I know you don't like talking about private matters, so if you don't wish to respond to some questions, I completely understand."

He nodded, and looked a little distracted as he enjoyed another lingering inhalation of his cigar.

"It's OK," he said. "Sometimes I can talk about Jackie and sometimes I just can't. It's OK to talk about her now, but tomorrow it may be different."

He was as relaxed as I had ever seen him. If he didn't want to answer a question, he just looked through me. But I loved listening as he talked about Jackie, her instincts, and her ruthlessness with music.

I asked him about their first meeting at Fou Ts'ong's house when, instead of talking, they played together. His dark eyes lit up with the memory.

"I was flabbergasted by her personality and her ability to be at one with the music. She *was* the music. When Jackie played the cello it was always to the limit. She had such a passionate relationship with music and such a sense of intonation that she was able to be totally reckless with the instrument. The cello had never met anyone like Jackie before."

We both laughed.

"You know, Mum was very hurt by all the criticisms: that she had pushed Jackie and forced her to . . ."

"Listen," he said, sitting forward in his chair. "Jackie never did *anything* she didn't want to do. She had a total conviction that her instincts were right, and never doubted herself for a moment. That's why her playing was so direct. It was as natural for her to play as to pick up this glass of water. You couldn't move her. Wild horses wouldn't move her if she didn't want to move . . ." He laughed heartily, as though a thousand memories were streaming through him. He paused. Another long draw on his cigar, which was now growing a precarious tip of ash.

". . . With most people you feel that only a part of their day is dedicated to music, practicing and performing. With Jackie it was the other way around. Her day *was* music, which left her with X number of hours to do something else. She spent all day long with music."

Danny explained his belief that sensitive people can be divided into "ear" people or "eye" people. There are those who stand in front of a painting by Picasso and have an intensity of emotion which they will never feel for a piece of music. And the other way around. Jackie was ninety-nine per-cent an "ear" person.

"But she had uncanny instincts for so many things other than music. She could come to an opinion about a person instantly and have him summed up in five minutes."

"You and Jackie were from very different worlds, weren't you?" He didn't respond.

"I mean, Jackie was an English country girl, not very worldly, and . . ."

He interrupted me. "Yes, and there was something very attractive about that . . ." He looked away. "I want to explain something to you." He leaned forcefully toward me, changing the subject completely.

"People think that music actually exists. The Elgar Cello Concerto doesn't exist! It's not like an object which, once you've created it you put in a cupboard and you can pick it up again tomorrow. It exists briefly in the composer's brain when he composes it, and it exists briefly in black dots on white paper when he writes it down. But it only *truly* exists each time someone plays it. Therefore, each time you play it, you have to realize that you are bringing those sounds into the world, physically, not metaphysically, sounds that do not otherwise live permanently in the world. Music exists in the moment of playing it and then it's gone; unless you keep it artificially by recording it, of course."

I was riveted.

"Jackie had an instinctive feeling about this. Whenever she picked up a cello and started playing she had an ability to bring the sound into the world in exactly the way she wanted to at that moment. That's why her playing was so spontaneous. She never had to worry about 'How do I do this?' She never had to think about it. She just felt it and it happened. She surprised me with every performance."

I told him we had reason to believe that Jackie's illness was caused by stress. This made him angry.

"That's not true, absolutely not true. It's not a strain to play three or four times a week if you are enjoying it. It is absolutely not true that Jackie was under stress. The real stress for her was when she couldn't play anymore."

"Do you miss her?"

He was silent for a while.

"Very much . . . I still get a funny feeling when I visit London, even now."

"Do you ever visit the grave?"

"No. I don't go." He shrugged. "But I don't visit my mother's grave either."

There was an awkward silence. A pianist started playing deafeningly loud jazz on the piano just behind us, shattering our intimacy.

It was time for Danny to leave. I thanked him and told him he had been wonderful to Jackie, especially through her illness. How had he coped with it? Once again, his dark eyes cast a penetrating look.

"It was horrible. I tell you how I lived through it. I lived through it because I couldn't have lived with myself if I hadn't. It would have been much easier not to cope with it, but I could never have lived with that."

In 1997 I went to a concert Daniel was conducting in the Albert Hall. Nico came with me and, before the performance, we found our way to the Green Room. I stood in the entrance. Danny turned and began to walk toward me but, catching sight of Nico, was momentarily transfixed. In many ways Nico looks very similar to Jackie. The impression I had was that Danny was stabbed by memories in an unguarded moment.

How Jackie, cut off from her playing, bore her last years I can hardly bear to think. No wonder she felt bitter and angry, while we all stood by unable to do a thing, as she sank inexorably into isolation and decline. I suspect that both her frailties and her proud, rebellious spirit made her almost unapproachable in her entirety by anyone.

EPILOGUE

Piers

1996, and at last, after all these years, Hilary and I wanted to visit Jackie's grave. As we drove toward Golders Green, neither of us spoke. We couldn't. The memories of the funeral were flashing back with great force and I was reliving the day. I felt like a guest, an accessory. I found myself wanting to shout: "Go away, get out, she's my sister, not yours."

Now, feelings of intense anger, sadness and loss were being mixed into a cocktail of painful tears.

Hilary

We walked in silence between the two little synagogues. I was momentarily shocked to see, leaning against the wall, a coffin trolley covered with a rather tatty black mantle. In my mind, it didn't belong there: it belonged inside. I opened the door to the synagogue where Jackie and I had last been together. Now I was alone with the pews and my recollections, but could still imagine Jackie's shrouded coffin. This was where I had poured out my heart to her and said goodbye.

I rejoined Piers, and together we walked slowly toward the grave. The golden letters of her name shone in the early autumn sunlight from the majestic blue-black granite headstone. Growing at the end of the grave was Jackie's rose, the rose she had chosen to bear her name from Peter Harkness, the rose-breeder. Her eyesight by then was so blurred she had selected it by scent alone. The pale creamy-pink blooms seemed a living memorial to Jackie's spirit—gloriously wild and free.

As I stood and looked around the cemetery, I began to feel troubled. Why was she here? No family, no friends, no beauty, no breathtaking view, nothing lovely to hear. I paused in my thoughts. She seemed cut off from every place she had loved. I wished she could have been with Mum.

Our family were all so close and dependent on one another that we developed the ability to know what each was thinking, removing the need for words. We inherited Mum's intuitive approach to life, and have always followed our instincts.

As Jackie's talent became more evident, the balance of our family life altered and we felt compelled to nurture both her and her colossal gift. Following Mum's lead, we all supported Jackie and watched as she shone in the spotlight. She became the center of our attention and was automatically and without question put first.

All my life, I have referred to Jackie as a genius, without truly understanding what it means. One day I looked in a dictionary. The first definition was: "A person . . . who, for good or bad, powerfully influences another," with a further description: "The personification or embodied type of something immaterial." Both of these certainly applied to Jackie.

It was that sense of something indefinable which drove us to revere her. The girl dressed in yards of blue silk, who came bounding toward us after a concert with her rather awkward and unfeminine gait, was very different from the person on stage, unearthing our deepest emotions.

As a family, we regarded her genius as natural, normal. Now I realize that geniuses are rare. They are not the same as other people, and it would have been impossible even to try inflicting an ordinary way of life upon her. She was driven by something from deep within her, and we had no option but to be borne along by her current.

Genius demands an unusual and specific environment in which to flourish, which, in itself requires genius. Mum's intuitive understanding and thorough musical training enabled her to provide the background Jackie needed. Dad, trusting Mum implicitly, provided the home and financial support.

Her genius made her vulnerable and this, in turn, induced the desire to protect her. Many men wanted to take care of her and fell in love with her golden looks, her wicked humor and the magnetism of her personality. As her fame spread, it seemed as if half the world wanted to look after her. She was idolized, both for herself and her gift. Her playing aroused ardor, indeed ecstasy. And the emotional response to her tragedy was equally fervent. Everyone longed to support her through her terrible illness.

Before I met Kiffer, I took it for granted that my job in life would be to care for Jackie wherever she might be. But falling in love with Kiffer was even more powerful and I was jolted away from my self-imposed destiny.

For a while I was free. But when Jackie called from America and turned to me for help, I immediately slotted back into the old pattern. Without question, I responded to her needs once again.

I thought I was doing everything in my power to help her, but her death left me with an overwhelming sense of failure. I couldn't save her.

Mum had the same struggle. In every detail, she had taken care of Jackie. When her child was eighteen, she had bravely released her from the nest into the world. The daughter for whom she had fought and given her life was ready to fly, and she let her go. At the time MS was diagnosed, Mum became the scapegoat. They said she had denied Jackie a normal childhood, a normal education, friends, had imposed her own unfulfilled ambitions upon her; no wonder Jackie was so unhappy, so stressed; no wonder, they said, she developed MS.

Poor, broken Mum, falsely accused, suffered for thirteen years before dying. She was crippled by criticism, at the very time she should have been showered with thanks. Jackie was adored, and her illness and death aroused great passions, just as her playing did and still does. It was Mum who "created" Jackie. Without Mum, there would have been no Jackie or her music to adore.

Mum never "pushed" Jackie. *Jackie* was the pusher, and Mum, like the rest of us, had positively to run to keep up with her.

As I stood beside Jackie's grave I pondered. Mum, in giving herself completely for and to Jackie, was as much a genius as Jackie herself.

Recently, Piers came across a quotation:

"No family should have less than three children. If there is one genius among them, there should be two to support him."

Piers and I stood at the grave in silence. Lying on the huge granite slab were several small stones, placed as a traditional mark of respect. I realized that for me Jackie was not here but in my memories and in the special places we had shared together. For Piers, though, it had been different. He had been denied a last private moment with Jackie.

After a while, he turned to me and said: "At last, I've been able to say goodbye."

We hugged each other and wept tears of reconciliation and relief.

"One day," I said, "we'll come back here, and leave a stone from each of our favorite places. And the stones will say: 'We were together—remember?' "

ACKNOWLEDGMENTS

Hilary du Pré and Piers du Pré are extremely grateful to their families and friends who have supported and assisted them in countless ways, and without whose help and co-operation this book would have been incomplete.

We offer especially warm thanks to Christopher Finzi and Lin du Pré, whose understanding and patience have allowed us the time we needed; to Daniel Barenboim for sharing many poignant memories of Jackie and for his kindness in granting permission to quote from Jackie's letters written before 1967; to William Pleeth, Jackie's "cello daddy," for his vision and time; to Lorraine Dixon for being the perfect PA to both of us; to the staff of du Pré plc for their support; to Penelope Hoare for her time, help and sensitivity; to Mark Lucas for his inspiration; to Howard Ferguson for his memories of Joy and Jackie; to Sylvia Spice; to Andrew Keener for his detailed discography; to Andrew and Gerry Pengelly for the many delicious meals, for their genuine interest, and for Andrew's thorough first reading of the manuscript.

Many thanks to the medical experts who were all extremely generous with their time, sharing their expertise and their memories: Dr. Bernard Hatchick, Dr. Dawn Langdon, Mr. Leo Lange, Professor Ian McDonald, Dr. Donald Paty, Julia Segal, Dr. Len Selby, and Mr. Anthony Wolf.

Thanks, too, to the Norwegian Embassy for allowing us to revisit Jackie's house in Pilgrim's Lane.

We would like to extend particular thanks to the many people who wrote to us, gave interviews and hospitality: John Anderson, Jeremy Ard, Lucy Balley, Stephen Banfield, Lady Barbirolli, Charles Beare, Kate Beare, Mary Billot, Commander Hugh Blenkin, Betty Bois, Neville Brazier-Creagh, Ruth Ann Cannings, Peter and Reggie Chelsom, Alison Clwyd, Gareth du Pré, Jeremy Dale

Roberts, Peter Denny, Patricia Edward, EMI, The Ernest Read Music Association, Gloria Evans, Judy Fox, Rabbi Friedlander, Robin Golding, Myrtle Grange-Bennett, Margaret Greep, Suvi Grubb, John Harding, Lord and Lady Harewood, Derek Honner, J. A. Howley, Jersey Museum, Godfrey Judd, Stephen Kovacevich, B. Le Fevre, Dr. F. Le Maistre, Sir Godfray Le Quesne, Mr. and Mrs. R. Le Sueur, Lord Coutanche Library, Tom Lori, Mary May, Dennis Marriott, John and Rita Mitchell, Christopher Nupen, Henrietta Otley, Melissa Phelps, David Pitt, Maggie and Joe Richardson, Diana Rix, Anne Sarre, David Sarre, Tony Scott-Warren, Ronald Smith, Sylvia Southcombe, Dr. and Mrs. R. Sternberg, Bill and Nancy Stuart-Williams, C. Sumner, Peter Thomas, Rufus and Elizabeth Vandespar, Christopher Vandespar, Malcolm Walker, Moray Welsh, Mary Wharlow, Laurence Whistler, Araminta Whitley, Elizabeth Wilson, Herbert Withers, Francis Zagny. It has certainly been our intention to thank everyone. But if, through oversight, there is anyone we have failed to mention, we offer our heartfelt apology.

We are grateful to The Literary Trustees of Walter de la Mare, and The Society of Authors as their representative for permission to reproduce verses from *Peacock Pie* by Walter de la Mare, and to Oxford University Press for assistance with *Romance* by W. J. Turner, which is included in the *Oxford Book of English Verse*.

Thanks also to the various media organizations referred to in the text for their kind assistance.

All the photographs we have included come from private collections and family albums.

Finally we are grateful to Terence Palmer for permission to reproduce his letter about Jackie's début, to Sylvia Darley for permission to reproduce Sir Malcolm Sargent's letter to the *Evening Standard*, to Mollie Brown for permission to reproduce Wilfred Brown's letter, to Dominic Cooper for permission to quote from the writing of his father, Martin Cooper, to the *Newbury Weekly News* for the quote on page 119, and to Zubin Mehta for allowing us to use his heart-felt words spoken at Jackie's thanksgiving ceremony.

Books consulted:

When Poland Smiled by Derek du Pré, Gee and Co Publishers Ltd.

Uncle Ernie, a biography of Ernest Read by Frances Zagny, The Ernest Read Association.

Jackie's First and Second Cello Books by Iris du Pré.

A Pathway to Dalcroze Eurhythmics by Ethel Driver, Nelson.

Joy Finzi, Tributes by her Friends, Private publication.

Daniel Barenboim, A Life in Music by Daniel Barenboim, Weidenfeld & Nicolson.

The First Ten Years of the Suggia Gift, The Arts Council of Great Britain.

The Lives of the Great Composers by Harold Schonberg, Abacus.

Treatment of Multiple Sclerosis: Trial Design Results / Future Strategy by W. I. McDonald, Springer-Verlag London Ltd.

The English Festival by Laurence Whistler, Heinemann.

The Great Cellists by Margaret Campbell, Victor Gollancz.

Jacqueline du Pré: a life by Carol Easton, Simon and Schuster.

Jersey in London by Brian Ahiev Read, Seaflower Books.

Jacqueline du Pré: Impressions, edited by William Wordsworth, Grafton.

DISCOGRAPHY

Even when an artist is no longer making records, a discographer's task is not unlike that of the painter of the Forth Bridge. Familiar studio recordings offer a relatively unchanging picture. But who can guess what tapes of concerts or other broadcast material lie in some attic gathering dust, ripe for issue, "unofficial" or otherwise? Therefore, the CDs of such material within the following list are solely those which are, or have been, commercially available before August 1997—although as I suggest in a moment, there is quite a bit more to be discovered by even the most half-hearted detective.

In the case of the approved recordings from du Pré's company EMI (and a pair of "one-off" releases from CBS/Sony and Deutsche Grammophon), I have decided to keep catalog numbers to a minimum. The record catalog never stands still. A recording appears, is deleted, then reappears with a new number and often yet another coupling. Jacqueline du Pré's 1965 Elgar Concerto has appeared in at least six incarnations, each with a different companion work. Continuing reissue programs and future music carriers may well double this figure before the coming century is a decade old. So, when a recording is available at the time of writing, a single current catalog number is quoted. When currently unavailable, a deleted CD or LP number is given.

Several people supplied information which eluded regular channels: Michael Anderson (former Chief Librarian at the Music Faculty Library, University of Edinburgh); my partner Peter Avis (whose collection of music magazine backnumbers supplied information missing from the files of two London orchestras); Jenny Johns (formerly of The London Philharmonic); Suvi Raj Grubb who, as du Pré's EMI recording producer, delved into his diaries to correct information published from erroneous record company files; Paul Orlando (Philadelphia Orchestra); and William Pleeth.

What of the gaps in the list? More than one pupil has spoken to me warmly of du Pré's Debussy Sonata. Perhaps microphones were present during one of the many times she played it (though I have so far drawn a blank). A similar case might be the Brahms Double Concerto with Zukerman and Barenboim, apparently relayed from the 1969 Brighton Festival. All BBC Promenade Concerts are broadcast, so it follows that somewhere, if not in the BBC vaults (where the list of retained recordings is less extensive than one might wish), there exists a recording of du Pré's 1965 Bloch *Schelomo* with Norman Del Mar (RPO). At the time of writing, her premiere of Priaulx Rainier's Concerto the previous year with the same conductor (BBCSO) has been kept.

When the BBC archives disappoint, there are the treasures of the National Sound Archive around the corner from London's Royal Albert Hall, where recordings can be heard by appointment. Donated off-air tapes, though variable in sound quality, offer much that might otherwise have simply disappeared into the ether. There is a vivacious BBC studio recording of the Ibert Concerto made in 1962 when du Pré was seventeen. (William Pleeth tells me that she never returned to the work; I wonder why.) A relay of Shostakovich's First Concerto from the mid-sixties (CBSO/Hugo Rignold), although magnificent in the slow movement and cadenza, finds her elsewhere impulsive and ill at ease with unhelpful conducting (bringing to mind Barenboim's famous lament in an interview, "she's hard to follow'), while a Schumann Concerto from a 1962 London concert with Jean Martinon offers a touching, if relatively unformed view beside the 1968 EMI account with Barenboim.

Her last-ever performance of the Elgar Concerto, on January 25, 1973 at the Festival Hall with Zubin Mehta, appears not to have been preserved by the BBC. A home taping reveals a heartbreaking emotional vulnerability with, on the whole, a technical command remarkably free from signs of illness. As for Jackie's Beethoven Triple Concerto, her Britten Cello Symphony, Hindemith and Walton concertos, they remain, until some attic discovery, delightful daydreams. Below, supplemented by a handful of

commercially-released broadcasts, is the work of less than a decade
in the recording studio.

                                    Andrew Keener, 1991, revised 1997

1961   March 22, BBC Broadcasting House, London
        FALLA (arr. Maréchal): Suite populaire espagnole
        HANDEL (arr. Slatter): Sonata in G minor, Ernest Lush
            (piano)
        (BBC Recording, Home Service program "The Rising
            Generation")
        EMI CD CDM 7 63165 2
        EMI CD CDM 7 63166 2

1962   January 7, BBC Maida Vale Studios, London
        January 7, BBC Maida Vale Studios, London
        BACH: Suite no. 1 in G, BWV 1007
        (BBC Recording, Third Program)
        EMI CD CDM 7 63165 2

        January 26, BBC Maida Vale Studios, London
        BACH: Suite no. 2 in D minor, BWV 1008
        (BBC Recording, Third Program)
        EMI CD CDM 7 63165 2

        July 10 and 11, Abbey Road Studio no. 1, London
        BACH: Adagio (Toccata in C, BWV 564), Roy Jesson
            (organ)
        BRUCH: Kol Nidrei, Gerald Moore (piano)
        FALLA (arr. Maréchal): Jota (Suite populaire espagnole),
            John Williams (guitar)
        MENDELSSOHN: Song without words, Op. 109, Ger-
            ald Moore (piano)
        PARADIS: Sicilienne, Gerald Moore (piano)
        SAINT-SAENS: Le Cygne (Carnival des animaux),
            Osian Ellis (harp)
        SCHUMANN: Three Fantasy Pieces, Op. 73,
            Gerald Moore (piano)
        EMI CD CDC 5 55529 2

September 3, Freemason's Hall, Edinburgh
BRAHMS: Sonata no. 2 in F major, Op. 99, Ernest Lush
    (piano)
(BBC Recording from the 1962 Edinburgh International
    Festival)
EMI CD CDM 7 63166 2

1963   March 17, BBC Broadcasting House, London
        COUPERIN: Treizième Concert à instrumens à
            l'unisson (Les Goûts réunis), William Pleeth (cello)
        (BBC Recording, Third Program)
        EMI CD CDM 7 63166 2

        August 22, Royal Albert Hall, London
        ELGAR: Concerto in E minor, Op. 85, BBC Symphony/
            Sir Malcolm Sargent (Henry Wood Promenade Concert)
        Intaglio CD INCD 7351

1965   January 12 and 14, Abbey Road Studio no. 1, London
        DELIUS: Concerto for Cello and Orchestra, Royal Phil-
            harmonic/Sir Malcolm Sargent
        EMI CD CDC 5 55529 2

        February 25, BBC Broadcasting House, London
        BRITTEN: Scherzo, March (Sonata in C, Op. 65),
            Stephen Bishop (piano)
        (BBC Recording, Music Program)
        EMI CD CDM 7 63165 2

        August 19, Kingsway Hall, London
        ELGAR: Concerto in E minor, Op. 85, London Sym-
            phony/Sir John Barbirolli
        EMI CD CDC 5 55527 2

        December 19 and 20, Abbey Road Studio no. 1, London
        BEETHOVEN: Sonata in A, Op. 69 and Sonata in D,
            Op. 102 no. 2, Stephen Bishop (piano)
        EMI CD CDM 7 69179 2

1967   April 17, Abbey Road Studio no. 1, London
        HAYDN: Concerto in C, Hob. VIIb:1, English Chamber/
           Daniel Barenboim
        EMI CD CDC 7 47614 2

        April 24, Abbey Road Studio no. 1, London
        BOCCHERINI: Concerto in B flat major,
        English Chamber/Daniel Barenboim
        EMI CD CDC 7 47840 2

        September 21, Abbey Road Studio no. 1, London
        BRAHMS: Sonata no. 1 in E minor, Op. 38,
        Daniel Barenboim (piano)
        EMI, unissued (see 1968)

1968   April 6, Abbey Road Studio no. 1, London
        STRAUSS: Don Quixote, Op. 35
        New Philharmonia Orchestra/Otto Klemperer, Herbert
           Downes (viola)
        EMI, incomplete (see April 9)

        April 7 and 8, May 11, Abbey Road Studio no. 1, London
        SCHUMANN: Concerto in A minor, Op. 129, New
           Philharmonia/Daniel Barenboim
        EMI CD CMS 7 63283 2

        April 9, Abbey Road Studio no. 1, London
        STRAUSS: Don Quixote, Op. 35, New Philharmonia/
           Sir Adrian Boult, Herbert Downes (viola)
        EMI CD CDC 5 55528 2

        Only when researching this discography was I able to
        confirm that the above recording existed. The sessions,
        scheduled with Klemperer on April 6 (see above), were
        brought to a halt by his withdrawal after a series of
        fragmentary takes. The octogenarian Boult, a recent
        EMI exclusive signing, replaced Klemperer at the Festi-
        val Hall performance two days later, while his Abbey
        Road run-through, at the end of a rehearsal for the

concert, was made releasable by my editing in brief moments from the Klemperer fragments. Had du Pré been allowed to return to "Don Quixote," the result would undoubtedly have had greater polish than we have here. But she had just four playing years left, and the work was never rescheduled. Here is an invaluable, if imperfect, snapshot of an artist in her prime.

May 20 and August 18, Abbey Road Studio no. 1, London
BRAHMS: Sonata no. 1 in E minor, Op. 38 and Sonata
   no. 2 in F major, Op. 99, Daniel Barenboim (piano)
EMI CD CDM 7 63298 2

September 20, Abbey Road Studio no. 1, London
MONN: concerto in G minor, London Symphony
   Orchestra/Sir John Barbirolli
EMI CD CMS 7 63283 2

September 24, Abbey Road Studio no. 1, London
SAINT-SAENS: Concerto no. 1 in A minor, New
   Philharmonia/Daniel Barenboim
EMI CD CMS 7 63283 2

October 22, Royal Festival Hall, London
GOEHR: Romanza for cello and orchestra, Op. 24,
   New Philharmonia Orchestra/Daniel Barenboim
Intaglio CD INCD 7671

This was the second performance of a work premiered by du Pré six months earlier at the Brighton Festival. The piece puzzled her. Its lyrical moments show the du Pré familiar to us from her playing of Romantic compositions, its tougher sections an altogether more anonymous personality, as if withdrawal were the safest option.

1969   April 1, Abbey Road Studio no. 1, London
FAURE: Elégie, Op. 24, Gerald Moore (piano)
EMI CD CDC 5 55529 2

This was recorded as part of a tribute by various artists to
Gerald Moore on his seventieth birthday. The original
LP (HMV SAN 255) also included Dvořák's Slavonic
Dance in G minor, Op. 46 no. 8, in which Daniel
Barenboim played the *secondo* part.

1969/70   December 29 and 30, January 3, Abbey Road Studio
no. 1, London
BEETHOVEN: Piano Trios in E flat, Op. 1/1; G,
Op. 1/2; C minor, Op. 70/1 ("Ghost"); Op. 70/2;
B flat, Op. 97 ("Archduke"); B flat. Woo39; Variations
in G on Müller's "Ich bin der Schneider Kakadu,"
Op. 121a; 14 Variations in E flat, Op. 44; Allegretto
in E flat, Hess 48; Pinchas Zukerman (violin), Daniel
Barenboim (piano)
EMI CD CMS 7 63212 4

The Piano Trio in E flat, Woo38 and Clarinet Trio in
B flat, Op. 11, Pinchas Zukerman (violin); Gervase de
Peyer (clarinet); Daniel Barenboim (piano), were
omitted from the above set when transferred from
LP to CD.
EMI LP SLS 789

1970   August 25 and 26, Usher Hall, Edinburgh
BEETHOVEN: Sonata in F, Op. 5/1; Sonata in
G minor, Op. 5/2; Sonata in A, Op. 69; Sonata in C,
Op. 102/1; Op. 102/2; Variations on "Bei Mannern"
Woo46; Variations on "Ein Mädchen oder Weibchen,"
Op. 66; Variations on "See the conquering hero
comes," Woo45, Daniel Barenboim (piano)
EMI CD CMS 7 63015 2

These are from recitals recorded by the BBC at the 1970
Edinburgh International Festival. The audience coughs
and splutters throughout, but these are wonderfully
spontaneous performances and du Pré's illness was to

prevent a studio cycle of these works just four months later.

November 11, Medinah Temple, Chicago
DVŎVÁK: Concerto in B minor, Op. 104, Chicago
Symphony/Daniel Barenboim
EMI CD CDC 5 55527 2

November 12, Medinah Temple, Chicago
DVŎVÁK: Silent Woods, Op. 68, Chicago
Symphony/Daniel Barenboim
CD CZS 5 6813 2

November 27 and 28, Academy of Music, Philadelphia
ELGAR: Concerto in E minor, Op. 85, Philadelphia
Orchestra/Daniel Barenboim
CBS/Sony CD MK 76529

This recording is edited from two concert performances
and rehearsal material and offers the most highly strung
du Pré/Elgar Concerto available.

1971   December 10 and 11, Abbey Road Studio no. 1, London
CHOPIN: Sonata in G minor, Op. 65
FRANCK: Sonata in A
Daniel Barenboim (piano)
EMI CD CDM 63184 2

This and the Beethoven below were recorded at
Jacqueline du Pré's last commercial sessions as a cellist
after a six month "sabbatical" away from the cello. The
recording was arranged at less than a week's notice after
intensive rehearsal.

December 11, Abbey Road Studio no. 1, London
BEETHOVEN: Sonata in F, Op. 5/1 (1st movement),
Daniel Barenboim (piano)
EMI, unissued

A single take with no repeats made at the end of the
Franck/Chopin sessions, this is all that exists of a
projected Beethoven cycle.

1972   July, F. Mann Auditorium, Tel Aviv
        TCHAIKOVSKY: Piano Trio in A minor, Op. 50,
            Pinchas Zukerman (violin), Daniel Barenboim (piano)
        (From an Israel Broadcasting Authority recital)
        EMI LP EG 27 0228 1

1973   January 1 and 6, Severance Hall, Cleveland, Ohio
        LALO: Concerto in D minor, Cleveland
            Orchestra/Daniel Barenboim
        (Edited from two broadcast concert performances)
        EMI CD CDC 5 55528 2

1979   October 5, Henry Wood Hall, London
        PROKOFIEV: Peter and the Wolf, Op. 67, Jacqueline du
            Pré (narrator), English Chamber Orchestra/Daniel
            Barenboim
        DG LP: 2531275

Available exclusively on Sony Classical compact discs

Music from the Motion Picture
HILARY AND JACKIE

The CD features:

ELGAR: Concerto for Cello and Orchestra in E Minor, Op. 85
> Philadelphia Orchestra conducted by Daniel Barenboim, Jacqueline du Pré (cello).
> Recorded live at the Academy of Music, Philadelphia, PA, November 1970.

BACH: Suite No. 2 in B Minor for Flute & Strings, BWV 1067 – 1. Overture.
> London Metropolitan Orchestra conducted by Barrington Pheloung, David Heath (flute).

Music from the score composed by Barrington Pheloung.
> London Metropolitan Orchestra, Caroline Dale (cello), Sally Heath (piano).

Iris du Pré's "The Holiday Song."
> Caroline Dale (cello), Sally Heath (piano).